WHO SAYS
FOOTBALL
DOESN'T DO FAIRYTALES?

WHO SAYS FOOTBALL DOESN'T DO FAIRYTALES?

How Burnley Defied the Odds to Join the Elite

Dave Thomas

Foreword by Alastair Campbell

First published by Pitch Publishing, 2014

Pitch Publishing
A2 Yeoman Gate
Yeoman Way
Durrington
BN13 3QZ
www.pitchpublishing.co.uk

A CIP catalogue record is available for this book from the British Library.

ISBN 978 1-90962-669-0

Typesetting and origination by Pitch Publishing
Printed and bound in India by Replika Press Pvt. Ltd.

CONTENTS

Foreword By Alastair Campbell 14

Introduction By Sean Dyche 17

Prologue 18

Moving On Up…
Burnley's Post-War Promotion Parades 25

July
All Aboard The Pensioner Special 38

A Good Day Out:
Burnley 4 Sparta Rotterdam 1 47

August
Adventures With The NHS:
Burnley 1 Bolton Wanderers 1 52

Ooh Are We Going?:
Sheffield Wednesday 1 Burnley 2 58

The Curse Of Amazon:
Burnley 2 Yeovil Town 0 63

A Boy Called Joe 69

A Joy To Watch:
Derby County 0 Burnley 3 75

September
We Shop At Tesco Not Harrods:
Burnley 1 Blackburn Rovers 1 80

I Turn My Back For Two Weeks:
Burnley 3 Birmingham 0
Leeds United 1 Burnley 2
Burnley 2 Nottingham Forest 1
Burnley 3 Charlton Athletic 0
Doncaster Rovers 0 Burnley 2 86

October
Waxing Lyrical:
Burnley 2 Reading 1 92

All Noses In The Same Direction:
Ipswich Town 0 Burnley 1
Burnley 2 QPR 0 99

Toothaches And Penalties:
Burnley 0 West Ham 2 109

Sean Dyche One Year On. 118

November
The Quest For Pie And Mash:
Millwall 2 Burnley 2 127

Pondering On The Nature Of Things:
Burnley 1 Bournemouth 1 134

Director Clive Holt Talks With Dave Thomas 140

Sean Dyche, An Obscure Poem And Family Trees. 142

Sean Dyche And Winter Arrives:
Nottingham Forest 1 Burnley 1. .150

A Letter From Old Bob:
Huddersfield 2 Burnley 1 156

December
Culinary Treats And Cometh The Kightly:
Burnley 0 Watford 0
Burnley 1 Barnsley 0 164

You Know It's December:
Leicester City 1 Burnley 1 170

December
Clive Holt Chats 176

We Don't Need Gaviscon And Henry Winter On Sean Dyche:
Burnley 2 Blackpool 1 179

Twas The Night Before Christmas:
Middlesbrough 1 Burnley 0
Wigan Athletic 0 Burnley 0 190

January
Goodbye 2013:
Burnley 3 Huddersfield Town 2 196

Into 2014 Cups And Re-Unions:
Southampton 4 Burnley 3 202

Breakfast With The Galacticos:
Yeovil 1 Burnley 2 208

Calm, Pragmatic And Down To Earth:
Burnley 1 Sheffield Wednesday 1 215

January/February
Ormskirk With Chums:
Burnley 0 Brighton 0
QPR 3 Burnley 3 221

February
A Seven-Year-Old's Big Day:
Burnley 3 Millwall 1 227

The History Boys:
Bolton 0 Burnley 1
Bournemouth 1 Burnley 1 234

It's Tough Being A Man:
Burnley 3 Nottingham Forest 1 241

March
A Bargain At The Crooked Billet:
Burnley 2 Derby County 0 247

Sean Dyche – A Man With Beliefs 254

Dyche, Moneyball And Rovers:
Blackburn Rovers 1 Burnley 2 261

Written In The Stars:
Birmingham City 3 Burnley 3 269

Massimo Massimo Wherefore Art Thou:
Burnley 2 Leeds United 1 276

Tasteless Sandwiches And Reggae Music:
Charlton Athletic 0 Burnley 3 283

Sean Dyche And Old-Fashioned Values:
Burnley 2 Doncaster Rovers 0 .290

Back To Earth With A Bump:
Burnley 0 Leicester City 2 297

April
Battered And Depleted:
Watford 1 Burnley 1 304

Barnes Makes The Difference:
Barnsley 0 Burnley 1 311

Everything Back On Hold:
Burnley 0 Middlesbrough 1 318

Blackpool Rocks:
Blackpool 0 Burnley 1 325

The Burnley Lord Mayor's Show:
Burnley 2 Wigan Athletic 0 331

May
Making Sense Of It All 338

The Beautiful Game, The Beautiful Season 352

Echoes Of, And Re-Writing The Past 365

The Co-Chairmen, Sean Dyche, And The Final Words 375

Final League Table 383

This book is dedicated to the memory of supporter John Markey and Victor Collinge of the Border Bookshop who was so helpful; two good friends.

Gordon Harris, a great player for Burnley, and Arthur Bellamy, an unsung hero and a lovely man I met several times.

The players in 2013/14: Tom Heaton, Kieran Trippier, Michael Duff, Jason Shackell, Ben Mee, Dean Marney, Sam Vokes, Danny Ings, David Jones, Michael Kightly, Scott Arfield, Ross Wallace, Danny Lafferty, Junior Stanislas, David Edgar, Ashley Barnes, Chris Baird, Kevin Long, Brian Stock, Keith Treacy, Alex Cisak, Luke O'Neill, Cameron Howieson, Steven Hewitt, Ryan Noble, Cameron Dummigan, Nick Liversedge and Jason Gilchrist.

The first-team staff: Sean Dyche (manager), Ian Woan (assistant manager), Tony Loughlin (first-team coach), Billy Mercer (goalkeeping coach), Mark Howard (head of sports science) and Alasdair Beattie (head physiotherapist).

Special thanks go to Alastair Campbell, Darren Bentley and Adam Riding in the Burnley media department, Mike Garlick, John Banaszkiewicz, Chris Boden and Daniel Black of the *Burnley Express*, Suzanne Geldard of the *Lancashire Telegraph*, Henry Winter of *The Daily Telegraph*, Juliette Ferrington at *Football Focus*, Tim Quelch, Matt Rowson at Watford, Dean Standing at Millwall, Tony Scholes, Tom Morton, Mike Smith, Ian Brookes and www.dnapeople.co.uk, Richard Walker from Watford FC's media department, David Blackburn, Tony Dawber, Clive Holt and www.sportnw.co.uk.

PART ONE

FOREWORD BY ALASTAIR CAMPBELL

WHEN Burnley were promoted via the play-offs in 2009 it felt like a miracle. Somehow – and this really is a miracle – as the 2013/14 season wore on, automatic promotion under Sean Dyche felt like it was never in doubt. It is a truly remarkable story.

Dyche can now rejoice in the chants of 'Ginger Mourinho', though I suggest we change this to 'salt and pepper Dychio' when we play Chelsea. But it is fair to say there was a mixed reaction to his appointment following Eddie Howe's departure back to Bournemouth.

Equally, as the season started, I cannot be alone in having thought that another mid-table finish would be the best we could hope for, with the season made or broken for many according to whether we managed finally to beat Blackburn Rovers after a drought lasting more than three decades.

Data can tell a lot of stories, especially in sport. Small squad, low wage bill compared with Championship big boys, small town with several bigger clubs within an hour's drive, limited funds for transfers, not a Qatari or Russian in sight; these are all data points pointing in one direction – the likelihood that an exciting end to the season was going to be a battle for survival rather than promotion. Oh we of little faith.

A lot of the credit must go to the board for the decision to hire Sean and for running the club in a sensible way. It is brilliant that we have a board made up entirely of Burnley fans. Barry Kilby was a hugely popular chairman and one of the highlights of our last season in the Premier League was the trip to Old Trafford and amid the anti-Glazer protests the chanting of 'only one Barry Kilby' and 'we've got more cash than you'. John Banaszkiewicz and Mike Garlick have been a great double act as co-chairmen and their passion for the club is never in doubt.

The players too – if I may make a statement of the obvious – have to take a lot of the credit. Go through the entire squad and you see stories of excellence and improvement. It was right that Danny Ings and Sam Vokes got all the awards and accolades for their goalscoring exploits but from back to front we had a team of players who played at the top of their game week after week.

To get a team playing better than the sum of its parts, to get players who had been six out of ten to regularly hit eight out of ten; that is down to leadership and management and that is down to Sean and his staff. Arsene Wenger once said, 'If the manager isn't the most important person at the club, why is he the one who gets the sack when things go wrong?'

Since Sean arrived, virtually everything has gone right and none of it was by chance. It happened because he and the team made it happen. He inherited a squad that had been doing OK without being brilliant. He made a small number of changes. But the fact is he got everyone playing better. There was no team they feared.

I am writing a book about winning and the winning mindset right now, looking at winners in politics, business and sport and seeing what lessons can be transferred from one to the other. Sean really instilled a winning mindset in the club. How many times down the years have we gone behind and thought 'that's it'? But even at Blackburn when we went one down, I felt we would come back and win. Following Burnley in the second half of the season was so exciting because players and fans alike were so full of confidence. This is quite a rare experience.

I have got to know Sean and his backroom team well and Gawthorpe is a buzzing place; professional, well organised and intense in a good way. Automatic promotion on the resources he had is a story worthy of its own book and I am pleased Dave Thomas is writing it and delighted to provide this foreword.

We know the year ahead is going to be tough. We know that we will not compete for the top spots. But we know we can punch above our weight as well. And we know that we can be very, very proud of our club and very grateful to the board, management, players and staff who made it happen.

Alastair Campbell
May 2014

INTRODUCTION
BY SEAN DYCHE

WHAT a marvellous season we have just enjoyed. This club has a rich history and I am delighted that we have been able to add another chapter to our remarkable story. I remember saying very early on that I couldn't promise results, but I could certainly guarantee we had a team that was competitive and would give everything.

The entire team has certainly done that; both the footballers on the field and my staff behind the scenes.

It's good to see that the story of the season has been recorded. Dave Thomas tells me that he only received confirmation that it would be put in print after the Wigan game, when promotion was assured, which left a month to meet the publisher's deadline.

These are diaries collated from the beginning of the season, in a non-serious kind of way. As the season progressed, Dave sniffed something special might be happening, the focus increased and the writing intensified.

I know that Dave has written other Burnley books, but he says this one has given him huge joy and satisfaction.

Now a memorable season is over and the next chapter begins as we look forward to the Premier League.

Everyone has enjoyed the collective success we've achieved, but football waits for no man. Having said that, I hope this book helps you and future fans to relive the season – ONE GAME AT A TIME.

Sean Dyche
May 2014

PROLOGUE

THIS is the 13th book and the third diary of a season I have written. It begins in 2013. The first was about the season that ended in 2003. The first was *It's Burnley Not Barcelona* and subtitled *The Search for Champagne with Beer Money*. That line belongs to Stan Ternent.

You could argue today that it is hardly beer money any more. The two co-chairmen, Mike Garlick and John Banaszkiewicz (it becomes much easier and saves a whole deal of ink to call him John B from this point on), have sunk millions into the club; so has former chairman Barry Kilby.

The 2002/03 season was one of the most bizarre you could imagine with the most unlikely scorelines, most of which brought tears to your eyes; a 6-5 defeat away at Grimsby, a 7-4 defeat at home to Watford were just two of them. There were plenty more. It was the first book I ever wrote and it had an immediate impact on the publishing world. The publisher went bankrupt within a few weeks of its appearance.

When I finished headmastering I'd always planned to write uproarious school novels that would make me a fortune with film and TV rights thrown in for good measure. That never happened. I'd phoned the guy who published the Barcelona book to see if he was interested in the hilarious school books about me being a frenetic head in a rib-tickling village filled with country characters, eccentrics, crooks and villains, and wandering livestock. He wasn't; but he was very interested that I was keeping a Burnley diary and said, 'Well you're a headmaster so you must be able to write and spell – and Burnley books sell OK so I'll publish the diary.'

When I sent it to him he said he couldn't possibly publish it because it was so libellous. So I took the dodgy bits out and more or less re-wrote it. And thus, it was published.

I was astonished to say the least and that, in a nutshell, is how I came to write football books instead of bestsellers, and am still poor. Not one has made me any money and I'm still not famous; in fact if I ever write a book about me, I shall call it *Still Not Bloody Famous*.

Russians Don't Land Here was the next diary and that was the season that Burnley had the run of something like 20 games without a win. There were no oligarchs with any money on the horizon to help out, and the jam jar on the boardroom mantelpiece remained permanently empty. It was drab stuff that season but there was no relegation.

That's the thing about this little club. It battles against the odds. It isn't Harrods, it's Netto. It has the smallest this and the smallest that, but manages to survive and get there in the end; it kind of sneaks under the radar. Sometimes you could use the word muddle. It's had more than one hairy financial moment during these last ten years. Even in the Wembley promotion season it escaped insolvency by the skin of its teeth thanks to director loans, crossed fingers, silent prayers and Wade Elliott's wonder goal.

In February when someone on one of the Claret message boards came up with this, the hairs on my neck stood on end.

Fulham are currently rock bottom of the Premier League and looking a club in crisis. Leicester City are runaway leaders of the Championship. Northampton Town are bottom in the entire Football League. Now the last time Fulham were relegated, Leicester won promotion, Northampton Town finished bottom of the entire Football League. Burnley also won promotion that season, 1993/94. Fate?

That's the thing about all football fans no matter what team we follow. These are the things we look for to give us strength and belief. To my dying day I'll still believe that it was written in the stars before the season began that Burnley would win promotion at Wembley in 2009. In the final four games Burnley did not concede one single goal. It was unprecedented. A penalty won the game at home to Reading in the play-offs when Andre Bikey lost his cool and his shirt. In the second leg, Steven Thompson and Martin Paterson scored two world-class goals they will never score again if they play until they are 100.

And in the Wembley final referee Mike Dean ignored two penalty appeals from Sheffield United that on any other day, any other referee might easily have given. That was the day I decided that destiny truly is written in the stars by the football gods. And here's another thing: 100 years ago this year Burnley won the FA Cup and five years ago this year Burnley won promotion to the Premier League.

Anyone who bought the two previous diaries will know that I'm not one for times of goals, or how many corners there were and endless reams of stats. What I love is the quirkiness of football, the build-up, the aftermath, the pies, the whole matchday experience, getting there, coach trips, coming home, what mood we're in, the things people grumble and groan about afterwards. This is a book as much about being a football supporter as whether we won or not.

But, as the book progressed and as little by little it became clearer that something remarkable was happening, one name was on people's lips more and more, Sean Dyche. Bit by bit what emerged was just what a remarkable man and manager he was. That is a story emerging through the book.

I am not the kind of person who will slag players off when they've had a bad game. I had enough bad days as a headmaster to know that if we turn up for work stuffed up with a cold we ain't gonna perform at our best, or if the newest bairn has been wailing all night and sleep is hard to come by, who wants to go into work anyway. None of us perform at 100 per cent 24 hours a day and even the best footballer can have an off-day. None of them turn up on a Saturday afternoon having chosen to have a bad game, fluff a pass, miss a golden chance or fall flat on their face. They are human beings.

Anyone expecting a work of great literature should look away now. These are just diaries joined together to make some kind of sense. They were written as the season progressed and have been tweaked to help the narrative. But not until the season was two-thirds through and Burnley were in the totally unexpected solid top-two position did the thought surface that something astonishing was happening and there might well be a book that could be cobbled together.

What I did do later was deliberately insert as many Sean Dyche articles as I could find so that his huge part in the story is covered as much as possible. Ian Brookes, for example, provided a fine analysis of his leadership skills that slipped nicely into the section about the Derby home game. There was a terrific piece in the Watford programme. Henry Winter wrote a superb article. By accident rather than design the reasons and picture might emerge as to exactly how this promotion miracle happened.

Occasionally I looked back at the original *It's Burnley Not Barcelona*. In that there were quite a few mentions of what was going on outside of Burnley in the wider world. There is less of that in this book. Towards the end of 2013/14 Vladimir Putin was flexing his muscles; Ukraine was a powder keg. Putin seemed the only person who could pull the plug on promotion, fans joked. Petrol was an astronomical price. People were struggling financially but somehow gates increased and away support was superb both in numbers and volume.

So, ten years on: that's a lot of water under the bridge, a lot of Saturdays, some joyful, some utterly frustrating and some just plain depressing. In 90 minutes you can go through the whole gamut of human feelings. In ten years you can multiply that by 500. Football should carry a Government health warning on the tickets.

We've had Stan Ternent, Steve Cotterill, Owen Coyle, Eddie Howe and now Sean Dyche. Every one of them maintained, at the least, the Championship status. Ternent took us there; Cotterill preserved it and gathered the players that Coyle inherited. Coyle, through sheer charisma, took them to a whole new level.

The 2008/09 season was memorable. Wembley and the win was a day none of us will forget for the rest of our lives. It was his triumph. But the Premier League season was painful after the brilliant beginning. Coyle's walkout and the manner of it midway through the season is something many of us will not forget for years to come. Howe came and went. His legacy was the group of players that Sean Dyche then worked on, added to, and inspired and motivated to another astounding and memorable season.

Ten years on: always hard up, even during the Premier League season because money was immediately deducted by the Modus administrators and the chairman's generous offer that handed out 7,000 free season tickets, the result of a pledge the previous season. Most of those ten years were under the chairmanship of the safe-handed Barry Kilby, who but for illness may well have been chairman still, though he remains on the board.

Now there is a co-chairmanship comprised of Burnley men, but London based, Mike Garlick and John B. And that's the thing, the board is rooted in Burnley, all of them, including the one man born down south but who moved to Burnley over 30 years ago and is now an honorary Lancastrian.

There was a time during the season when living in Leeds I watched from close up the mess that Leeds United had got into (yet again). It was when the Italian but Miami-based Massimo Cellino was involved in the takeover from the Middle East people, Gulf Finance; the joke being that Leeds had the only millionaire owners with no money.

Thank the Lord, I pondered, that little Burnley is based on good Lancashire soil not the shifting sands of Bahrain or Dubai; that our directors speak with broad, earthy, local accents not Russian, Malaysian or Italian. Burnley: where we eat Lancashire hot-pot and cow-heel pie not tagliatelle and Mediterranean sun-dried tomatoes. At other clubs the scouting network might stretch as far as China. At Burnley it might get as far as Skipton, Barry Kilby once famously said.

This is the club of Bert Freeman, Halley, Boyle and Watson, Bob Kelly, a young Tommy Lawton, Alan Brown, Harry Potts, Jimmy McIlroy, Colin MacDonald, Jimmy Adamson, Leighton James, Frank Casper and Martin Dobson and that's just a handful of the great names that the club has produced. Then there's the greatest of all chairmen, Bob Lord. If you wanted to erect a statue of one of them you'd be stuck for choice.

Turf Moor has seen title winners, cup winners, European football, great teams, wonderful players and great victories. Tradition and history pervade the ground; the bricks and mortar are saturated with a distinguished past. And yet from the stands at Turf Moor you can still see the rows and rows of terraced houses and chimney pots that stretch up the hillsides until they reach the moors. Turf Moor is part of all that.

And this season with nobody really noticing, and against all the odds, there was another glorious story. Pre-season bookies' forecasts had Burnley among the favourites for if not relegation, then certainly something in the bottom six. But Sean Dyche did something quite incredible with the players at his disposal. It was his triumph although he will no doubt modestly point to players who were willing to sweat blood, give their all, never give in, and pursue wins with a dedicated and professional relentlessness, the latter becoming the buzz word towards the end of the season when people said they couldn't wait for the next game.

All that is true enough, but what he did was fashion a team in every sense of the word where the whole is greater than the individual parts, and for certain it was a team that included a backroom staff second to none in keeping those players fit and well.

But then what drama unfolded. With just ten games to go and a cushion of ten points and in second place, injuries kicked in. The experts had said all season that Burnley would never manage to make the finishing line ahead of the pack once injuries and suspensions took effect.

But on and on the season went with none to worry about until come the end of March, first Danny Ings, and then Kieran Trippier fell by the wayside. Dean Marney was suspended for two games and then most cruel of all, Sam Vokes collapsed in a key game after just a few minutes with a cruciate ligament injury. Next was Junior Stanislas with a hamstring strain. And there were still seven games to go with Derby County menacingly behind.

There was a blip when Leicester came and won. Even with a comfortable points cushion, the Burnley fan is nothing if not nervous. An implosion was just round the corner. The northern mentality is suspicious that good fortune is fleeting and will disappear. The school of hard knocks was founded in Burnley. Another home defeat to Middlesbrough and even with the healthy points cushion more nerves began to kick in as Derby kept on winning behind us.

But all was well. There were no more twists in the tale, another win at Blackpool and then on 21 April 2014, Wigan were dispatched 2-0 in front of a crowd of over 19,000 and Burnley had secured a place in the Premier League. The 'Moneyball' team had succeeded. Over a full season the league table does not lie and success was earned without favour or fortune.

The writing is almost a reflection of the way the season went. What began as a straightforward, certainly not serious, light-hearted diary for my own amusement is the basis of it, albeit amended and edited once the late decision was made to publish. But what began with no great degree of seriousness and the basic hope of a final respectable place in the division slowly morphed into something more focused and intense as the realisation grew that something special was happening.

And then after the fairytale had run its course. Next, there was a serious attempt in the final chapters to examine just how all this had happened. For days afterwards we looked at the final league table and just shook our heads in awe and amazement. Against all the odds something remarkable had happened. This is the story.

But first, Tim Quelch provides some historical perspective.

Dave Thomas
May 2014

MOVING ON UP…
BURNLEY'S POST-WAR
PROMOTION PARADES

1946/47

BURNLEY'S restoration to the First Division began one year after Second World War hostilities were concluded. These were the austerity years with Britain reeling from an Allied victory; battered, barren and bankrupt. The common cry was, 'We're so short of everything,' as food, fuel and clothing were rationed in order to feed a national export market needed to reduce the nation's wincing £3bn war debt.

According to Labour's monastic Chancellor, Sir Stafford Cripps, it was a time of self-denial. It was a message picked up by the popular 1946 film, *Brief Encounter*, in suggesting that family duty should take precedence over affairs of the heart.

It was perhaps apt then that the promotion-winning Burnley side of 1946/47 should be managed by the dour, censorious and ascetically-minded Cliff Britton, and captained by a highly principled ex-policeman, Alan Brown. Brown was a member of the international Moral Re-Armament League which maintained that moral recovery was a prerequisite for economic improvement. He was an authoritative, sturdy centre-half, who organised his team's 'Iron Curtain' defence with unstinting rigour.

In that arctic winter of 1946/47 when production halted, homes iced up, and the shivering British residents took to their beds in balaclavas and heavy woollens, Mr Brown's boys froze out their opponents, conceding a miserly 29 goals in their 42 league games. Burnley proved equally resilient in the FA Cup in progressing to an unseemly sun-drenched final at Wembley, where they lost narrowly, in extra time, to Charlton Athletic after a gallant, if attritional, display.

Britton never relaxed his disciplinary standards on or off the pitch. With his team 5-0 in the lead at West Ham, and with promotion assured, he surprised one appreciative Burnley director by berating a Burnley player for a sloppy pass. Realising the importance of sport in raising the morale of those afflicted most by these lean times, Britton insisted that each of his players had 'a duty to entertain the hard-working men and women of Burnley', often taking a new apprentice to the top of a hill overlooking the smog-filled town, where, with a biblical-like sweep of his arm, he would demonstrate the intensity of his conviction.

Britton frowned at smoking, abhorred the consumption of alcohol and was apoplectic if he found any of his players inhabiting what he considered to be 'ne'er-do-well' snooker hall haunts. Despite the flair of his flying amateur winger Peter Kippax, the deftness of inside-forwards Harry Potts and Billy Morris, and the explosive shooting of Jackie Chew, it seemed entirely appropriate that Burnley's 1946/47 promotion campaign should be achieved parsimoniously.

Burnley's promotion ushered in a 'Golden Age' in the club's history in which the groundwork undertaken by Alan Brown, on his return to Turf Moor in 1954, as a far-sighted, innovative coach and manager, paved the way for the Clarets' First Division championship under Brown's successor and former team-mate, Harry Potts, in 1960.

1972/73

Like his former mentor Alan Brown, Jimmy Adamson was a highly gifted coach. In fact, he was so good he was offered the England job before Alf Ramsey in 1962. Adamson refused, preferring to extend his playing career, which had culminated in a Football Writers' Association Player of the Year award in 1962. Like Brown, Adamson also captained a victorious Burnley side, guiding his team to the Football League championship in 1960.

Burnley's blunt and outspoken chairman, Bob Lord, was concerned about losing Adamson after the internationally-acclaimed coach ended his playing career in 1964. Lord hoped he might tie Adamson to the club permanently by assigning him a coaching role alongside Burnley's championship-winning manager, Harry Potts. But it was not long before the pair fell out over training drills, tactics and team selection. The club atmosphere soured with players unsure who was in charge.

In February 1970, Lord felt compelled to act. He replaced the kindly but tactically naive Potts as team manager with the solemn, studious Adamson. Potts was 'pushed upstairs' as general manager, where he remained unhappily for two more years before leaving the club in June 1972.

Whether coincidental or not, it was then when Adamson's Burnley players began to spread their wings. They reached top spot in September 1972 and remained there for most of the season. Enjoying better luck with injuries, Adamson could regularly play his strongest side. The defence was strengthened by the acquisition of classy England full-back Keith Newton and by the inclusion of Jim Thomson in central defence, allowing the elegant Martin Dobson to operate as a roving turret in midfield.

Deft playmaker Doug Collins came into his own as did the scrapping, fetching and carrying workhorse Billy Ingham, and the versatile Geoff Nulty. Up front, Paul Fletcher and Frank Casper formed a potent partnership, assisted by Leighton James's scorching pace, deadly crossing and powerful shooting.

In seizing the Second Division championship just ahead of Queens Park Rangers, Adamson's team secured 24 victories in their 42 league fixtures, losing only four games.

Alas, the cost of replacing an obsolete stand and keeping Burnley competitive at the highest level proved ruinous. Despite netting over £1m in transfer receipts from outgoing young talent, including Dobson and James, Burnley were relegated in 1976 saddled with debts of around £400,000 (around £12m–£15m today) with approximately £40,000 being lost each week. Following a stormy 1-0 FA Cup defeat by Harry Potts's Second Division Blackpool in January 1976, Adamson paid for this failure with his job. Despite Potts's briefly successful return to Turf Moor a year later, without Adamson's attention to detail professional standards fell, as did fitness levels and tactical awareness.

After the abolition of the maximum wage in 1961, the club's 'sell to survive' policy could not be relied upon to guarantee solvency. Once that artificially levelled playing field was removed, Burnley were less able to compete with the bigger, richer city clubs in attracting gifted youngsters. With the local economy continuing to languish, by 1980 Burnley found themselves down, if not yet out, in the Third Division.

1981/82

At the top of the singles charts, UB40 ('One in Ten') and The Specials ('Ghost Town') railed against the economic and social malaise gripping Great Britain. In Burnley, its last deep coal mine at Hapton had closed in February, and its last steam-powered mill, in Briercliffe, was destined to shut shortly. Unemployment levels were between 18 and 20 per cent. Although it was once the world's leading producer of cotton cloth, Burnley had become less like the cradle of English industrial revolution as its casket.

This was a valedictory occasion at Turf Moor, too, with the final flowering of its once famous youth policy. It was fitting then that a former product of that proud process should be in charge – local lad Brian Miller, another star of the glorious class of 1959/60.

Three of Burnley's Third Division championship-winning side of 1981/82 went on to play regularly in the First Division – full-back Brian Laws, centre-back or midfielder Michael Phelan and flanking midfielder Trevor Steven, who was also capped by England.

Meanwhile, apprentice Lee Dixon was waiting in the wings hoping that a big club might recognise his immense promise. Other former youth team graduates played leading roles or bit parts in Burnley's promotion success too, including full-back Andy Wharton, strapping centre-half Vince Overson, penetrative midfielder Kevin Young, and nippy winger Phil Caverner.

However, after a dismal home defeat by Swindon on 3 October 1981, watched by a meagre crowd of 3,377, Burnley seemed destined to exit the Third Division via the trap door rather than as champions. But a startling reversal of fortune began a week later.

Manager Brian Miller was indisposed with appendicitis, but his deputy, Frank Casper, came up with a winning plan. It involved deploying the regal if veteran Martin Dobson as a sweeper, allowing progressive full-backs Laws and Wharton a licence to advance.

The new system worked like a dream. Burnley defended redoubtably and broke quickly. Wharton and Young scored in a stunning 2-1 victory. While six out of the next seven games were drawn, a 3-2 win at Bristol City in late November revealed how good this young side was.

Here, the undoubted star of this switchback game was 18-year-old Trevor Steven. Seemingly oblivious to the frenetic tackling and heavy surface, Steven oozed precocious class. Always composed and precise in his passing, he nonchalantly freed himself of any trouble with a feint here, a drop of the shoulder there, and a dab on the accelerator. He continually changed the direction of play, twisting one way, and then another, looking for runners, rolling out inch-perfect passes to the Burnley wide men and prodding teasing passes through a thicket of City legs. It was obvious then that this Berwick boy was destined for the very top.

Northern Ireland international Billy Hamilton and Steve Taylor scored the crucial goals, but at contrasting ends of the age continuum, Dobson and Steven epitomised Burnley's irrefutable class.

Not even the horrific events of the Falklands War disturbed Burnley's relentless acquisition of points as the club raced to the line, seizing the Third Division championship ahead of rivals Fulham, Lincoln City and Carlisle United. And yet within 12 months it all went horribly wrong. Despite reaching the League Cup semi-final and the quarter-final round of the FA Cup, Burnley's 1982/83 league form was wretched, resulting in their immediate relegation. Miller and his successor Casper were held culpable as the club turned to an outsider, John Bond, to revive its fortunes

1991/92

However, Bond's appointment proved disastrous. True, he was unlucky with injuries but he was guilty of discarding the talented youngsters too quickly. Meanwhile the board allowed the cost of their replacements to spiral out of control. There seemed far too many cheques and not nearly enough balances. The club became almost bankrupt, forcing a fire sale of its remaining young assets, and leaving it to face the traumatic 1986/87 season with just 13 professionals, comprising the lame, the grey and the green.

The embattled club board turned once again to its stoical, ever-faithful servant, Brian Miller, to avoid the looming rocks. But by 9 May 1987, Burnley faced relegation to the Conference, and possible liquidation. Only a desperately tense victory in the final game of the season, plus Swansea's defeat of Lincoln, saved Burnley's bacon.

However, the near-death experience galvanised both town and club. Attendances rose and the TSB rediscovered its capacity to say 'yes', enabling Miller to strengthen his hand. Incredibly, just 12 months after confronting oblivion, Burnley progressed to the final of the Sherpa Van Trophy at an almost packed Wembley. It seemed inconceivable that the club would ever play again in front of an immense crowd of 81,000, with 30,000 supporting Burnley.

However, the recovery momentum stuttered thereafter. Miller was once again replaced as manager by Frank Casper, but, apart from guiding Burnley to a Fourth Division play-off place in 1991, Casper was unable to deliver promotion. After a hapless defeat by ten-man Scarborough on 28 September 1991, Casper resigned to be replaced by his deputy, Jimmy Mullen. Mullen's impact was immediate and astounding as Burnley won their next nine league games. By Christmas his reinvigorated Burnley side was top.

The secret of Mullen's success was his employment of a more direct style of play which capitalised on his players' pace, power and potency. His wide men, John Francis and Steve Harper, frequently broke at lightning speed, setting up copious chances for the mobile and marauding strikers Mike Conroy, Roger Eli and young Graham Lancashire.

Meanwhile, Burnley's robust back four, in which centre-backs Steve Davis and John Pender were outstanding, authoritatively barred the door, assisted by the more defensively-minded Andy Farrell and the box-to-box raider John Deary in central midfield.

On 2 May 1992, a Turf Moor crowd of over 21,000 acclaimed Burnley as the Fourth Division champions, the title having been secured at a crammed Bootham Crescent, York, four days before. Burnley, like Wolves, had achieved the rare distinction of winning all four divisional titles.

The 1991/92 championship season remains as a treasured memory for many long-standing Burnley supporters. After the bleak times which had preceded it, this was the ultimate restorative victory. The country had been racked by rising unemployment, record bankruptcies and resulting civil strife with hooded joy-riders 'burning rubber', with apparent impunity, on the mean streets of Cardiff, Birmingham, Oxford and Tyneside, but in equally troubled Burnley, the long-awaited ascension of the Clarets granted a welcome distraction, and a sense of hope.

1993/94

After a season of consolidation in the Third Division, manager Jimmy Mullen looked to progress further, signing creative strikers David Eyres and Kevin 'Rooster' Russell, and industrious midfielder Warren Joyce, son of former Claret Walter. Former Everton and Stoke star Adrian Heath led the line, having been recruited a year before, as had inspirational goalkeeper Marlon Beresford. With ex-Aldershot man Adrian Randall also beginning to demonstrate his undoubted ability as an attacking midfielder, Mullen's team was attractive and dangerous pushing forward.

However, it was less convincing when under the cosh, notably when playing away. One supporter commented, 'The contrast between home and away performances has been startling; at home, confidence abounds, the ball is passed to feet, space found, superb crosses put in and wonderful goals scored. Away, there is no space; long balls are hoofed out of defence to our isolated forwards, while the opposing strikers are allowed glaring gaps.'

With Eyres, Francis and later Ted McMinn largely hugging the flanks, and Randall proving little help to an oppressed defence, the under-populated central midfield was frequently overrun. Nevertheless, Burnley's impressive home record garnered enough points to scrape a play-off spot, resulting in a two-legged semi-final tie with a free-scoring Plymouth team which had completed its fixtures 12 points ahead of Burnley, having thrashed Hartlepool 8-1 away in their final game, while Burnley were losing 4-1 at already-relegated Exeter.

There was little doubt that Peter Shilton's men were expected to reach Wembley. After securing a dour 0-0 draw in the first leg at Turf Moor, it seemed as if the Pilgrims thought that the result was a foregone conclusion. The Devon club had even arranged their Wembley trip before Burnley arrived at Home Park.

To add deplorable insult to insufferable complacency, Burnley's black winger, John Francis, became a target of venomous racial abuse. It was perfect justice, then, that his immense speed and assured finishing should turn the tie in Burnley's favour after Plymouth had taken an early lead. After Warren Joyce had scored Burnley's decisive late third goal, a Wembley final against Stockport beckoned.

The play-off final proved to be a stormy affair with Stockport having two of their players dismissed for violent conduct. Thanks to a sublimely-struck goal from David Eyres and a scuffed one by right-back Gary Parkinson, Burnley made their numerical advantage count, but there was considerable uncertainty as to whether the club would be strong enough to retain its place in the second tier.

And despite 12 additions to the squad, including four loans, Burnley were relegated 12 months later. Although Jimmy Mullen hung on to his post for much of the following season, a poor New Year run resulted in his resignation, whereupon he was replaced by Adrian Heath.

In the four seasons which followed relegation in 1995, Burnley faced the prospect of relegation in three of these, with the closest call coming at the end of the 1997/98 campaign when former England international Chris Waddle was in charge. Only a home victory over Plymouth in the final game rescued them although, as in May 1987, Burnley were indebted to a result elsewhere in making their narrow win count.

1999/2000

With Waddle resigning a few days after the 1997/98 season ended, former Claret Stan Ternent was chosen to succeed him. Ternent had impressive coaching experience at Sunderland, Crystal Palace and Chelsea and had helped guide modest Bury into the second tier. However, Andy Payton apart, Ternent was unimpressed with Waddle's signings and set about making sweeping changes.

Having been granted a larger transfer kitty by new club chairman Barry Kilby, who took over at the end of 1998, Ternent paid substantial fees to acquire former Burnley centre-half Steve Davis and dynamic midfielder Micky Mellon. Other notable signings included goalkeeper Paul Crichton, creative midfielder Paul Cook, scrapping combatants Lenny Johnrose and Ronnie Jepson, and the versatile Graham Branch and Gordon Armstrong.

However, shocking consecutive home defeats by Gillingham (5-0) and Manchester City (6-0) in late February and early March 1999 seemed to threaten Burnley's third-tier status and Ternent's tenure. Fortunately, Ternent retained his pugnacious resolve, while chairman Kilby kept his head.

Both were duly rewarded as Burnley completed this difficult season with a ten-match unbeaten run with prestigious victories at Stoke (4-1) and at home against Premier League-bound Fulham (1-0).

The momentum this late run created was then carried forward into the following season. In Steve Davis, Mitchell Thomas and Ian Cox (signed from Bournemouth in January 2000), Ternent assembled one of the strongest defensive partnerships in the division. He had two tough-tackling but progressive full-backs at his disposal in West and Armstrong, enabling him to play three or five at the back.

Blessed with a selection of forceful, energetic box-to-box midfielders, including Mellon, Johnrose, Branch and youth team graduate John Mullin, Ternent could accommodate the wing wizardry of Glen Little and the assured playmaking of Paul Cook to increase his attacking options.

Up front, Ternent continued with the successful pairing of Andy Cooke as target man with the ultra-predatory Andy Payton, although the ex-Palace, Arsenal and England star Ian Wright was signed in February 2000 to boost Burnley's goal-power, helping the club to secure automatic promotion behind Preston North End. At Turf Moor, the frenzy of Wright adoration bit much harder than the so-called 'Millennium bug'.

Sustained by his trio of burly defenders and a fearsome ball-winner in Kevin Ball, Ternent's Burnley narrowly missed out on play-off places in the ensuing two seasons. By then a new striking partnership had been established between Gareth Taylor and Burnley's first £1m signing, Ian Moore, prompted briefly by Paul Gascoigne during the final games of the 2001/02 season.

However, the financial collapse of ITV Digital hit the club's resources badly forcing it to make severe economies, including the sale and lease-back of Turf Moor and the Gawthorpe training ground. Thereafter, the club was more concerned about hanging on to its second tier status than in progressing to the higher division. Consequently, Ternent's contract was not renewed at the end of the 2003/04 season, after the Clarets had narrowly escaped relegation. Instead, the Burnley board of directors turned to Steve Cotterill, a young, promising manager who was accustomed to performing well with slender resources. Cotterill did well in ensuring that Burnley became hard to beat, trading frugally in the transfer market, but he seemed to be drained by the constant effort of beating the retreat. After a dire home defeat to Hull in the autumn of 2007, Cotterill left the club by mutual consent to be replaced by St Johnstone's enthusiastic manager Owen Coyle.

2008/2009

Helped considerably by additional investment, Coyle was able to strengthen the club's attacking prowess, bringing in Scunthorpe striker Martin Paterson, Manchester United's wide midfielder Chris Eagles, and Cardiff's target man Steven Thompson, alongside promising Dundee United central midfielder Kevin McDonald.

But arguably Coyle's greatest contribution to Burnley's success was his indefatigable positivity which inspired a good team to both believe in, and play above, itself. Coyle's enthusiasm and inspiration was so infectious that his players became convinced that they could beat anybody, including the best opposition in the land, as they did in the 2008/09 cup competitions when eliminating Fulham, Chelsea, Arsenal and West Bromwich Albion, and in almost overturning a 4-1 deficit against Spurs in a pulsating League Cup semi-final second leg at Turf Moor.

Coyle led by example, choosing to play alongside his rising stars, such as Jay Rodriguez, in reserve team games, providing them with a constant stream of encouragement and occasional advice. Tactically, he made a crucial change, too, by moving veteran right-back Graham Alexander into a holding central midfield position to help shore up Burnley's sometimes suspect back line and in enabling defence to be turned into attack quickly.

Thompson's job was to hold the ball up in advanced positions allowing his rapidly advancing midfield colleagues, such as Robbie Blake, Wade Elliott, Chris Eagles, Joey Gudjonsson, Kevin McDonald or Martin Paterson, to inflict damage with their quick feet and powerful shooting.

A late surge in form saw Burnley reach the play-offs, having thumped Bristol City 4-0 in their final game. One of the division's front runners, Reading, were beaten in both semi-final legs, with spectacular strikes from Paterson and Thompson at the Madejski Stadium. Elliott then produced another stunning shot to defeat Sheffield United at Wembley.

Despite registering a 1-0 victory over Manchester United in their opening Premier League home game, brought about with a blistering volley from Robbie Blake, Burnley were far too vulnerable on their travels.

Up until Christmas, only their excellent home form kept them in with an outside chance of survival. But early in the New Year, their charismatic leader Coyle decided to jump ship in favour of relegation rivals Bolton Wanderers. The effect on the players' morale was devastating. Having been encouraged by Coyle to believe in themselves, his departure seemed to signal that they were not good enough. Coyle's replacement, Brian Laws, seemed powerless to stop the slide. Successive home defeats to Blackburn (1-0) and Manchester City (6-1) at Easter emphasised the hopelessness of their chances.

Back in the Championship, Burnley found themselves well behind the leading clubs, Queens Park Rangers and Norwich City, although still in with a chance of reaching the play-offs. But the prospect of achieving this took a nosedive after a diabolical home defeat by Scunthorpe during the festive period. It spelt the end of Brian Laws's period in charge.

Eddie Howe, the bright, young Bournemouth manager was appointed as his successor. Despite making a number of important signings, including striker Charlie Austin, central defender Jason Shackell and full-backs Kieran Trippier and Ben Mee, Howe was unable to improve Burnley's prospects of promotion. Meanwhile the Premier League booty was slipping away, requiring the club to plan increasing economies in order to break even, meaning a lower player wage bill and a smaller squad.

For the 2012/13 season, the 'parachute payment' was halved, reducing from £16m to £8m. Despite an uplifting start with a 2-0 victory over Coyle's recently-relegated Bolton, results fell away quickly with Burnley shipping far too many goals. However, it was something of a surprise when Howe requested a release from his contract only a few months into the season, citing family reasons. Little did anyone realise, then, that with Howe's departure and Sean Dyche's subsequent appointment, history was about to be made.

Tim Quelch
May 2014

PART TWO

July

ALL ABOARD THE PENSIONER SPECIAL

THERE were the usual thoughts. The new season almost upon us; here we go again. The addiction continues. This season none of us expect anything of note. Survival maybe and retain the Championship status and we can count ourselves fortunate. That'll do for us.

The last of the parachute payments and after that what's to come, slow decline? The experts and the bookies have us down maybe even for the bottom three and the dreaded drop. It's an unfair world, little Burnley, penniless, David versus Goliath. McCann and Paterson gone, Jensen released, heroes of Wembley 2009 and that magical promotion.

We have our season tickets again. You do what you can.

It was a first ever trip to the south-west coast of Ireland for me and Mrs T. Prior to this there'd been a fleeting visit to Carrickfergus and Belfast up in the north; and many years before that to Dublin when me and a pal went. That pal was John Helliwell, he of Supertramp.

In our youth, we used to scour the market stalls of Manchester for jazz records on Saturday mornings. There was a little band at school, he played saxophone and I played piano. He practised and practised and I didn't. He stuck to his lessons and I gave up. He became a millionaire and megastar of the 1970s and I became a poor teacher and writer of football books that make no money. There's a moral in there somewhere.

It was a 6.30am start from Turf Moor – with the usual crowd and some new faces as well. Zimmer frames, bus passes, walking sticks and things with wheels were in plentiful supply. I'm not mocking – I'll be 70 myself next year.

We see some of the crowd just the once a year and you just pick up where you left off. Thirty-three people made the trip and had the hotel had spare rooms there might have been more. We'd left Leeds at 5am and drove over the tops on a gorgeous morning to see the moorland covered with cotton grass. Pendle Hill poked out of the mist that covered the vale and Burnley below. None of us began that journey with anything other than a good few days in prospect. None of us had any idea that this would be a season that would develop into a monumental journey with magical stops along the way.

The talk as we progressed along the motorways (along with Rocky shouting down the coach 'When's the next brew?') was of what happens next at this football club. The ground buy-back was a plus; the exit of key players a worry. Pato and McCann gone and other players, of lesser value tis true, had been told they could clear off. Charlie Austin had been on the verge of signing for Hull City but then the deal was called off when the medical showed problems with his knee according to Steve Bruce.

In truth it produced a no-gain situation for everyone, leaving Burnley with a player who could walk free in a year's time even if he stayed and ran his socks off and scored 30 goals. Then no doubt, dodgy knee or not, the offers to him would come flooding in. Or, it gave Austin a tricky decision as to whether to play safe and sign the new contract offered by Burnley. And for Burnley – £4.5m would not be heading their way.

While we were in Ireland, Championship clubs like Reading and QPR were allegedly sniffing round trying to sign him on the cheap for £2.5m. Minus the pay-out to Swindon it would leave Burnley with a paltry amount that would barely last a couple of months. Didn't the directors say at one stage we did not need to sell? At that price we hoped not.

The first pre-season friendly ended in a 1-0 defeat at Morecambe. Opinions varied as to whether it was a tad disappointing; or it didn't matter because it was just a glorified workout and fitness session in the evening heat. Maybe I'm old-fashioned but Burnley 1 Morecambe 0 looks better than the other way round, and wins breed confidence. The inevitable questions were asked about the manager. There had been times during his first months at the club when things had seemed uncertain and lacking in promise. With just a handful of games to go the bottom three beckoned.

Replacements for departed players had been hard to spot other than four new goalkeepers. Then there was the mystery of full-back Joseph Mills signing permanently with the surprising news that it had been part of the loan deal a year earlier. And yet with Dyche he had hardly figured in the first team. A hero of the promotion year, Brian Jensen, was another to depart, muttering (allegedly) that there had been little interest in his testimonial year. There had been talk of a testimonial game – it seemed to be following the same path as the proposed Jimmy Mac testimonial game some time earlier; nothing happening, until Jensen tweeted that things might be in the offing.

Through the preceding weeks we'd worried or grumbled about this and that; membership of the EU, the euro, Syria, the vacuum that is Nick Clegg, the bloomin' cold spring, the state of Nigella Lawson's marriage. For anybody heading to Egypt for a holiday in the sun it wasn't just the Germans who might be snaffling the sunbeds – now you had to watch out for the Muslim Brotherhood getting there first.

A couple of things were never off the news – the royal baby and Wayne Rooney, would he or would he not stay at Manchester United? Frankly I didn't give a jot. And then there was that wonderful sporting weekend when the Lions stuffed Australia in Sydney and then Murray won the Wimbledon final. That was truly mint. I had a tear in my eye and a lump in my throat and the last time that happened was Wembley 2009 at the final whistle.

Nobody grumbled on the coach at the wonderful weather. It was brilliant from start to finish other than a few clouds appearing from time to time. We saw Ireland at its glorious best; green, verdant and largely empty until you reached a small town here and there. The Irish Sea was flat and still; the journey to Cork on largely vacant roads.

From our hotel bedroom window we could see Blarney Castle poking up through the trees. We climbed up the hundreds of winding stone stairs on the morning of the game against Cork to get to the top and the famed Blarney Stone. Up and up and round and round this narrow staircase we went inside the walls hanging on to the safety rope; the same steps where men in tights swashed and buckled, and years ago one guy killed his brother and then he himself was murdered by his son in order to inherit the castle. They didn't mess about in them days. Little tiny rooms lead off from the stairway where evil deeds and skulduggery took place, when pillaging was a respectable profession.

When you get to the top you skirt round the battlements and because the roof caved in years ago it's now an awfully long drop to the ground floor. At the stone you lie down on your back and twist and bend and end up half upside down with your head over this drop of hundreds of feet down below. A guy hangs on to you and then you kiss the stone. Mrs T couldn't quite reach it and kissed it with her nose. It hasn't increased her gift of the eloquence, but she says she can smell things a lot better. This stone is supposed to be one half of the Stone of Scone; or the other tale is that a local vicar years ago thought, 'Now here's a way to make some money, bring on the tourists.'

Blarney is a nice little place with a few brightly-coloured shops and bars dotted round the village green. On one side of that there's the enormous old Woollen Mills now converted into a huge three-floor shop, and other parts of the mill are now a pub, a vast stone-floored restaurant and then the hotel. On the other side of the green are the castle and the gardens.

Coaches pile in; people pile off, all through the day in both mill and castle. When we wound our way up the castle stairs there were Americans in front of us and Australians behind. Blarney is big business, but trust me, all done in the best possible picturesque taste and somehow it still seems unspoiled.

It was the weather for shorts and a whole range of chubby knees were on show. John Smith and Barrie Oliver revealed knees that hadn't been seen since the Coronation. The chef came out of the kitchen and I could see him totting up the chops he could get out of them.

We took a stroll round the village after breakfast on the first day. A few Garda were lolling about waiting for a café to open or a crime to avoid. The castle has a Poison Garden filled with stuff like hemlock, cannabis, heroin, opium, wolfsbane, belladonna and birthwort. Poisoning the neighbours was a popular sport in medieval days. It needs special permission to grow some of this stuff in there today but the Garda raided it one night and took a few plants away.

As we strolled round the street one guy sitting on a wall bid us good morning – at least I think that's what he said – it was almost unintelligible. A little further on was a small chap with an orange beard, in a green suit and sitting on a mushroom. He grinned and nodded so I smiled back. I never gave it a thought but then quickly realised: hey that's odd, green suit, orange beard, surely not. But when I turned round just seconds later he'd vanished. Now then: I'm not one for making things up but I thought the way he suddenly disappeared was pretty spooky and left me wondering…

The coach left for Dingle at 10am for a day out. The Dingles in Dingle on the Dingle Peninsula, we had to make the pilgrimage. The journey took us through Ireland at its best. Eric demonstrated that it is indeed possible to drive a ten-foot wide coach down an eight-foot wide country lane. The roads wended and weaved this way and that, up hill and down dale, through mile after mile of fields and farmland. Sometimes a view of the sea, creeks, rivers and estuaries opened up.

Through the villages we went; Tralee, Trala and Traladiddle, Ballybunion and Ballyawful. Signposts pointed to Kilkenny, Killarney and Kilwilly. Macroon was the biggest that we passed through, a long main street lined with bars and shops and cottages. They have the habit over there of painting every building they can in the brightest, most garish colours possible, so gaudy you need sunglasses. Blues, crimsons, purples, yellows, reds, you name it and then the window frames are painted in something else, usually the opposite, but equally psychedelic. It's like driving through a technicolour cloud of LSD. It's as if people find a shed filled with old paint tins that need using up and think, 'Jaysus Paddy, this'll look grand.' Do this at home and you'd have the town council jobsworths telling you to cover it up or demolish the house.

'Grand' is the word everyone uses. 'How are yer this mornin'?'

'Ah oi'm grand.'

'Good mornin' Seamus, 'tis a lovely day 'n all.'

'Ah ter be sure, 'tis grand alroight.'

'Good mornin' sor and would yer loik the full breakfast?'

'Ah yes that'll be grand.'

Dingle on a rainy day no thanks, but this was a day of warm sun and blue skies. It was grand. It was packed, the place doing a roaring trade. On a normal day it's just a quiet fishing harbour. We took a boat trip round the bay to see Fungie the local dolphin who has lived there for 30 years. For an hour this creature, as big as a Mini, swam, dived, leapt and plunged for our entertainment. He'd come alongside the boat and then disappear. I swear he puts on a deliberate act and a performance and has done this for years. The bugger knows though, just when you're about to click the camera, he vanishes to pop up on the other side of the boat. It was the first time I'd heard a dolphin blow a raspberry.

In the evening back at the hotel there was old-time dancing and familiar Irish songs with Finbar O'Shuffle and the McHooligans. Rocky Mills, one of Burnley's most colourful supporters – and loudest (on his best behaviour most of the time) – and Rockette did some fine gliding around. A few of the elderly locals turn up every Sunday for this musical treat. Young folk on our trip were hard to spot and before anyone says, 'Oi cheeky sod just watch what yer saying', I'm a pensioner myself.

Anyway we fitted in quite well on this musical evening. The night before, after dinner, we'd sat out in the warm, balmy air putting the world to rights and wondering what the season would bring. Bottom half of the table was the general consensus.

Matchday was Monday and a chance to wander round Cork after some shopping in the Woollen Mill in the morning for those who had any money. I'm cross because I decided not to buy another claret and blue scarf. Plenty more in the club shop you might think, but this one was rather swish and superior in cashmere, and reduced from some fancy high price.

On yet another blazing day there was a temperature of 30.5 in the city. Cork is a kind of mini-Dublin and the open-top bus tour took some of us round the city's narrow streets and along the riverside. Others headed for the Guinness dispensaries. From the upper deck of the bus we could look down on claret shirts and travelling fans congregating outside the pubs. It made you remember there was a game that evening.

These pre-season trips are special. For me the game is not the priority; it's the 'holiday', the meeting-up with old chums, meeting new ones, the big breakfasts, seeing new places and then if there's a win it's a bonus. The weather made it all totally special.

There was indeed a win. We were dropped at the ground, Turners Cross, at 5.30pm. Turners Cross is the home of Cork City, sponsored by Clonakilty Black Puddings. Some went to the pub for the free drink provided by co-chairman John B; some went in early to read the programme and eat our sandwiches. The players were out warming up in the still-blistering sun and we, knowing no different and with ageing eyesight, and they being on the far side, thought it was Burnley.

'Yes that's Wallace,' said Mrs T. 'There's Austin.' We watched approvingly as the goalkeepers went through their routines thinking they were our new ones that we'd never seen before. 'Looks good,' I said as one of them made some smart saves. And then Burnley came out.

Having discovered that these were the Cork guys that we'd been admiring, one of their goalkeepers came over clad in black and with black tights to our touchline with the job of lobbing crosses over for his buddy to catch. Behind us sat Lynne Barkess and her gang, the golden girls, all of them pensioners. We were only a few seats away from the poor lad in tights. It's not long since Cork were penniless and the lad's tights still had holes in them. This loud voice belted out from behind us, a voice that could fell trees a hundred yards away.

'D' yer know yer've gor 'oles in yer tights?' He didn't hear or pretended not to. The voice yelled out again.

'D' YER KNOW YER'VE GOR 'OLES IN YER TIGHTS?'

This time he heard and turned round sheepishly. A Burnley accent at 10,000 decibels would sink a battleship. He rubbed his ears. Suddenly he had a migraine. The golden girls mocked him shamelessly and offered to mend them for him. Craftily he shifted his position so that he was ten yards further down the pitch out of harm's way.

Lynne was with her father who was also on the trip, 90-year-old Harvey O'Hara. What a fantastic fella. He's watched Burnley since before he can remember. He saw Tommy Lawton. He worked down the mines in Burnley as a boy. He joined the Army in the Second World War and became a commando. He jokes he knows exactly where he was on the beach on D-Day, 'Sixth from the end on the left.' These guys are heroes.

The squads went in; the Cork goalie presumably making a mental note to raid his girlfriend's tights drawer. Burnley came back out with new man David Jones. Trialist Scott Arfield played the whole game and in the second half in the middle of the park had a storming game. Danny Ings was in little genius mode. Ross Wallace pinged over the crosses. Austin looked classy. Shackell, with Kevin Long and then Michael Duff, looked solid. Mee joined Mills on the injured list after coming off worse in a 50-50 tackle. Treacy showed again that somewhere in there is a damned good player who could run a game commandingly if he wanted to. Hewitt didn't do much wrong and looked a bit meatier than he was.

Chris Gibson, Burnley FC's catering director, after he had stuffed himself on chips and gravy at half-time, fell asleep for the second half. All in all we looked a class act for long spells and then found out afterwards this was only the Cork City second team.

What was impressive was the number of Irish Clarets there. One of them lived just 20 minutes from the ground and three or four times a year comes over to stay in Harrogate and then gets to a match. Another guy from Longford was staying in the hotel.

It was a 7am breakfast on day four and an 8am departure. I guess most of us could have stayed longer. There have been some memorable pre-season trips. This was one of them. The sea was still like glass and the return ferry journey smooth and calm. If it's Cork again next year, put our names down now Joyce please. The whole trip was just – grand.

Truth is we saw nothing to make us think, 'Hey we got a team here that might do something.' Our thoughts remained the same. This will be a season to cling on and hang tight. 'And after this season,' we worried, 'there's no more parachute money, so gawd 'elp us.'

A GOOD DAY OUT:
Burnley 4 Sparta Rotterdam 1

THE passing away of Bert Trautmann at the age of 89 meant that another of the truly great names of football was gone. He played in an FA Cup Final for Manchester City with a broken neck for the final 17 minutes and really was one of the all-time great goalkeepers.

A former German prisoner of war imprisoned in England in Ashton in Makerfield; at the end of the war he had no wish to return to Germany and settled in the area before becoming the goalkeeper for St Helens Town. In October 1949 he signed for Manchester City but it was Burnley who had expected to sign him.

Trautmann was ill in bed on 6 October in his lodgings when two officials from City arrived and more or less wore down his resistance. His confidante and father-figure Jack Friar, with whom he lodged, was absent and was unable to prevent the signing. When he returned he was astonished to hear what Bert had done with Burnley in the background desperate to sign him.

The following day the Burnley chairman sent Trautmann a letter expressing his astonishment. Trautmann and Friar were expected at Turf Moor on 8 October to sign for Burnley. It's thought they had already talked of obtaining a job at the NCB in Burnley for Bert, as 'aliens' were only allowed to play part-time for professional clubs at that time. The letter expressed surprise and had the chairman known what City were up to, he would have been to see Trautmann before them to make sure of his signature.

When I sat down for the Sparta Rotterdam pre-season friendly game at Turf Moor, the seat was once again owned by the club thanks to the 'buy-back' group who amassed the £3.5m to re-purchase the stadium.

I'm in the group that applauds it. For me the ground is the heart and soul of the club, it's the whole history thing that gets me. I'd hazard a guess too that the people who funded it would have been swayed to invest in the ground, but less so for any youth development where the prospects of another Rodriguez emerging seem to lessen each season, or the funding of players for a promotion push. Regarding the latter what would £3.5m buy? Two half-decent Championship players and their wages for two seasons; not much, is it?

But the ground is iconic, an emblem, a symbol of all that the club has been through. And tangible too, a visible sign that this club is not in dire straits just yet. Look what's happened to Coventry City. That might be an extreme example; the detailed origins of it are clearly explained in Paul Fletcher's Coventry chapter in *Magical*.

Of course a few people asked, and not without reason, what eventually happens to the bonds and the bondholders. Both capital and interest are repaid over seven years. The rent payable to Longside Properties and then Lionbridge (anonymous owners registered in the British Virgin Islands), always seemed to me to be dead money, especially as the club, not the landlords, was still responsible for maintenance and upkeep. I always thought it should have been a priority purchase with the Premier League money.

And as for the few people who were suspicious of the whole thing regarding who makes what out of it all; I know two of the bondholders well, and for sure they won't be making a fortune out of it, plus seven years is a long time to get your money back. And: the repayments to the bondholders are less than what the club was paying in rent.

I'd been in once or twice during the summer and seen the work being carried out on the pitch. On the last visit, two groundsmen were slowly walking up and down the turf with a fertilising machine. A group of schoolkids was up in the Bob

Lord Stand being given a tour. If it was me I'd have been asking them to work out how far these two guys had walked by the end of the afternoon fertilising session. 'Can we use a calculator?' they'd have probably asked these days. 'Or phone a friend?'

People on the Irish trip were none too confident about the coming season with memories still clear about how Burnley had almost flirted with the bottom three the previous campaign, but new man David Jones provided a bit of a boost. Few if any dared think of a top six place; most expected us to be dallying with the bottom half of the table.

Dane Richards was gone; so far out of his depth that probably all of us were scratching our heads as to why he was ever signed in the first place – on the strength of a cut-price video in a clear-out sale at Poundstretcher was a strong story. George Porter was sent out on loan, another one where we all asked, what was the point of this one? The chairman reported that moves to sign Charlie Austin on the cheap hadn't even been considered.

Overall, the pre-season results had been good and included decent wins at Cork City, Carlisle United and Tranmere Rovers. As well as the four new goalkeepers the other arrivals were Ryan Noble, Scott Arfield from Huddersfield on a free and eventually Jones. Out had gone McCann, Paterson, Jensen, Porter and Richards.

Sometimes I think I should have been a food critic. On one of my football book-hunting forays to Victor's Border Bookshop in Todmorden the other day, me and my pal Pete called at Hebden Bridge to visit Sid's Muse Record Store up Market Street; that's the Tod road on the way out of town. Now this used to be the tiniest little shop and independent music store with barely room to swing a cat but after the floods of 2012 Sid and Valeen had a sit down, a big think, and made a big decision. They'd knock the back wall through, install what flood defences they could, double the size of the place, retain the music side of things, and on the other side of the room open up a little café; thus making the Muse Music and Love Café.

It is now thought to be the only music café in Yorkshire of its type. Sid's musical knowledge is without parallel; Valeen's food-making is exceptional. It astonished me to hear they received nothing from the insurers for the flood damage, but they sank their own money into it and boy if you're passing by, love music and food, then call in for a treat in this little jewel of a place. You can check it out at www.musemusicandlovecafe.co.uk.

Sid and Valeen will sit and chat about music or food and we watched a procession of people come in as if they were old friends. The café means you can sit and listen to the music you love while you eat or have the best hot chocolate in Hebden Bridge, a hot choc described as 'richer than Pink Floyd, smoother than George Benson and more luxurious than Sade'. Pete and I had a warm curried vegetarian pasty, a slice of quiche and a mix of three house salads after we had been to Victor's bookshop: and in the background great music.

The Sparta game was worth seeing. The sun was baking hot, beating down on most of us in shorts and sunhats. A hundred or so Sparta fans in red-striped shirts added noise and colour. They drank and mixed in well in the pub over the road. Jimmy Adamson had dallied with the idea of managing Sparta after he was sacked at Burnley.

The details of this are in the Adamson book *The Man Who Said No to England*. To cut a longer story short Jimmy realised he didn't want to be separated from his wife and family and after just a few weeks came back. One of the things he left behind was a small notebook in which he had jotted down all the details of his time there so it became a key part of the Sparta chapter. It was a fascinating 101 things you have to do as a manager.

Meanwhile Sparta provided a good workout for Burnley in what was a properly competitive game. It wasn't all kid-gloves stuff. They are currently in the Dutch Second Division which maybe took some of the gloss off the resounding 4-1 Burnley win. But you can only beat what's put in front of you and Burnley duly did – and in truth could have scored eight or more had the goals gone in that their slick play deserved.

There were moments of intricate Harlem Globetrotters stuff that was a joy to watch from a team (and it looked like a team) that was organised, quick and inventive – and in temperatures where it would have been far more sensible to just sit on the grass and eat ice-creams. 'Quick and inventive', not words we'd used much in the last season.

Sparta took the lead, players like Vim Van Vonk, Wit de Van Driver, Crescendo Van Berkel, Wip Van Winkle and Jeremy de Hooter combining well to set the early pace. Unfortunately for them it lasted just minutes as Burnley equalised with an Austin header that the watching Andy Lochhead would have been proud of. Then for long spells it was party time. Marney was head and shoulders the man of the match with a cracking display.

The day was finished off at Nino's on the way home with chums. With my food critic hat on, the lasagne there was superb and plentiful. And so was the totty. Processions of them came in; bright young things, pert, perky, polished, pretty, pouting, average age 20 maybe, in all their flimsy, dolled-up, giggling, where's-the-men finery. But it was the shoes that got me. We could have held up cards with marks out of ten. They tottered in on a variety of stilts masquerading as stylish footwear that looked fantastic but upon which most of them could barely walk in a straight line.

Now call me an old dinosaur but to look good, you need footwear on which you can glide, sashay and proceed into a room with a slinky style that oozes nonchalance and says, 'Hey boys, how's this for an ass?'

But darlings, it does nothing for you if you wobble all over the place, stumble into things, have to hold the nearest chair, or look as if you're some kind of novice skater. All in all, it was a good game at the Turf and a free cabaret and shoe-show at Nino's.

Now that's what I call a good day out. The Burnley performance was impressive but none of us thought for one minute that this could possibly be any kind of a special season.

August

ADVENTURES WITH THE NHS:
Burnley 1 Bolton Wanderers 1

I WAS ruminating the other day. The sun was out; the garden chair was invitingly comfortable, the birds were chirruping, 'taties, broad beans, cucumbers, courgettes, peas, runner beans, onions, tomatoes all thriving. Blackcurrants and redcurrants all picked and in the freezer. Just like *The Good Life*, all was well with the world. I just couldn't resist having a good ruminate.

I decided a number of things in my little head; that no prison sentence was too harsh for the bestial couple who murdered little Daniel Pelka; that people like Cameron and Clegg are just not from the same planet as me, the bedroom tax needs a damned good rethink; that Ricky Gervais is about as funny as a dead hedgehog; that *Frasier* and *Dad's Army* are my best ever TV shows and that I never get tired of watching *Lonesome Dove*.

I'd also had some adventures with the NHS. I'd had a carcinoma thingy removed some time ago and in the Cameron/Clegg Utopia my regular check-up was four months behind schedule because of a backlog. To complicate things there was another of the buggers on my neck. My doc bless him got me in there pretty damned quick. It was a Nigerian guy doing the ops – he'd come up from London for a week to help Leeds clear the backlog before jetting off to the USA to do plastic surgery;

he said the NHS was in a shambolic state and he'd actually be better off in Nigeria.

Nice guy but he didn't get my little joke. He was asking what conditions I suffered from and finally enquired did I have a pacemaker – no, I said, a Peugeot. There wasn't even a smile, not a glimmer; and then he wasn't too chuffed when my phone in my pocket rang, while I was on the slab, laid out flat, and he was just about to make the first slice into my numbed neck.

Nobody ever phones me on my mobile. Nobody loves me, I don't care. I haven't had a call for weeks and even that was from the guy who rings to ask if you have ever been sold one of those PIPS or whatever it is they're called and I always yell down the phone and tell him to f**k off. So I decided I didn't need to switch it off; the odds on someone calling were a million to one. And it bloody rang. 'I'll leave it,' I said. 'It'll probably be Carol Vorderman. She rings me all the time. She can wait.'

I always get to Burnley eventually when I ruminate and in the course of recent events I'd had some dealings with the club. Those dealings left me pondering just what a knife-edge the club was on. Of course it has to make some money to pay the bills, and cope with critical cashflow; but how best to do that? Charlie was sold… I guess we all knew it was coming. We're a selling club and have to live with that.

That was reinforced at the Adamson book launch in the club shop the other day. Sean Dyche came along and he'd just seen Charlie sold and he opened the Adamson book at random on the page where the club had just sold Dave Thomas – but went on to win the Second Division title. So Sean spotted that and joked that maybe it was some kind of omen for the season ahead. We all agreed that nothing changes in as much as Burnley must sell to survive and I was struck by how unfazed he was with a sort of, well, OK we'll just get on with things. A very likeable, sociable guy I thought. Big, solid fella too… the sort that when he was a centre-half for Chesterfield, centre-forwards would have just bounced off him.

The basis of Burnley Football Club it has always seemed to me is that it is small, friendly, and woven into the fabric of the town. The town is small and as such it has a firm identity and Burnley has always been seen as a community club. From the surrounding hills you can see it below, nestling in the town, fitting in like the piece of a jigsaw puzzle. 'The club for its people' or 'the people's club' somebody once said, possibly Dave Edmundson; the club was struggling then and the begging bowls went out.

It's a parochial club. It isn't an Arsenal or a Manchester City or Manchester United where the bulk of fans are faceless and anonymous. It isn't a club that tourists from Japan or the Middle East have on their lists of places to visit while they're in the UK. Sure we have people who travel to games from far and wide, from way beyond Burnley. The list is endless; but they are people who are in the main either Burnley, or East Lancashire, born and bred; or a smaller number of people who have somehow built up a connection with the club even though they were born miles away. These people are not part-timers or one-off visitors. They are cast-iron regulars; albeit slowly dwindling perhaps as costs go up and up.

The little 'do' we had in the club shop was another indication though that these almost impromptu social things are where the club can open itself up a bit. Where else could you get six ex-players and the manager to call in just for an hour and chat away with a glass of wine? The guys from the 1970s are a special bunch. Jimmy Robson was there too – the man who scored the 1962 FA Cup Final goal.

The letter I got from David Miles, who wanted to order a book in North Carolina, was special too and brought me out in goose bumps. I love getting letters like these and it's one reason why I write books. It sure ain't for the money. There he is over the Atlantic and it turns out he's originally from Todmorden, same as me, and I was astonished to read my mother used to teach him at Roomfield Junior School.

It was a long letter filled with references to things from our youth and even the old and ancient Todmorden Amateur Operatic Society, for which he used to play the trumpet. I had one starring role in *Magyar Melody*; it must have been 1960 or thereabouts and I had one line to say and I fluffed it every night for a week. That was when I accepted I was never going to be a Hollywood movie star.

He recalled streets we both knew, Billy and Roger Birch and other people whose names sounded familiar. He saw his first game in 1952 when he was five.

The opening matchday meant that at last there was cash coming in, a little bit of the pressure off now that there was some Charlie dosh. Charlie was gone to QPR but John B in his programme piece was writing about how 'we want to do better this season and really go for it' and I couldn't quite equate that with the willingness to sell Charlie.

In the claret corner were those who argued he had to be sold while he was still worth something. In the blue corner were those who said this season was the last real chance with the final para payment to hang on to him and 'really go for it'. But one thing was clear, we thought; you can't sell Austin and then 'really go for it'.

Unless of course you spend all the money on a replacement – and if you do that what was the point of selling him in the first place? There was much wringing of hands and furrowed brows as rank and file folk discussed what would happen without the key goalscorer.

I came across a few lines in a book I was reading, *Hatters, Railwaymen and Knitters*, that struck a chord. They could have been written by any fan at any club, 'First day of the season, five words that mean the world, five words that let us breathe again. Five words that represent hope and radiate optimism; the sun is out, our shirts are new and anything can happen. This is August, our month, one whose dictionary definition in our minds reads: noun, start of new football season. Even just rolling the word around our mouths conjures first days gone by and the fiery glow of chance.'

You wondered what Sean Dyche might have been thinking. He'd made much of the success of the pre-season training but now it was all for real.

One manager, Neil Warnock, admitted that the first game of the season was always a nervous one. All of them are nervous, but the first is particularly so. You think you are ready but you don't really know until that first game. And above all, you can't beat a good start.

The attraction for the first proper game of the season was Bolton Wanderers. Burnley had had a good pre-season with four wins and one defeat. Bolton had had a lousy pre-season, nothing but defeats and one draw. In May, Bolton had announced their main sponsor would be Quickquid, a payday loan company. Phil Gartside had expressed delight in the partnership and hoped it would bring 'some real fun to matchdays'. Right Phil, people in debt to companies like this along with the infamous Wonga, have loads of fun trying to pay off their debts.

Greg Hohnstein, head of Quickquid, had also expressed his delight and hoped it would bring 'opportunities in the wider community'. A month later the deal was dropped as a result of adverse criticism and fans' reactions.

A 12.15pm kick-off on the opening day, was that a first; all to do with the celebrations for the 125th anniversary of the Football League. The day fine, pitch immaculate, 'wear your colours' the club asked, Australia fighting back in the Ashes, Rooney still at Manchester United, Fabregas at Barcelona and Bale at Tottenham, who cares a fig.

Picnic in the car park, Mrs T had packed a bag of salmon and cucumber sandwiches. I looked longingly at the healthy pies and hot dogs in the kiosks.

Back to the glossy programme, Barnsey's fanzine, hundreds of people buying the new Adamson book (yeah right Dave), crowds outside the pub over the road in the sunshine, anticipation, expectation, a touch of first-day nerves; fish out the season tickets, through the turnstiles, up the stairs, see familiar faces along the concourse, up the next stairs and out into the daylight. What a sight…fabulous…but…rows and rows of empty seats.

A 1-1 draw was maybe about right and Dyche overall was pleased. Bolton were a strong, big side. Eagles was crisp and sharp, darting about, and made their goal; why boo him? He served Burnley well.

It was Burnley who went ahead in a game that was fast-flowing and entertaining but the groan-factor was ever present.

Burnley had ten corners, all of them so predictably identical without variation or disguise; from not one did we ever look like scoring. And the shooting: abysmal and shots went over the bar or wide with infuriating regularity.

The approach play was frequently great to watch but too often Trippier's skills down the right were cancelled out on the left by the donation of the ball to a Bolton player. Jones and Marney excellent in midfield, Long and Shackell strong at the back, Stanislas a threat, Ings with Vokes battled manfully against the Bolton giants. There was little to suggest that any kind of a special season might unfold.

The attendance was dreadfully low even with over 2,000 from Bolton. Even taking into account that the game was live on TV, that August is holiday time for many, the swathes of empty seats, even with some of them available at just £12.50, were a reminder that the club might struggle this season to fill them. It was 6,000 down on the opening game last season when Bolton arrived for the Coyle grudge match and the circling plane with its banner that had us in stitches.

You can argue until the cows come home that this club needs to sell players to balance the books; but seats don't fill up unless there is a top-six place and a real hope of success. And for that you need good players…on a good wage or they won't give you a second thought…and for that you need high ticket prices…and then there comes a level when people can't afford them…so fewer season ticket sales…attendances decline even more…and so it goes on…ad infinitum.

Somewhere there has to be a cut-off point. People in Burnley hesitate at the idea of paying anything over £30. That's a lot of money for low-income families to find. The general consensus was that a bottom half of the table final place was the best to be hoped for. A few mentioned a top-six place, but more out of hope than conviction.

OOH ARE WE GOING?:
Sheffield Wednesday 1 Burnley 2

IT was a few days before the first game of the season and Mrs T (who I love dearly) had spotted what I'd hoped she would not spot; that Burnley were at York in the League Cup. 'Ooh, are we going,' she asked. 'It's only a bit more than 20 miles from Leeds.'

I'd groaned and muttered something about did she really want to go… it was a horrible place to go, all permits and stuff, it was easier parking in Leeds City Square, and other sundry reasons for giving it a miss.

Don't get me wrong, if I could press a button and be transported to an away ground without any hassle I'd be happy to go. I love the away trips with the supporters' club. We're off to Millwall with them in November. I treated her to the Cork trip. But, I'm no longer a great fan of driving to away games, battling with motorway hold-ups, having to find somewhere to park, sitting through what last season were frequently thoroughly drab games, waiting ages to get away, and then driving all the way home again. My protests were all to no avail. She wanted to go. There was no escape. I couldn't even say it would be difficult to get tickets. It was pay on the gate.

And as if that wasn't enough, she looked through the programme before the Bolton game. 'Ooh,' she said. 'Did you know they're at Sheffield Wednesday next Saturday?' Well of course I bloody knew but I'd kept quiet. We've been to Wednesday a few times before. Gawd, we were even there when we lost in the FA Cup semi-final in 1974. I saw them get hammered in an FA Cup replay years ago, too, sometime in the 80s.

'Why aren't we going?' she said. 'We usually go… don't we, we are going to go aren't we?' It was the time-honoured tactic of wearing me down. It was agreed that we would go on condition that she paid and battled with the online booking system.

And thus it was that the decisions were made to go to two away games that I'd been keeping quiet about and hoping she wouldn't notice until about an hour before kick-off whereupon she would have said, 'Ooh you didn't tell me Burnley were playing tonight,' and I'd have said, 'But darling I'm sure I did… didn't I?'

'I'll make bacon sandwiches,' she said. 'We can go early and find a parking space in York.' Thus it was decided and I do like bacon sandwiches. That was the clincher. And then I thought it would be good to see the site of the great promotion triumph of 1992, the place that people go all misty-eyed about and speak of in such awed voices, where Johnny Francis slammed home the goal that ended all those years of torment and suffering. It would be a pilgrimage, like people make to Lourdes or historians make to Agincourt.

York is flat so I thought all I need do is head round the northern ring road, turn down into York, head for the Minster but before getting there look for the floodlights. It worked a treat. Parking problems: no bother; by some fluke we found a street where you didn't need permits. A very kind bloke confirmed, 'Yes that's the ground, walk down that street and there's a chippy, and then you can go in the pitchside bar.' How very nice.

The bacon sandwiches went down a treat and then we walked round the ground and down a little way into York wondering if it's always gridlocked.

The site of Bootham Crescent had previously staged cricket for 50 years. Nearby was Asylum Lane (now renamed), and the site of the old lunatic asylum. For steam train enthusiasts the ground is a bit of a mecca. Over the tunnel is the restored nameplate of an old York City steam locomotive with the name 'Minster Men' inscribed over a golden ball.

As we walked to the ground we saw a line of old crimson railway carriages with faces hanging out of the windows. Some of them had 'steam train nut' written on their foreheads. Wisps of steam rose from above the trees, the polished loco gently simmering. We hurried over and there was a gleaming old steam engine at the head of the carriages, filling up with water. It wasn't allowed to do this in York Station so they'd rigged up a hose from somewhere across the fence syphoning off someone's water.

In the setting sunshine the ground looked clean, neat and trim. It was a reminder of what little grounds always looked like; homely, slightly ramshackle, eccentric, and higgledy-piggledy but well-cared for – a bit like the old city itself. At the end where Super John scored his goal I stopped to think; that this was a goal scored only just over 20 years ago that began the road to where we are today. Perhaps I should have bowed my knee in tribute and kissed the terrace. I was an absent supporter during the seven years of suffering and famine so I can't wear the badge. Today I feel I missed out on something truly heroic.

The game was a good'un, Burnley like Real Madrid for the first 25 minutes and could have been 3-0 to the good. Then York took over, belying their lowly wages, dominated and battered the back four. Shackell repelled all boarders, all hands to the pumps, some desperate defending. York must have gone in at half-time thinking 'this game is ours in the second half'. Out they came and carried on… but post-Howe, Burnley are made of sterner stuff these days and fended them off again. And then class told. One by one three more goals went in as Burnley scored almost at will, finishing the game strong and dominant.

Sean Dyche said his men had 'manned up' after the York onslaught… hmmm… naughty Sean… he'll have the Liverpool FC politburo after him… doesn't he know that 'manning up' is on their list of things not to say because it's sexist. Absolutely bloody daft: can pirates not say 'man overboard' or can a sinking captain not say 'man the lifeboats'? Do I tell my little grandson there's no such thing as a 'fireman' and Fireman Sam is banned at Anfield? One thing I'd do if I was Sean… I'd be on the phone to York about their storming left-back. The lad could play a bit.

The Claretsmad topic 'Would you be happy if the Charlie money was spent to improve the academy and not on his replacement' was one of the best discussions for years. It was measured, reasoned, fair, and was most certainly a resounding 'no'.

Investing more money into the youth set-up is for me a total waste of money now. The last player of any value to emerge, Jay Rodriguez, was five years ago. The two newest hopes, Steven Hewitt and Cameron Howieson, don't even get on the bench. Young players go out on loan one after the other and are then released. The debate was united on one topic; that without the maintenance of the first team and investment in it, then League 1 would inevitably beckon by a process of simple natural selection.

One comment stood out, 'By not improving the first team squad based on this sale, the board are now dangerously testing the patience of even the club's most adoring fans.'

Maybe there will be a signing, we thought, but the signs were against that, and an 'undisclosed fee' simply made many think it was probably a low figure for Austin that the club was reluctant to reveal.

The message was clear; that we all needed a boost, something to make us think we could still compete, that we were not just drifting, that the promotion and the year in the Prem did count for something; that we could recover from the Laws appointment fiasco, and then the bland Howe period. If cuts had to be made, could the club continue to haemorrhage money on youth development? Could it really afford the ever-growing army of playing support staff? It showed how little we knew. By the season's end we'd be lauding that backroom staff.

So there we were at Sheffield, down the M1, down the A61, pay to park the car in a convenient spot, pay for a programme, pay for the two tickets, another coupla gallons and 12 quidsworth of petrol gone, because despite all the frustrations, despite all the pessimism, and all the moans and groans, BFC is in your blood and it's been there so long that it's an addiction. It's fortunate that as a doddering old pensioner it doesn't cost me as much as others. So I could afford it and that's why I continue to attend. But, increasingly, others couldn't when money was so tight.

The attendance in the away end was far less than others there in the recent past, another indication of ever-dwindling support and difficulties finding the money to pay for these trips. But what a boost the 2-1 win was for all of us needing an injection of optimism and regeneration of fervour. It was a fantastic display of grit, bravery and courage, particularly in the second half when Wednesday pushed, shoved, elbowed, playing balls into the box and balls over the top with incessant menace. The aerial bombardment was relentless. Up close to the defenders we watched them battle and fight to the end and hang on to the points that were won in the first half.

It was a game of three periods. For the first 20 minutes Sheffield were like greyhounds out of the traps. For the next 25 it was Burnley dominant, in control and they scored twice. And then came that second half of backs-to-the-wall defending when Heaton, Long and Shackell were magnificent. Even under the constant pressure, there were good chances for Burnley to have scored again. Marney, Trippier and Vokes were equally superb throughout the game.

During that second 45 minutes when Burnley defended the end nearest us, we saw every block, every last-ditch tackle, some of them breathtaking, every header; we felt every bone-jarring collision, winced at every bruising encounter and breathed constant sighs of relief when danger was cleared and whenever Heaton pounced on the ball or made a stunning save.

Burnley caved in just once and with the score at 2-1, the nerves and tension doubled, every minute felt like two; and then to prolong the agony there were SIX minutes of extra time. We groaned. It seemed Burnley must capitulate but ironically those extra minutes presented least danger as Burnley played out the game and I'll swear blind that the weird little referee with the matchstick legs didn't play the full six. The players were shattered by the end. If they have a Saturday night out on the town by God they'd earned it.

'Well done Mrs T,' I said to her. 'Two games you made me go to and we won 'em both.'

THE CURSE OF AMAZON:
Burnley 2 Yeovil Town 0

SOMETIMES I curse Amazon. It's just too easy to press a key and buy another football book. Little grandson's room is piled high with them on top of the wardrobe. The bookcase at the top of the stairs (minstrel's gallery in the brochure) is all football books. The office is filled with them, on the window ledge, on the floor, on the shelves, under the desk, behind the door. In the bedroom the table has a stack of them waiting to be read – and another two arrived this week.

Down below in the basement old stuff goes to the charity shop to be replaced by football books and programmes and magazines, heaped up next to the homemade marmalade, plum jam, chutneys and crates of Bollinger. The shelves groan under the weight.

I thought the David Peace *Damned United* book was outstanding in its 'differentness' and style so I bought his new one, *Red or Dead*. With the success of his other books, Peace is in the J.K. Rowling bracket inasmuch as a new book is an event. He is a 'name' and his subject Bill Shankly is a name. Thus *Red or Dead* is already number seven in the top Amazon bestsellers. Four of the others, incidentally, are cookery/diet books.

At 700 pages it's a monster of a book. If you buy a copy you'll see exactly why it's 700 pages. It's written in the style of a Janet and John school reader, or the old Ladybird Peter and Jane books with endless word and short sentence repetition. Interspersed with all this are passages of dramatic powerful stuff.

By coincidence I'd got as far as page 180 before we set off for the Sheffield Wednesday game. The bit I'd just read could have been written specially for that match. Liverpool had just beaten Everton 5-0 and Shanks addressed his troops. Burnley had just beaten Wednesday in a pulsating game and Dyche entered the dressing room:

> After the whistle, the final whistle. In the dressing room, on the benches. Still in their kits, still in their boots, the players heard the footsteps in the corridor. Bouncing, dancing, Sean Shankly waltzed into the dressing room, around the dressing room. From player to player. Patting their backs, shaking their hands.
>
> 'You were magnificent boys. Magnificent. Every one of you, boys. Every single one of you. I could not have asked for more. You have answered back every comment, every question with a magnificent display of total, team football. From the back to the front, from the left to the right, every one of you boys. Magnificent I tell you, boys.
>
> 'That is one of the best displays of football I have seen in my life. And no one here today will have seen a better display, a better example of team football in this country since the war.
>
> 'Playing like that, playing like you can, we will be champions again. We will win the cup again. And we will win the Cup Winners' Cup too. We can win them all, boys. We can win them all. So now you go out there tonight, boys, with your heads held high. And you walk among the people of this city. And you listen to what these people will tell you. Because to a man, they will tell you the same as I'm telling you now. You are the best team in England.'

The other one that arrived was by Daniel Gray with accounts of his visits to different grounds in different parts of England. As soon as I knew there was a Burnley chapter, I pressed the one-click buy button. *Hatters, Railwaymen and Knitters* looks at 13 towns that host a football team. He chose Burnley as one of them. As an Englishman living in Scotland he took the view that he could return to England as a traveller and see it through objective eyes.

Focusing on the Burnley v Bolton game when Owen Coyle returned with his team in the opening fixture of 2012/13 made it all the better. Lucky for me; I can salt the chapter away in the filing cabinet to use in the next No Nay Never anthology whenever that might be. I have this thing about writing a trilogy; three books in the set but not a fourth. That's mainly because I know a series of three is a trilogy but I haven't a clue what you call a series of four.

Gray immediately gave his permission and I added it to the permission letters relating to Brian Laws's book, Peter Swan's book, and a fascinating book called *32 Programmes*, in which a poor hen-pecked bloke is commanded by his wife to reduce his precious programme collection to just 32; that's all the room there is in the suitcase before they move to the USA. Two of his programmes involve Burnley games – fascinating stuff. It's a book that's so simple in its basic concept that you wonder why the hell you didn't think of that. So that's the challenge to all progophiles; what would you choose if you had to prune your collection to just 32 if you've got hundreds of them?

Permission too came from Brian Jensen to add the final chapter of his book to a profile of the big man. It's a book and chapter that makes some revealing comments about the Laws/ Premier period. It seems Beast was none too pleased with the attitude of some of his team-mates during that time, though he doesn't name them. Judging by the displays in the home defeats against Wolves, Portsmouth and Blackburn, it was probably most of them.

The news before the banana-skin Yeovil game was gloomy. It had trickled out late in the week and then there it was in the chairman's programme notes on matchday. For the year ending 30 June 2013, the club would be posting an £8m operating loss. It was a jaw-dropping figure and much as most people know that the club is leaking money, gates are slowly falling, that directors' loans play a huge part especially at critical cashflow times, that player wages eat up vast percentages of the income; nevertheless this was a figure far in excess of anything suspected.

In hindsight it made the Charlie Austin sale all the more important and understandable and the whisper was that the fee was in the region of £3m. No wonder he had to go. It begged the huge question – just what happens when soon there were no more parachute payments and annual income was solely what would come via tickets and commercial income? From a £3m profit at the end of June 2012, to an £8m loss in 12 months; most reactions on message boards, that by and large went into meltdown, were of disbelief. One or two tried to make some sense of it.

For years, without director loans, the club would have faced administration more than once. Today, should the co-chairmen decide they've had enough and walk away from the club and want their loans back, it would be in instant dire straits. Between them they have loaned the club in excess of £10m over the last three years, much of this I would guess because of cashflow problems at the end of season and through the summer.

On Radio Lancashire later in the evening Mike Garlick was optimistic that the club would be in a break-even position by the end of the current season. He didn't elaborate but it wasn't rocket science to work out that drastic surgery would be needed in the absence of further parachute payments, to get staffing costs down when ticket and gate receipts would amount to little more than £3.5m.

Without considerable increases in commercial, catering and retail income, it was hard to imagine a total income anywhere near big enough to sustain the present club lifestyle. And, looming over all of that was the prospect of one day having to repay over £6m owed to directors. What happens if ever they decided they'd had enough (and who could blame them?) and chose not to invest yet more money was not hard to imagine.

Out of the hundreds there was one message board post that stood out, 'I just feel it's a real shame that the first manager we've had since Coyle, who seems to know his a*se from his elbow, is the one to suffer.'

Money in short supply, an £8m loss, the last of the parachute payments, a threadbare squad, Charlie Austin gone. You could be forgiven for abandoning hope. Top two, impossible; top six, highly unlikely was the consensus. If only we'd had a crystal ball.

It was good to get back to the green bit and the Yeovil game and surmise that a win would cheer us up a bit. And it was my six-year-old grandson Joe's first game. Yep, I was doing my bit to drum up support and it was an extra £5 for the club coffers. We'd bought him a new shirt and shorts the other week – goodbye 40 quid or something in that region. We went in today and spent another £30+ on him.

It was a game in atrocious conditions that until the latter stages seemed to be taking us all to an early grave. The sun had shone most of the week but this game was on as miserable a day as you could wish for. Mid-August and up in the rarefied atmosphere of row eight of the Upper James Hargreaves, we sat and shivered and covered our heads from the wind and cold and rain that drove in. Even the pigeons stayed indoors.

Injections of sweets, buns (three), Fruit Shoots, and a sausage roll kept Joe at least semi-alert. He loved Stan's (his name for him) yellow boots and was thrilled at Treacy scoring, not because he knew much about him, but because his other granny is called Tracey. It was Bertie Bee, not the goals, that had him laughing and chortling.

For the first 45 minutes the word dreary would not go amiss. Ironically as the rain intensified in the second half the tempo picked up and the ball fizzed about with a bit of venom. Tackles became a bit spicier; the yellow card increasingly waved about. With Jones giving a midfield masterclass, alas Wallace and the yellow-booted Stan were about as effective as a rubber hammer; they were subbed with 16 minutes to go. A win seemed a forlorn hope.

But on came Arfield and Joe's new hero Treacy. Gawd, what a relief when Treacy's goal went in. We've let some soft goals in at Burnley over the years and today at last we scored one when the Yeovil keeper seemed to punch the wicked, swerving cross that was heading for the top corner into his own net via the crossbar. Within minutes, an Arfield thunderous shot that was heading for Park View Chippy hit Vokes and cannoned in. Yeovil capitulated completely and by the end the score could have been doubled. Warmed by the goals, we headed for the exits, not only winners but in possession of third spot in the table. In the car Joe's sagging spirits revived quickly with copious supplies of Hula Hoops and cheddars.

The Jimmy Adamson night went down a treat. It was a free night thanks to the sponsors. Gerry O'Gorman and his band were terrific, boy can they play a bit; the pie as mouth-watering as ever. I had a phone call from talkSPORT in the afternoon. 'Hello is that Dave, this is talkSPORT.' I was chuffed to bits, my little head thinking great, an interview, some publicity for the book.

I went into overdrive, rabbited and gabbled away about Adamson, Lord, Potts, broken dreams and the guy who had the football world at his fingertips and then walked away from it all when he was only 51. On and on I went. God I'm on't wireless, I thought, I'm famous at last. It's about bloody time. Sales would double. And then the guy got a word in.

'That sounds great, but,' he said and then paused. 'But all I want to ask is, do you have Dave Burnley's telephone number.'

So much for being bloody famous.

A BOY CALLED JOE

DEAR Keith Treacy: You have a new admirer. My six-year-old grandson came to his first game on the Saturday we played Yeovil. During the game we fed him sweets, cheddars, Hula Hoops, sausage rolls and buns to keep him cheerful while the heavens opened up and the winds cut through our thin summer coats and chilled us to the bone.

It wasn't the greatest of games but it sure livened up a bit when you and the other lad, Arfield, came on. A number of things intrigued Joe. First there was the sight and the antics of the mascot Bertie Bee. It taught me not to underestimate the importance to little people who are just six years old of this fat, swaggering creature dressed up as a bumblebee.

Us oldies might just shrug our shoulders at it and say, 'Well I suppose in today's game we have to have these things.' But I realised on Saturday that Bertie does in fact have a real role to play and the kids love him.

Secondly, it was the colour of the football boots that got Joe all wide-eyed. Jimmy McIlroy and John Connelly never wore boots the colour of a Dulux catalogue; so me being me, a bit long in the tooth and a bit of a traditionalist, dinosaur some would say, I've always looked at today's fancy boots and wondered what iron-man Dave Mackay would have thought or Tommy Banks and Roy Hartle. I reckon they'd have made a beeline for anyone in green or blue boots and kicked them into the stand. Anyway, Joe loved them, so much so that on Monday this week we had to get him a pair of vivid orange-striped trainers.

We were shopping for new school shoes for him. We hadn't the heart not to get him the trainers. He particularly liked the yellow boots that Stanislas was wearing. Personally I thought it looked like he was wearing a banana on each foot, but then when ah were a lad we all wore enormous brown boots that came up to our shins, with studs six inches long, and not until we had rubbed them with dubbin for six months were they fit to wear.

On Friday afternoons at Tod Grammar school we'd clatter down Ferney Lee Road in them to Centre Vale Park. We sounded like weavers in clogs going to the mill. I tried to explain to Joe what dubbin was. He said it was the silliest word he had ever heard. I said you should have seen the boots and then remembered I could show him some.

On Thursday night at the Adamson book 'do' Steve Kindon gave me a pair of gigantic, ancient boots mounted on a plinth that weighed a ton. They were signed by Jimmy Adamson. Steve is a big, strong bloke so he lifted boots and plinth in the palm of one hand while holding up the roof with the other. When I copped hold of them my knees nearly gave way. They were so big you could have put a hundredweight of coal in each one and sailed them down a canal.

Back at home when I showed Mrs T and said I don't know quite where to put these she just stared and said in utter astonishment, 'What the f*ck are those?' The last time I heard such language was when she went to have a hairdo and when she came back and said, 'Do you like it?' I asked her was it finished yet and when was she going back.

I said the boots would look nice on her dressing table as a feature, maybe with some plastic flowers stuck in them. If looks could kill we'd all be in the 1882 today having a wake. Anyway, at the moment they are in the lounge on the hearth. For novelty value and as a talking point they equal the condoms the club gave away a while back; the ones with the picture of Graham Alexander on. What a claim to fame that is, or a good question on that TV show – *Pointless*.

Anyway, it was when your goal went in that little Joe got really excited mainly because we told him your name was Treacy. Well his eyes opened wider and wider and he was well chuffed. The reason being that his other granny is called Tracey and this in the head of a six-year-old is just a piece of the magic that helps make up their little worlds. He couldn't wait to tell her.

Since then, and I am not making this up, you are his favourite player. And this I think, in fact hope, will be a bit more inspiration to you in your search for fitness and a return to a frame of mind that is focused on being the skilful, talented footballer that we know you were, and seem determined now to be again. It's clear that Sean D has played an important part in your rehab. If for nobody else, then do it for him and little Joe.

There's this expression 'battling with off the field demons' that's been bandied about. We always assumed it was a liking for a drink or two, and then another drink or two. What we didn't know was that these demons also included personal domestic issues, needing to be with family in Dublin when things were tough, and battling for access to see your daughter. If you've been involved in court procedures it's draining, hardly the best background if you want a good night's sleep, either.

If you've been down in the dumps, a bit depressed, then the last thing you need is folks telling you to snap out of it. Depression is something nobody can just click a finger at and it disappears. Once people know about things they become incredibly understanding and many can identify with the same problems. Most people are patient and tolerant and want others to get their lives back on track when they know they are struggling.

'When can I go again?' said Joe. I guess, for various reasons, it won't be until October. By then who knows, you could have cemented a first team regular place. He'd be well pleased if we said you were playing. If it's at Stan's expense, you'll have to borrow the banana boots. With you in yellow boots he'd just be overwhelmed.

The other thing is this: the club is skint. Sean D so far has only brought three new players into the first team; Tom Heaton, David Jones and Arfield. And they've been cracking signings. Getting you back to full fitness and playing like a match-winner would be like having a fourth brand new player, and at no real extra cost.

It's clear that the rest of the players are backing you now. Michael Duff was commentating on Clarets Player and said how the players were encouraging you. That's great. What's coming across is that there is a spirit and camaraderie in this group of players. We saw it at York and then away at Sheffield. It's a small group of solid players that together is making a real team.

Nobody is a Messi but the sum of the parts makes it a close-knit side that might just do a bit more than any of us anticipated. If we bemoan the lack of a real flair player, the Robbie Blake-type player that can produce the magic moments that win games, then the goal you scored against Yeovil was one of those unexpected magic moments that has fans standing up roaring. We'd love more of that. It takes a lot to get me on my feet (bad knees I'm afraid), but by gum that goal did.

Mike Garlick told us fans what the picture is. It won't have escaped you players I'm sure. The club isn't awash with money. There's no more parachute money after this season. But if football is all you know and it was you that said, 'I'm too stupid to do another job,' then the thought of another contract at BFC must surely provide yet more motivation. And jeez, you're only 24. The interview you did that was in the *Telegraph* was eye-opening and brave.

Mind you despite the serious attempts of several good folk to explain things to me I'm still confused by these money issues. I could do with a sort of idiot's guide to finances in the next programme; some simple definitions of what's what. What's the difference between debt and operating losses for example? Is some of the £8m 'loss' not really a loss like you and me sometimes lose £8m of real cash under the settee, or on a slow horse, but is some of it to do with theoretical losses to do with depreciation of assets and amortisation – and what are they when the cows come home; are they the same thing?

Depreciation is, I think, if a player is an asset and three years ago cost £300,000 on a three-year contract, it means that each year he goes down in value by £100k. So that is entered as part of the operating loss. But it's not real money. It's this theoretical money. Similarly the same rule applies to buildings and equipment – the new tractor at Gawthorpe, the new players' rooms, for example. It's just the way some things go down in value and you can enter this in the profit and loss account.

Somebody once tried to explain amortisation and I had to go and have a lie down. If I've got it right, amortisation is just the decreasing value of something over time, and an £8m operating loss doesn't actually mean you owe £8m. Thus, within hours of the programme piece by the chairman that caused mass shock/horror/panic/wailing and gnashing of teeth among us rank and file thickies, another interview revealed that it was not as bad as we should imagine, because things were on track for a break-even scenario at the end of this season with the Charlie sale and more director loans.

But, and this was my uneasiness, all the while the debt to directors is increasing and will increase further during the coming season to get the operating loss reduced to zero. Currently at over £6m, what will these loans be by June 2014? And if one or more directors become fed up of all the flak they take (and who could blame them when its they and not us who stick their heads above the financial parapet) and want out, and want repayment of their loans from a club that has no money, then what the hell kind of mess are we in then? That's the worry for me; not controllable operating losses but the underlying debt that won't go away.

Much has been made of the six and a half per cent interest on loans that directors make. But here's the thing: a commercial loan would cost ten per cent, maybe more, and the lenders would want repayments on the dot, bang on time. Directors can waive repayments, and they do, if things are tough. But worryingly, that interest does accrue and adds to the club debt.

Joe stayed over last night and this morning found me tapping away on the computer writing this letter. 'What you doing?' he said. I said I was writing a letter to Keith Treacy 'cos I'd heard he was a bit down in the dumps. He looked puzzled when I asked him if he knew what amortisation meant.

'Don't be daft Pop Pop,' he said and asked, 'Will Treacy score another goal like he did last Saturday? I hope he does.' Then he skipped off down the hall looking for Buzz Lightyear. 'And can I have some toast – please?' yelled the voice as it raced away. 'And can I watch *Cars 2*?' How wonderful to be six, I thought.

If, 60 years from now, Joe remembers his first game, he'll think of a few things I bet: yellow boots, Bertie Bee and his hero called Keith Treacy and the cracking goal he scored. Dear God Keith, you'll be 84 then so the thing is; make sure that in the next ten years you can store away a treasure trove of football memories to look back on – and don't forget a little blonde-haired lad called Joe who decided, on 17 August 2013, that you were the next best thing to Buzz Lightyear and *Cars 2*.

If that doesn't cheer you up, nothing will. And: if you've no idea what amortisation is then join the club.

A JOY TO WATCH:
Derby County 0 Burnley 3

WE had a week away, heading for Kent, travelling down on the day of the Brighton game; resisting the temptation to head for the game there. A good decision as it turned out with a 2-0 defeat. On the return journey home it would have been no great problem to make a detour to Derby but we decided not to. Bad decision: a marvellous 3-0 win and by all accounts a near-perfect performance. The goals went in as we trundled up the M1 making the dullest bits of the drive through the 50mph limit zones bearable.

The praise came thick and fast: 'an all-round superb performance and a joy to watch'; 'tremendous away performance'; 'as complete an away performance as I've seen from a Burnley team'; 'a very special performance'; 'best performance I've seen for a long time, superb display'.

In between those two games Preston were neatly disposed of in the League Cup but there were reports of chaotic scenes at some turnstiles as people tried to pay at the gate and the decision to keep both upper tiers closed for the local derby was roundly criticised as some people gave up the attempt to get in and went home.

Clips of the Derby game showed what a superb goal Ings scored with a burst of acceleration that took him past defenders as if they weren't there. His celebration 'dive' was worth the entrance fee on its own – I seem to recall Graham Alexander did a similar routine once or twice. Vokes's goal was the result of a defender's clearance hitting him on the head and ricocheting in like a bullet. You wondered if they practise this at Gawthorpe.

On the way out of the game Derby fans were overheard saying that his performance was the best they'd seen from a centre-forward. Derby fans must be sick of Burnley arriving at Pride Park and winning year after year.

The penalty decision by the referee following Shackell's superb, perfectly timed tackle was one of the worst refereeing decisions you could see. Had Derby scored from the penalty it could have turned the game. Ings's disallowed goal was easy to shrug off when you're winning 3-0 and afterwards you can make light of it. But disallowed goals like this can have a huge influence on the final league position when goal difference can be the decider between sixth or seventh place. It happened years ago when Stan T almost took us to the play-offs.

End of August: three wins, one defeat and one draw and Burnley sitting nicely in third spot. It would have been a supreme optimist in July who would have predicted this. The message boards were a mixture of optimism and caution, but there was agreement on one thing; that there is a clear team spirit and bond that exists between this bunch of players. The best teams are exactly that, a team, a group, where the sum is greater than the individual parts. Early forecasts that the season would be a real struggle made the sight of Burnley in third spot all the sweeter.

I sat glued to Sky's coverage of the transfer window countdown. Over the previous weeks it must have been a rare person who wasn't bored rigid by the sagas of Bale and Real Madrid, Rooney and Chelsea, Suarez and Arsenal, Fellaini and Manchester United.

Up bright and early on deadline day: little Joe sleeping over, his school hadn't started because roof repairs weren't completed. Switch on Sky: the anchor people at their desks, reporters at all the major training grounds, the sun shining everywhere but cloudy Leeds; Wenger telling the one assigned to Arsenal to expect a major surprise. Fourteen hours to go. Cardiff City reported to be sniffing around Burnley's Trippier.

Bale's agent, looking tanned out in sunny Spain, informed us that this particular transfer was done and had taken 110 days. Apparently Burnley had once been linked with him on loan when he was bench-warming at Spurs. Bale told his adoring fans that Spurs would always be in his heart. I read an article some weeks ago that since he'd had his sticky-out ears pinned back his confidence and performances on the pitch had increased dramatically. For £85m I'd have any bit of me pinned back you'd care to mention.

Six hours to go and no sign of Jim White, who is to deadline day what Robin Day once was to election night and what David Frost was to *That Was the Week That Was* and David Jacobs to *Juke Box Jury*. That was sad news about them both passing away; each of them part of my vanished youth. But nice to see the Beast, Brian Jensen, back at a club, Bury. He served Burnley well.

Sky used the word 'extraordinary' for the millionth time since breakfast. Would Arsenal get Demba Ba as well as Ozil? Would Man U get Herrera? Barmiest bid must surely have been the £6m offer that Coyle made to take Jordan Rhodes from Blackburn to Wigan. Since Blackburn allegedly paid £8m for him to Huddersfield in the first place, the logic of this silly bid escaped me.

Chairman Dave Whelan later denied the bid, adding to the mystery, and also announced the Everton offer for James McCarthy was ridiculous.

Following all the news every now and then through the afternoon, I thought the biggest set of numpties on view seemed to be the chumps at Liverpool's training ground. It's usually the goons at Stoke who take this award.

But where was Jim White – the usual anchorman? The *Telegraph* had a nice paragraph about him, 'Sky's earl of excitement, their high priest of hyperbole, Jim White has made deadline day his own in recent years, serving a valuable if unintended purpose for the viewer. Warmed up recently by touring the country in a helicopter for Sky's '92 Live' feature. As a general rule, the more screen time White is getting, the less there is actually happening.'

I flicked back to the newsdesk at 7.30pm and Jim was there at last, all spruced and scrubbed up, beaming away, presumably there to crank up the excitement during the final hours like Peter Snow does with the swingometer at General Election time.

Meanwhile: Chelsea had agreed terms to send Demba Ba to… but wouldn't say where.

8.30pm: dusk falling round the nation and Abdul Razak (who the hell is he?) left Manchester City. Norwich wanted Ricardo Vaz Te from West Ham. I settled for a cuppa Te and a ginger biscuit. BIG NEWS! Fellaini handed in a transfer request at Everton in a sneaky brinkmanship move to force a deal. Watched an hour's TV, an episode of *Ray Donovan* we'd taped.

10.05pm: the nation in pitch darkness except for floodlights at training grounds all over the country. Arsenal fans competing with Liverpool's for the title of prize idiots. The big surprise: no live interview yet with Harry Redknapp through the window of his car. The Ozil deal still not sorted because of protracted complications and time was running out. Claretsmad website offline – service unavailable; Jim White uses the word 'extraordinary' for the millionth time.

Burnley fans in the know tweeting that Michael Kightly might be a great under-the-radar signing by Dyche. The Burnley first team is off on a golf bonding trip to Scotland. Plans to rename Deadline Day to Agents' Day announced. Both Burnley journalists, Boden and Geldard, tweeting that Michael Kightly could be on his way from Stoke. Pursuit of Ashley Barnes of Brighton was 'now dead in the water'.

10.25pm: and a beaming Jim White in dark suit, crisp white shirt and yellow tie proudly announced, 'Arsenal have got their man. Ozil is now an Arsenal player.' The Arsenal fans behind 'our reporter at the scene' were having a gurning competition. Still couldn't load up Claretsmad.

10.40pm: Gareth Barry drives into the Everton training ground. Everton have first refusal on Romelu Lukaku of Chelsea. Claretsmad now loading but slow. 'This is really exciting,' says Jim White. Harry Redknapp at the QPR training ground since 8.30pm in the morning with deals in the offing. 'Don't go away,' implored Jim.

Five minutes to go and Jim had Ian Holloway on his mobile. 'Wow it's all happening,' he cries, looking like he's having an orgasm. Meanwhile McCarthy could be on his way from Wigan to Everton; no mention of Fellaini and Man Utd. Will Burnley get Kightly?

BONG…BONG…BONG: the bells of Big Ben began to chime out 11pm. The window was closed but Jim, still irrepressible and exuberant, tells us that dozens of deals that have been started will now have folk scuttling round all over the place to get the paperwork sorted and finished. 'That was amazing,' he says. And then minutes later, voice decibels an octave higher, 'Here's confirmation Mario Fellaini has gone to Manchester United for 27 and a half million pounds – WOW.'

Everton have gained McCarthy, Lukaku, Barry, and won Bradford West from Labour and Orpington from the Conservatives.

11.20pm: the icing on the cake; Harry Redknapp (with two gains) on his way home stops the car, and is interviewed through the open window. 'Quite amazing,' says Jim.

And then the news that all Burnley fans had been waiting for – Sean Dyche had pulled a rabbit out of a hat. Michael Kightly had indeed signed a season-long loan deal. Twitter in meltdown mode because the consensus was that this was a good signing.

Jim sent us over for an update to the West Brom training ground where the fans gathered there comfortably took the award for the dumbest-looking. The Herrera to Man U deal was off with the rumour circulating that the guys dressed in black suits who arrived to do the deal were imposters.

It was at this point that I could feel the will to live slowly evaporating. The last dregs of energy helped me switch off while Jim was on his mobile to yet another manager and Bryan Swanson at the Totalizer was in full flow, pleased as punch because the Fellaini deal took the day above the £600m mark.

Bed: and I dreamt I was doing keepie-uppies in the Bernabeu with Gareth Bale. Perhaps I should watch less TV and get a hobby. That was a long, long day.

September

WE SHOP AT TESCO NOT HARRODS:
Burnley 1 Blackburn Rovers 1

I'D had great fun avidly checking Amazon first thing every morning looking where the Adamson book was in the charts. To my astonishment one morning it was top of the FA section, beating by just one forehead a Rooney book. And this was with little or no press coverage either nationally or locally, or promotion by the club. Neither had local radio showed the slightest interest. And yet this was Jimmy Adamson, one of the club's greatest servants, a legendary player and one of the finest ever coaches, a title winner, FA Cup finalist, Footballer of the Year in 1962, manager of one of Burnley's finest ever teams, and the man who said no to England.

In Kindle-land it dropped to second and then back to first again and then for much of the week, there it was up in the heady heights of number one. The last time I felt as proud was a year ago when the Paul Fletcher book was top of the charts for a week in Bacup.

And then along came the Clarke Carlisle book extracts in the *Daily Mail*.

Some while back I'd had lengthy conversations with him when writing *Entertainment Heroes and Villains*. I had interviewed him in his home and then in a subsequent phone call had offered, if ever he was interested, to help with any book he felt like writing. I actually said that tongue in cheek. It was obvious way back then that he would be a prime candidate for adoption by a big publisher; he had a huge story to tell, and that was even before he became chairman of the PFA, a TV pundit, appeared on *Panorama*, and was making acclaimed documentaries.

He was erudite, ultra-professional in all he said, and highly articulate. It was therefore with some surprise that in the extracts I read, I found he had fallen into the trap of using foul language and crude sensationalism in his book. As soon as you see a book described as 'blistering' you know what kind of book it's going to be. The excerpts were indeed blistering – and then some.

This was not the Clarke Carlisle that I had talked to at some length. This was not the *Panorama* Clarke Carlisle, and I couldn't help thinking that here was the chairman of the PFA, respected in the media, but was now reduced to writing a book that seemed to be a vehicle for settling old scores, one being with Kevin Blackwell, and calling other people 'shithouses'.

Maybe his book would top the footie charts. I didn't doubt it will be a 'good read' in the same way that Stan Ternent's book was a 'good read', as was Peter Swan's *Swanny*. It would undoubtedly tell it like it is and fly off the shelves. But I hoped he wouldn't shoot himself in the foot.

I've ghosted four books and in three of them I've held back the people involved from going overboard when writing about people they wanted to slaughter. If you have a copy of the Harry and Margaret Potts book, the background to that is that all Margaret wanted to do was have a go at her mother-in-law at every opportunity, on every page if she'd had the chance.

A libel action is only ever a careless sentence away if the target is alive and well. To me, it just isn't worth the hassle. You don't have to call someone a 'shithouse' in print. The facts always speak for themselves; let them tell the story, let the narrative do the job and it's soon clear if someone is a 'shithouse'.

As it turned out the rest of his book was better than the *Daily Mail* sample. It gets off to a good start and the account of how Eddie Howe had no further use for him is sad and disquieting, almost cruel in fact.

I ploughed on with the David Peace tour de force *Red or Dead*. It took two postmen to carry it up the steps and we had to take the door off the hinges to get it in. It's an unconventional style for an adult book:

> Bill opened the book and began to read. Bill finished the page and turned to the next. Bill read that one. Bill got up and made a pot of tea. Bill walked to the cupboard and took the jar of tea down. Bill got the spoon and spooned three spoons of tea-leaves into the teapot. Bill walked to the kettle. It had boiled. Bill turned off the gas. Bill picked up the kettle and poured hot water into the pot. Bill let the tea-leaves settle to the bottom of the pot and flavour the hot water. Bill put the lid back on the teapot.
>
> Bill walked to the pantry and got the milk. He put the milk bottle down. Bill picked up the teapot and poured the strong tea into the cup. He let the few tea-leaves settle to the bottom of the cup. Bill poured milk into the cup. Bill added two spoons of sugar. Bill sat down with his cup of tea and with his little black book. His book of names, his book of dates, his book of results. He looked at the names and the results and the dates. Then Bill closed the book.
>
> Bill took a sip of the tea. Bill put the cup down into the saucer. Then Bill opened the little black book again and studied the names and the dates and the results. His book of names and dates and results.

A publisher friend of mine gave up the effort of reading it. But he said how much he enjoyed hearing it read aloud at an authors' luncheon when it came across as a sort of intense literary rap. I managed to get to the end of reading it. After about page 520 it livens up a bit when Bill lays the table for breakfast and cleans the oven.

Don't get me wrong. It's a monumental work, but you'll either become addicted to it, or be driven mad and not get past page 30.

The co-chairmen's open letter to fans was a nice gesture. It was general, wide-ranging and clearly from the heart. Of course it was low on specifics; how could it be otherwise in this first instance? The real worry that the came across was the amount owed to directors (£6m+ I believe) and we wondered what happens should one or all of them need it back quickly.

The chairmen wanted to usher in a system of better communication and transparency but it coincided with the curious case of Saigonclaret's wish to make a substantial donation to the club. This is the user name of a Claretsmad contributor and on CM he posted that he had offered several weeks earlier to make a fantastic £10,000 donation to the club in memory of his mother.

This wonderful offer had been made with the proviso that he wanted it to go to something specifically identifiable, such as the training facilities.

It was sent to one of the officers at the club who replied immediately that time would be needed to consider the potential options. And that was the last thing that Saigon heard for weeks. It left him in a dilemma. Should he email someone else? Should he withdraw it? There was alas the faint possibility I suppose that the club saw it in the same way we view those letters we get from a long-lost Nigerian cousin telling us that if we get in touch we can share in the money he has discovered is owed to us by the Bank of Nigeria and all we have to do is send them our bank details.

As a result, Saigon again got in touch with the same officer at the club who had indeed passed on the information and was surprised and apologetic that Saigon had received no reply from the management people further up the ladder. But there was a happy ending when representatives of Claretsmad met with one of the co-chairmen on behalf of Saigon and astonishingly the donation was increased considerably.

And then it was the Blackburn game, the 100th meeting; the last match before me and Mrs T vanished to Kalkan thereby missing some corkers including Leeds. A beautiful day, win and we'd go top, (top, Burnley?) and the Adamson book was still top of its bestseller Amazon chart. Win and we'd have a bottle of fizzy I promised Mrs T in a moment of impetuous generosity.

As we drove over the tops, the helicopter was buzzing around. As we drove down the hill nearer the ground the empty Blackburn coaches were pulling away. The club shop down to its last two Adamsons, the buzz outside tremendous, even the empty coaches were abused as they drove by.

The crowd disappointing: some had come from Sweden, some from Norway, the guy next to us constantly on his phone to his brother in Australia. But less than 16,000 there. The game on Sky but the ticket prices remained high when common sense said reduce them to the lowest category because of the TV coverage. How many casuals could pay the top price, well over £30, especially when it was on TV and money is tight?

This is Burnley, not Barcelona. We shop at Tesco, not Harrods. In fact a lot of us shop at Poundstretcher. The chief exec eventually responded to criticism by saying at a fixture like this there were extra policing, stewards and seat repairs to pay for.

With 15 minutes to go we thought the game was won after Stanislas had scored a contender for goal of the season, a fantastic and intricate passing move of one-touch football involving several players to set up a stunning shot, drilled low into the corner from 30 yards. It zipped across the ground like a missile.

We really thought this was it after a non-show from Blackburn other than one great shot tipped round by Heaton and some vicious in-swinging corners.

The first half was simply one-way traffic but at half-time there were no goals to show for it. There was nearly a wonderful start to the game when a goalkeeper clearance cannoned back towards the Blackburn goal from 30 yards off a Burnley leg. It could have gone in, but was a few agonising feet wide. After that the Burnley approach play was a delight to watch, chances and attempts came and went, but just would not go in.

Blackburn were more in it in the second half, a second half that was stop-start, niggly, more physical and with no real moves of note, but just when you thought this was heading for a 0-0, up came Stanislas from the bench to smite his perfect strike. Turf Moor rocked round three sides with dancing and singing, and the hugging of strangers, but was mute on the fourth. Mayhem, euphoria, a crescendo of noise and pent-up passion released like the explosion of a volcano. This is it, we thought, this is bloody it, after all these years.

But football is cruel, unfair, unjust, and kicks you in the teeth. Arfield suddenly under pressure from a dodgy pass, he in turn, why oh why, plays a suicidal pass back into the area. Jordan is lurking but Duff gets there first, sweet relief and no danger, but then smashes the ball into Jordan's shins whereupon it loops into the net almost in slow motion.

A tale of two ricochets: the first for Burnley in the first few minutes so close but just wide; the second for Blackburn goes in. Other than the one shot and the succession of wicked corners, that was all Blackburn did all afternoon.

In the evening Arfield apologised to all Burnley fans on Twitter. But the goal was just one of those things, just rotten luck, misfortune, a fluke and we at BFC over the years have become well used to that. Jammy buggers, we moaned as the final whistle blew, especially as Ings, through on goal near the end, past his man, nothing but the green, green grass of home in front of him, was cynically brought down from behind; a red card for the culprit, but scant consolation for the goal and the win that was prevented.

We didn't go top. There is a theory Burnley used up all their luck for the next five years in the run-in to promotion in 2009. But at least the Adamson book was still there, top, Amazon Kindle, £3.63. We left for home, if not impressed by the result, definitely by the performance. Maybe we could cement a place in the bottom half of the Championship after all. How were we to know that much better than that was in store?

I TURN MY BACK FOR TWO WEEKS:

Burnley 3 Birmingham 0

Leeds United 1 Burnley 2

Burnley 2 Nottingham Forest 1

Burnley 3 Charlton Athletic 0

Doncaster Rovers 0 Burnley 2

WE had a couple of weeks in sunny Kalkan and what happened? Five wins on the trot, including the first match in October. What the hell was going on, I wondered?

We flew out while Birmingham were demolished 3-0. That was a result I kind of assumed might happen although not by a nice comfortable three goals. The texts kept coming in from our chums in Burnley (the Sutcliffes of Towneley – you must have heard of them) as we enjoyed the complimentary 90-minute white-knuckle ride from Dalaman to Kalkan. I always thought Greek taxi drivers were bad enough in their huge Mercedes limousines; but give a Turk a white minibus on the now completed dual carriageway super-highway and a kind of Indianapolis 500 streak emerges in the male Turkish psyche. But 'completed' doesn't mean smoothly finished.

The four of us were the only occupants of a 15-seater luxury model that had us bouncing and rolling around like peas in a can as it hit ridges and potholes in the super-road at 80mph and overtook anything and everything in its path. All this was in the dark with blinding headlights ahead and unlit cars at least 30 years old emerging at junctions, or suddenly appearing in front of you with no rear lights. We wondered if our two weeks would be in the apartment (luxury with pool) or in Emergency Ward 10 in Fethiye.

Somehow we made it unscathed and emerged from the minibus with rubber legs and having left curiously damp patches on the seats. What a good driver though, to drive all that way one-handed, with his phone in the other, glued to his ear.

We used the same apartment as last year, and the Leeds United season ticket holder next door became my new best friend.

He emerged on our first full day, beneath a large wide hat, draped in a towel, from the apartment next to us. Significantly for both of us, the next Burnley game was at Elland Road. We exchanged pleasantries.

'By gum those legs are very white. You must be a Leeds supporter.'

John meanwhile, to his credit, was living proof that not all Leeds fans think they have a divine right to live in the Premier League. Like many fans, the universal football supporter, at many football clubs, like many of us at Burnley over the years he has questioned the sense in buying a season ticket when so often we have been submitted to displays of dross and boredom week in week out. He is as baffled as the rest of us when asked, 'Why have you got no money?'

'Because we have the only Arab millionaire owners with no money,' he replied.

He was far from happy. Elland Road is no Xanadu, he declared. He has lived through all the daft years of Leeds's financial problems and the chaos of the way it has been run.

By the day of the game, we were on pins. He because he fully expected to be beaten, and me because I really did think there was the chance of a result, the way things had been going. We sat by the pool, sun beating down, (5pm in Turkey), views of all the boats and gulets heading back into the harbour half a mile below us, with an iPad that his Mrs had brought, and drinks. By all accounts Burnley's display in the first half was Barcelona class, but we had no sense of that from so far away.

'Oh dear,' said his wife, slightly tickled; (she is not a football fan and is annually amused when he says he will not buy another season ticket). 'I daren't tell you; it's 1-0 to Burnley.' He groaned. Half-time came and I did a quick 200 lengths (it was a small pool).

Picture the scene when she told him it was then 2-0 to Burnley. Game over we thought, until Leeds pulled one back and then we both sat and squirmed; me wanting the whistle to blow, him wanting the equaliser.

'You'll not be buying another season ticket then,' his wife said to him, somewhat unnecessarily, I thought. The day then took a slightly surreal twist when a large tortoise emerged from the flower bed, looked at us, did a u-turn and ambled back into the greenery. In the supermarket later in the evening I saw they had Mumm champagne. It was tempting… a Burnley win at Leeds and the Adamson book still at number one. At £60 a bottle we thought not and settled for Angora white at four quid.

We caught the goals in the sports bar and as each one went in I let out a loud 'YEAH'. A guy turned round in front and stared, in fact it might have been a glower. With a sour face he muttered something along the lines of, 'Humph it won't last.' In the short conversation we had it turned out he was from Blackburn, miserable sod. My huge smirk wouldn't have improved his mood. I smirk a lot. I'm a heavy smirker.

Tuesday was another game. With our Leeds chums we headed towards a rooftop restaurant. Lamb stuffed with spinach and apricots for me, and then back at the apartment the iPad said it was 1-1 at half-time. 'We'll have to get one of these for next year,' said Mrs T. Forest are one of those Billy Davies sides that can turn up and get a result. They didn't this time and the 2-1 final score meant it was three wins on the trot.

Saturday: Burnley at home to Charlton and Leeds away to an improving Millwall. The sports bar heaving with Manchester United fans watching one big screen and a 2-1 defeat at home to West Brom; and on the other side a horde of Manchester City fans watching City lose at Aston Villa. I reckon old Fergie knew what he was doing when he retired and saw the writing on the wall. This was a poor United side and how they won the title last year is still a mystery to me.

Meanwhile, Burnley stuck their three goals in against Charlton and Leeds conceded them at Millwall. It was a fair bet I was the only happy person in that bar other than the lass who gratefully took her bloke's credit card and headed to the jewellery shop across the alleyway determined to make good use of it. So second we went in the table. I looked around to see if the Blackburn guy was in the vicinity. Sadly, he was not. Perhaps it was as well. I'm trying to give up smirking. I used to be on 40 a day. But second in the table, whoever thought this would happen?

Sunday: I couldn't believe it, so it meant a walk down the hill in the morning to get the Sunday papers to make sure it was true and sit reading them with a coffee in the Café del Mar, a fabulous little place with what I call the Beckham chairs. It's filled with huge, plush ancient sofas with crimson upholstery and old bowed legs. If you ever saw Maurice Setters play you'll know what bow-legs are. Jimmy McIlroy hated playing against him.

Shelves are filled with Turkish antiques, pots and pans and *objets d'art* covered in dust. Carpets and tapestries hang on the walls. And at the front are two huge upholstered wing-back chairs from which you can read the papers, and watch the passers-by heading down the narrow cobbled street. As soon as I saw them I called them the Beckham chairs.

In the evening came the best steak and chips I've ever had, in a posh harbourside restaurant called Trio. The downside was the smarmy waiters and a haughty front-of-house guy who I could have happily smacked. But the food's the thing. Akin's is the place to eat in Kalkan and feel properly comfortable with great food and friendly staff who entertain you with Turkish jokes like:

> Akbar was walking along the lane with his camel. In the distance he saw a stranger approaching. As they passed, the stranger spoke, 'My word that's a fine donkey you have with you.' Akbar, rather puzzled, replied, 'Pardon

my friend, this is not a donkey, it's a camel.' 'I know,"
replied the stranger. 'I was talking to the camel not you.'

We always visit the market in Kalkan. It's once a week and
a whole street at the top of the town is closed off and buried
beneath huge shady canopies. Beneath them are dozens of stalls
manned by shady dealers. You cannot go past any stall without
being entreated in pidgin English to buy whatever they are selling
usually at 'cheaper than Asda prices'. I always stop and look and
ask, 'Do you have any Burnley shirts?' It shuts them up a treat.

A text arrived. To my surprise it was from another Burnley
supporter, Harry Gardner, now retired, and who heads to Kalkan
for three-week stints. He'd heard from a total stranger that me
and Mrs T were also in town. That stranger could only have been
(I worked out) the guy I'd talked to for a while on the boat trip we
did. I'd been eavesdropping when he'd been talking about having
been a former professional footballer at Portsmouth.

I went over to talk to him and it turned out he'd only played
twice for Portsmouth in the early 1950s before being sold
to a club up north. He must have been in his 80s by now of
course but looked fit as a fiddle. Astonishingly one of the two
games he'd played had been against Burnley and he could still
remember being up against the two full-backs, Harold Mather
and Arthur Woodruff.

We reminisced about the good old days when we were all
poor. We were so poor in our house we didn't get the Betterware
man calling at the door. It was the man from Worse-for-Wear.

Anyway, Harry and I met up at the sports bar (where else?)
and watched the three Charlton goals, each one a peach; poor
crowd though and the sub-10,000 gate against Birmingham
must surely have set alarm bells ringing at Turf Moor Towers.

There was not a drop of rain for the whole two weeks, endless
blue skies and hot sun, but the very last day, departure day,
Burnley at Doncaster, brought rain spots and overcast skies. Taxi
due at 5pm to the airport and the prospect of another English
winter ahead. Rain on fast Turkish roads, not good, the roads
now greasy and treacherous, the second complimentary white-
knuckle ride in prospect.

Having negotiated our way through two accidents, the airport was a blessed relief but by now a massive electrical storm was ominously flashing and blasting all over the skies above and around us. It was so spectacular you could have been forgiven for thinking this was an attack by aliens from another galaxy.

With a 9.10pm departure time it meant we wouldn't get the Doncaster score until we landed at Leeds/Bradford. Doncaster: like Barnsley a place I'd vowed not to visit again, usually the scene of miserable defeats and poor performances. And since when had Burnley ever won five on the trot?

Over our heads the storm worsened with continuous massive lightning lighting up the sky almost permanently. All flights were either diverted or grounded. Our plane was now sitting indefinitely on the runway at Rhodes where it had been diverted. Ah well. Gin and tonics and slices of pizza, and the bonus of texts letting us know the Doncaster score.

Bloody hell, winning 1-0 with a Vokes penalty. 'Vokes…taking penalties' we both exclaimed at once. The storm raged incessantly as we sat by the huge departure-lounge windows looking out over the runways as we thought this is what Armageddon will be like. Not a drop of rain but just relentless sheet lightning and tempestuous winds blasting across the runways.

Another text arrived; 2-0 and an own goal, by now the game surely over and Burnley clear top, the storm clearly abating, the lightning receding into the distance. And the first sign of life outside as a plane landed to the cheers of the waiting crowds. Another 30 minutes and ours came in. The 9.10pm departure became well after midnight but by now it was confirmed, Burnley had won 2-0 and were top of the Championship.

We go away for two weeks, turn our backs and they go and win five on the trot and go top. Turkish delight I suppose you could say. 'You just know what'll happen on Saturday against Reading, don't you?' said Mrs T.

I knew what she meant. Five wins on the trot and top of the league, nobody ever saw this coming. But this is Burnley, we thought, we've no money, a tiny squad, small crowds, and in a league where the QPRs and Leicesters and Wigans should stroll to the top places. At Burnley it can't possibly last, we declared.

October

WAXING LYRICAL:
Burnley 2 Reading 1

THREE days of rain on our return from Kalkan. And not just any old rain, this was buckets and torrents of the stuff. A few things lightened the gloom however; top spot in the division (I kept looking at it and blinking), Ings selected for England under-21, and Sean Dyche named Manager of the Month for September; *Downton* is back, and a delightful letter from someone who had just finished the Adamson book. Getting letters like this is one of the pleasures of writing:

I have just finished reading your recent book about Jimmy Adamson which I collected from Turf Moor on the day of its launch along with a nice glass of wine and the pleasure of a chat to Mr Jim Thomson – a grand bloke. I have found the book absolutely fascinating.

Jimmy was my all-time favourite player. I always felt some affinity with Jimmy's career as my first ever visit to Turf Moor coincided with Jimmy's home debut on 24 February 1951 against Spurs who went on to win the championship of the old First Division. Result: Burnley won 2-0. Jacky Chew scored them both and Alf Ramsey played for Spurs that day. I was only just gone 14 then and had pestered my father for weeks to take me to Turf Moor. I seem to remember changing buses twice and a pie dinner at Burnley market.

I have enquired many times about Jimmy since I became a senior citizen and season ticket holder but no one seemed to know much about him anymore. So, it was a thrill to see him one last time at the opening of the Adamson Suite. I confess to a tear or two on that day.

My friends and I came to Turf Moor as often as we could (when we were not playing ourselves) including the famous replay against Bradford City when the ground was full to bursting, with allegedly, a few thousand getting in without paying.

Sometimes nowadays, during a dull period of play I see Jimmy in my mind's eye breaking up an attack with a clean tackle, and moving forward to give another immaculate pass (does anyone know how to make a clean tackle and stay on their feet anymore?).

To some extent I understand Jimmy falling out of love with the game he graced for so long. I too am sick of the cheating, diving, rolling around as if pole-axed; then running round like headless chickens if they manage a tap-in; a game that has made millionaires out of some very ordinary players. We saw the best of it when the game was played with two wingers and the ball was moved forwards, when the likes of Billy Elliott and Jimmy Scoular could flourish. Those two would last about five minutes with today's referees. But they were wonderful footballers too. I could go on – perhaps it's just old age.

Anyway many thanks for a superb book which has been a joy to read, filling in all the gaps for me. It was a delight.

Yours sincerely, Raymond Geldard

Jimmy Scoular: 'what a player' my Uncle George always used to say many years ago when I was only a nipper. George was a Geordie and saw Scoular play for Newcastle many times. Prior to that he had played for Portsmouth and Jimmy Mac still tells the story that when they first played against each other and Jimmy was just making his way in the game, Scoular crunched him out of the field of play with a snarling and ferocious tackle so that Jimmy ended up near the perimeter wall in a crumpled heap.

'Take that you little Fenian bastard,' snarled Scoular, standing over the stricken Jimmy.

'But I'm a Protestant,' replied a quivering Jimmy.

As soon as he heard this Scoular was mortified and, helping Jimmy to his feet, and putting his arm round his shoulder, assured him that he was terribly sorry for his mistake, and would never ever tackle him like that again.

'A footballing volcano,' wrote Ivan Ponting in Scoular's obituary. 'He tackled like a runaway coal wagon, and was prone to explosive eruptions of fury. It was said of him that he played as if he hated everyone on the field, demolishing opponents, bawling out team-mates and confronting referees.'

Enormously muscular, Scoular had legs and thighs the size of tree trunks. Such things seem to have been bred out of the modern footballer, now built for speed and athleticism. Andre Bikey was the nearest I've seen in physique to the legendary Jimmy Scoular, especially that snarling moment when he ripped his shirt off. When he played for Portsmouth, Newcastle fans labelled him a 'dirty bastard'. When he moved to Newcastle, they described him as 'robust but fair'. Such is the football fan.

The night before Reading we caught up on the two new *Downton* episodes. We love it. Lord Crawley was as gormless as ever, Lady Mary in episode one took the word miserable to new heights, and Lady Cora's face, as she lay in bed, when she discovered her maid, the devious O'Brien, had walked out without giving any notice, was worth the entrance money alone when she suddenly realised she would have to dress herself that morning. Mrs T has a similar expression she displays when I say I won't be able to bring her the first cup of tea in bed.

It's hard to imagine that people really did live like this (and worse) in the upper echelons, so out of touch with real life. Apparently the Cleggs and Camerons still do, with no idea of the price of a loaf even. With programmes like this, *Strictly Come Dancing* and *Homeland*, plus Dave Wynne's blog on Facebook, the winter becomes bearable.

Saturday: star date 5/10/2013: the rain gone temporarily, season tickets dusted off, the piggy bank raided for ticket money for West Ham and Millwall, Kalkan already a fading memory, Mrs T looking longingly at Viking River Cruises, me looking nervously at prices; and Reading next game.

A bad omen when we had to turn back to Leeds after a few miles because both of us had forgotten our phones; the curse of modern life is that you think they're essential. A bad omen when I heard we hadn't beaten Reading since the 2009 play-offs. And as the old saying goes there's many a muck-up between a mickle and a muckle.

The game tentative in the early stages, a bit of probing and fending like two wary fencers; each side neat and tidy, spruce and clean-looking in immaculate kits on a billiard-table playing surface; all of us on pins wondering would this be the end of the fine run that had taken us to the top. Top spot brings its own pressures. Could they handle it? Could they rise again to the occasion? Were they overachieving? Were we expecting too much? Would the bubble burst after so many fine wins?

Slowly but assuredly Burnley imposed themselves. The tempo picked up, the attacks increased; the slow waltz became a quickstep. Possession the key, passing the ball around from the back and then the penetrating ball forward, or played out wide. One-touch passing movements, little triangles, close control and then a superb Trippier diagonal ball that eluded the defenders and there was Ings to strike it home. Belief grew in crowd and team. And this is a team, a proper team, with balance, work-rate, passion, commitment, energy, creativity, with a strong midfield, and the two centre-backs at the top of their game.

Duff, like a fine wine that matures and improves with age, produced the tackle of the season in the first half, the full-backs defended with zeal and bite, Trippier getting forward when he could, Marney and Jones complementing each other perfectly. And the forwards: Kightly balletic and pacey; Ings, he of the twinkle-toes and quick feet, a Will o' the Wisp, now you see him, now you don't; Vokes another imperious performance playing out of his skin, and Arfield the willing workhorse, the fetcher and carrier, quick to get back, quick to break forward.

And then Tom Heaton: what a signing. All the way home on talkSPORT, Stan Collymore was banging on and on about Joe Hart and his current form and is there any competition? Well yes there is and he's between the sticks at Turf Moor but he won't be looked at because we're not fashionable. This guy has that priceless quality, presence. Just a few keepers have it, most don't.

The latter can still have great games every now and then; but the ones that possess it are worth a goal start and can be the difference between winning and drawing, or drawing and losing. His tip over the bar was the only save that was spectacular; the others, always in the right place at the right time to make them look easy, a sure sign of a good keeper.

The first half drew to its close, hands stinging from the number of times we'd applauded a move, voices raw from the incessant cheers and yells of appreciation. It could have been 3-0 had Ings not snatched at a golden chance that he dragged wide. And an Arfield header went across the goal with the keeper beaten, but went just wide.

Reading could have had no grumbles if by the 70th minute they'd been four or five goals down. Only their goalkeeper kept the score down, with some stunning saves, to something that left us all a bit nervous until Vokes scored. We're at the stage now where we assume that both Ings and Vokes will score each game.

Burnley took their foot off the pedal a wee bit and Reading increased their possession stats and a bizarre goal gave them hope. A bullet header from their big Russian guy back across the goal ricocheted in off Shackell's knee and he could do little about it.

There were still several minutes left in a game that could have been dead and buried, so that it became tense and uncertain until Burnley took control in the final minutes and played out the game with the crowd willing the ref to blow the whistle until at last he did.

The players elated, the crowd singing and cheering, win number six against a fancied side that was in the Prem last season; Dyche jubilant after the game, extolling the virtues of his 'group', the new buzz word.

'I am thrilled,' he said. 'I am waxing lyrical for the first time,' he added; saying that this was one of the best performances since he has been at the club. And why shouldn't he feel proud? Last season there were indeed some dull games, but it was not his team and in it were sub-standard players that he probably knew had to be shifted out, plus one who thought he was far better than he really was and even had the gall to ask for a pay rise.

Today, this was HIS team made up of shrewd acquisitions of real quality, Heaton, Jones, Arfield and Kightly, all of whom have bedded in with the remaining players as if they've been at Turf Moor for years.

I'd love to have been there at Dyche's team talk during the week when he spoke about expectations and the great athlete Ed Moses who remained unbeaten in 122 races over ten years. What did Moses think each race? What was his mental mindset? What did he think after 50 races, 70 then 90? It made me think of Al Pacino and the *Any Given Sunday* 'inches' speech. I'll guess that Dyche with that voice of his that sounds like sandpaper rasping on a nail file does a pretty good team talk.

We too drove home waxing lyrical. The bubble is still inflated and there is already a sizeable gap between top and seventh place. Of course there is a long way to go, the season is only a quarter over; optimism is dosed with realism. Cover for key positions is scant. The question was asked all the way down the stairs as we made our way out, 'Can they keep this up?'

Barely a minute on *The Football League Show* summed up national interest.

We had the two-week break to enjoy the astonishing sight of a worthy Burnley at the top of the Championship. And this was a long way removed from the struggles we all envisaged at the start of the season.

It came as no surprise to Sean Dyche, however, that Burnley were top after the run of six straight wins.

'Did I expect us to be top of the league? Why not, who's to say it can't be Burnley? And it is Burnley,' he said. 'Did I expect us to be top of the league? I'd be a liar if I said I did expect us to be top of the league. But, there's always a belief system in me that says anything's achievable.

'It's how hard you're going to work at it, how hard you're going to plan for it, and see if it can get there. There are no guarantees within that. You're in a business where you have to believe. You don't get to be a footballer without believing in yourself. I think your own expectation is that you want to go as far as you can in your career.

'Now as a team you try to bond that together with your beliefs and get them to believe further. I like what we're doing at the moment. I'm enjoying it but I know there's a lot more to change and work on. It's nice for the all-round situation. It's good for the fans, good for the players, good for the club, and all coming off the back of what I thought was a terrific performance against Reading.

'All of a sudden, you have got an interest in Burnley, cameras are here and I've just got Manager of the Month. All of these things go into the melting pot, being top of the league.

'And next we need to keep that clarity and focus on the game, and go and deliver another fantastic performance.'

ALL NOSES IN THE SAME DIRECTION:
Ipswich Town 0 Burnley 1
Burnley 2 QPR 0

MRS T and me have always fancied the trip to Ipswich on the supporters' coach. The long journey in comfort, the camaraderie, the banter and a place we've never been to all made it tempting. But I belonged to the group that looked at ticket prices before deciding. And Ipswich ticket prices were £23 for the over-60s – no thanks; £26 if you paid on the day if I understood it right. Contrast that with Millwall at £14.

Little Joe had been asking could he come to another game so I got him a ticket for QPR. The Burnley virus was now well and truly embedded in him. Mind you he might just be a bit puzzled if I buy him one of the new BFC beach towels. They're black and gold – Wolves colours. I just wondered, was this the beginning of a move to make Burnley's away colours next season black and gold?

Burnley progress under Dyche has so far been phenomenal. Is it only 12 months ago that Eddie Howe upped sticks? The reasons for his departure were genuine enough and no one could possibly regard him in the same light as Owen Coyle. Howe left after Burnley had gathered 11 points from ten games. Twelve months on before the Ipswich game there were 26 points from 11.

With such a poor run of form at the end of 2012/13 we could all have been forgiven for thinking that the current season would be a long, hard slog. Only in the penultimate game was Championship football preserved.

Top spot in mid-October amazed us all. Dyche attributed it to a number of things; having the squad for his own brand of pre-season training, the expansion of sports science, re-aligning the scouting structure, improved fitness, the introduction of his own philosophy and the acceptance of his ideas. And on top of all that, every signing he had made had been a success and was a first-team member. Howe brought in some damned good players, but so many of his others were at best peripheral, and at worst a waste of money, and ended up being the ones Dyche shifted out.

Saturday at last, Burnley hadn't won at Portman Road for over 40 years. The Beatles and *Abbey Road* topped the charts. Harold Wilson was Prime Minister. Martin Dobson recalled the occasion and remembered that the 1-0 scoreline could have been far more. When you go so long without a win at an away ground you think that this time the run is sure to be broken simply because of the law of averages. Such runs cannot go on forever.

It was an afternoon when you do a few odd jobs to pass away the time while the game progresses at the other end of the country. By all accounts this was a dull and dismal encounter according to Dickie Davies on Sky.

A few garden tidying jobs, a bit of hoovering upstairs, a couple of forms to fill in and then as I'm trimming my moustache Mrs T lets out a yell. The scissors missed my nose by a whisker. Eighty minutes and Burnley scored with a deft Arfield header from some distance, provided by a Trippier cross, just minutes after Charlie Austin had scored for QPR at Millwall to put them in the lead. It might not have been goal of the season but Sean Dyche surely provided one of the quotes of the season when he was talking about the one-club mentality, 'All noses are pointing in the same direction.'

At last: the spell broken with a 1-0 win. More than 600 travelling fans were there to see it on a damp and drizzly day; the first win there since January 1970. By all accounts this was not a vintage performance but it took them two points clear at the top. Millwall equalised against QPR and even sweeter – Blackburn lost at home. Shackell was again reported to be outstanding and with such good defensive cover Heaton 'had virtually nowt to do again', said one eyewitness.

Message board comments were of the disbelieving kind, 'Would have been happy with a draw'; 'still pinching myself that this is happening'; 'but it's not down to luck because this is an honest-to-God good side'; 'unbelievable'; 'yet another week gone by with me saying to myself, surely this can't get any better and then it does'; 'I can't stop looking at the table.'

The tweets twittered away on Twitter: 'Astonishing stuff from Dyche's army'; 'Running out of superlatives for Dyche and the team'; 'Best start to a season since 1897'; 'Smashing records all over the place'; 'Loving being a Burnley supporter at the moment.'

By some weird and wonderful coincidence, the skies above Burnley in the evening were just about the most stunning ever seen; all manner of colours from burnt orange to gold to sepia to red and yellow. It was almost mystical especially when the most spectacular gigantic rainbow appeared over Turf Moor. Were the football Gods telling us something?

Afterwards, the debate that took place was; is this a better team than that of 2008/09, the team that won promotion at Wembley? Both are 'teams' in the full sense of the word where each player complemented the other, and when the pieces of the jigsaw fit together.

The general consensus was that the current team has a far better workrate, every player working their socks off for 90 minutes, a greater tenacity but far less individual flair. Coyle's side had Eagles, Blake and Elliott, players who could turn a game in an instant. Questions were asked: about the better partnership, Caldwell and Carlisle or Duff and Shackell? What would be the better strike partnership, Paterson and Thompson or Vokes and Ings? What is the better midfield, Alexander and McCann or Marney and Jones, the better goalkeeper Heaton or Jenson?

Solidarity, work-rate, parsimonious defending and unity are perhaps where the current side is better. With Caldwell's team you always felt that defensively you were never safe until you'd scored at least two goals. With the current group you feel that few sides will score more than once. Clarke Carlisle said in an interview that he thought the start to the season had been brilliant, that Dyche's side was way ahead in terms of professionalism and technical skills.

In honour of Harry Redknapp's visit with QPR I dug out my battered copy of Tom Bowyer's book *Broken Dreams*, his study of 'the corruption and greed' in football. In chapter nine he covered Redknapp, particularly at West Ham and with particular regard to the sale of Rio Ferdinand to Leeds United. Redknapp was emphatic that he never deserved the soubriquet 'Readies Redknapp'. There is no question that Redknapp is one of the great characters of the game and Bowyer writes about him with what almost seems to be a degree of wry affection. He describes him as 'raucous'; 'pugnacious'; 'the former barrow boy and aspiring second-hand car dealer'; 'a living symbol'; 'portraying all the traditions of English football'; 'football and money were Harry Redknapp's preoccupations during his seven years' management at West Ham'.

'At the end of the day no-one gives a monkey's about you once your career is over so in my view you should make the bucks while you can,' is a Redknapp quote. 'If there's a chance to earn a few quid, take it because it doesn't last forever,' is another.

Haggling over the price of a player was, in 'Arry the 'Ammer's opinion, the epitome of astute business. Bowyer only touches on Redknapp at Portsmouth. I love the cover of *Harry's Games: Inside the Mind of Harry Redknapp*, where he is pictured in the style of a hitman from *The Sopranos*. Truth is Redknapp has almost assumed the hallowed mantle of a 'national treasure' these days.

The promotion of the forthcoming game had been relentless. Sean Dyche and Tom Heaton were ringing absentee fans. 'I like the look of Burnley, I must be honest,' said Harry. 'Life has been blown back into Turf Moor and the town,' said Dyche.

'It's gonna be one of those days,' I grizzled while driving over to Burnley. Traffic queues, lights, hold-ups in Hebden Bridge and Todmorden made it a journey of not far short of two hours to do just 40 miles. On top of that I had a rotten nagging toothache and was unable to get a dental appointment for another week. You could forgive me for thinking that the gloom would continue at Turf Moor with QPR upsetting the run of wonder-wins.

Oh me of little faith: when will I stop being a glass-half-empty bloke? This was another brilliant victory by the homespun little guys against the swaggering city slicker money-bags with a team filled with 'names' and ex-Premier players. It was Bank of Dave versus Bank of England.

This was a classic game, in front of 16,000+ people, with everything you needed to make it one for the scrapbook. There was a first half of cat-and-mouse stuff but Burnley were making more of the effort to win. Burnley got into their stride of pressing, passing, raiding, holding, containing, retaining, thrusting, and at the back solid and other than one occasion as good as impenetrable.

QPR were staid, unimaginative, unambitious and rarely threatening. Every time I see him I think Tom Heaton is worth a goal start. He fills the goal, he commands the players and plucks balls out of the air for fun. In front of him he has a rock solid defence and in midfield and up front the players quick enough to turn defence into attack in a flash.

But no goals and the longer the game went on the more you wondered if this would be a frustrating 0-0 draw. Not so: a move of bewildering precision, of lightning pace, of simple first-touch passing, a goal of beauty created by quick-thinking players that cut open the QPR defence like a surgeon's scalpel. This was Barcelona, Real Madrid, Arsenal quality; yes, it was that good. Before you could blink there was Ings like a blur clean through to score from six yards. Of his newest goal celebration the less said the better.

The villain as ever was Joey Barton; booked already, he was then penalised for handball. Now I might be wrong but I thought handball was an automatic yellow. The card stayed in the ref's pocket. The crowd howled for the red. In the second half Barton was hit on the head by a bottle thrown by an idiot from the crowd. Lee Hoos called this section of crowd 'numpties' in an earlier interview for damage caused to plastic seats. But Barton's head was made of stronger stuff, nobody knows exactly what, and this time there was no damage at all from the full bottle of Coca-Cola.

Villain number two was mascot Bertie Bee, sent off for offering the linesman a pair of glasses. Specsavers will be desperate to buy the photo. The newspapers couldn't decide which was the funnier, Optometrist Bertie, or Barton being hit by the bottle.

After the first goal QPR came into the game strongly; Burnley seemed to be caving under the rising pressure. There were some close moments including one open-goal miss that would have levelled things. Barton, villain-in-chief and seemingly PA to the referee, was then involved in Burnley's second and nerve-calming goal. It was bad-guy Barton who ended the tension when it was Ings again who secured the points. Barton chopped him down and Ings himself converted the penalty with consummate ease. Again, no yellow card for Barton; but credit to the guy, he later tweeted that Burnley were deserved winners and nary a mention of the lump on his head.

There were no villains in the Burnley team. Treacy was in for Arfield and did supremely well. A ball across the face of the goal in the second half was the pass of the game. Ings slid in but was a centimetre short. If you scored them out of ten how could you give anyone less than a nine? And Charlie Austin: anonymous, never in the game, 'Shackelled' you might say, can't even recall him having a shot.

'Arry 'Arry what's the score?' sang the crowd, lapping up the occasion.

Little Joe was with us for his second game. I reckon he's learning about football quickly. In between chocolate buttons his little voice piped up when the referee gave a free kick when two QPR players tripped up over each other and a Burnley player got the blame.

'That referee doesn't know what he's doing Pop Pop does he?'

This was a referee who gave out more cards than a postman at Christmas. Joe, only six, is gonna be OK as a pundit and he came away well pleased that his favourite Treacy had played. But as for the rest of us, wondering if this was really happening, all we could think was, 'Pinch us we're dreaming.'

When Lee Hoos took over as chief executive officer it's reasonable to suppose that he imagined his job would be to oversee the finances of a struggling club and keep them in the black while it endeavoured to survive in the Championship. Thoughts of being top of the division were probably far from his head. He was interviewed by Jamie Smith for the No Nay Never website (www.nonaynever.net), a piece I have been kindly given permission to reproduce here:

Hoos's entrance into football was perhaps a little more unusual than most, being brought into Fulham after a spell working for Mohamed Al Fayed.

'Obviously I'm not from around here. I'm from a little further west. I got a law degree. I was working for UPS, being groomed for a job in either legal or public affairs,' Hoos told us. 'I thought I wanted to be an environmental lawyer but then I worked on the 1992 Clean Air Act and thought this is the most boring thing I could possibly imagine. So I did that and after a while just said to myself, look I'm happy to go up to Baltimore and work in Maryland working in human resources.

'HR is great because it combines both the legal part with the people part. I was working there at UPS, being groomed for a job in public affairs and I got a call out of nowhere from a head-hunter who said that Mohamed Al Fayed was looking to recruit and he came across my name. I've never figured that out. He likes to fire a few people, so maybe he thought having an American lawyer was best.'

After 18 months working for Al Fayed, Hoos got the chance to move to Fulham, where he helped set up the club for the Premier League by building the off-the-field infrastructure.

'It was actually Kevin Keegan that brought me across to Fulham. Kevin said that the biggest problem with Newcastle when they got promoted to the Premier League was that they were so far behind. They were in the Premier League on a Second Division infrastructure. So my job, I had the greatest job in the world, was because I had the legal background and the HR background.

'They said to me, we want you to set up the infrastructure of the club so that it's one step ahead of the football. At the time I joined them they would have been in what is now League 1, so I set up a Championship infrastructure. Then when they got promoted I was already working on a Premier League infrastructure. So I was always trying to be one step ahead of the game. That's nice when you have the money to be able to do that.'

Hoos explained that his time at Fulham taught him the need to look at everything, noting how he took inspiration from clubs all the way up the football pyramid, citing the sports science work by Arsene Wenger at Arsenal as helping to move football forward. 'Since then, it's become the norm. That was my job: set up the infrastructure at Fulham, learn how a football club works, both on and off the pitch, which I think put me in good stead for other jobs I've had.'

After an eight-year spell at Fulham, Hoos moved to Southampton where he spent two years as the club's ownership changed hands. When Rupert Lowe returned as owner in 2008, Hoos then took the job at Leicester City working for Milan Mandaric, where he helped to sell the club to the Thai consortium that still owns the Foxes. Hoos parted ways with Leicester after three years and spent the summer on holiday back in the States before hearing of the vacancy at Turf Moor.

'I came back here in the autumn, thought I'd better look for a job and somebody called me and told me about this job. And I knew Barry Kilby. Barry is sound as a pound and I've got a lot of respect for Barry,' Hoos said, revealing that the former chairman is looking really well as he continues his recovery from cancer.

Hoos explained he took the job as he wanted to work with a more 'structured' board in place, adding that he enjoyed working with Eddie Howe who was then manager at Turf Moor. However, the chief executive noted how the Clarets' form on the pitch soon headed south when Howe's mother fell ill resulting in a difficult period for the manager and the club.

'The fans just see what's on the pitch. They sometimes forget that we talk about the club. The club is all of us together, 300 people. Every human being has strengths and weaknesses when things aren't going right in their life. It can affect your job. The same thing happens in football. We like to think they're superhuman beings and the human side doesn't affect them, but it does, it has a big effect.'

Hoos then gave an insight into the process when a new manager is appointed, revealing he keeps a constantly updated file just in case one is required, just as when Howe left Turf Moor to re-join Bournemouth a year ago. Sean Dyche was described by Hoos as being the perfect fit for Turf Moor after a season in charge of Watford.

'I have a list of what I'm looking for; this is how we rate the person in regards to those particular properties, and one of the big ones was that because this is a work in progress we needed to build something. He was absolutely perfect for the job because he's got the youth academy background in terms of youth development. He had a presence and energy that he was able to bring to the job.

'Fans want a name. They like someone they recognise. They all wanted a name. I know Ian Holloway was the name that was being touted around because they know the name. But I'll bet you after Ian Holloway left Leicester, because he got Leicester relegated, when he was first appointed at Blackpool the fans weren't saying hey, great, what a great appointment. They were saying oh my God this guy got Leicester relegated what on earth is this guy doing here? Some managers can be very successful at one club, but not at another. It's just the environment. It's just the mix of the club.'

Hoos also spoke of how the fit between players and the club can also have a big impact on whether or not they turn out to be successful, citing young players like Scott Arfield who have come in at a relatively low cost but have immediately had a positive effect on the team.

'If you look at the lads this year, there's a real spirit out there, a real sense of togetherness. That helps. That picks them up. There's a lot to it. I always think the culture of an organisation is important. People talk about it like its wishy washy HR talk and a lot of times it can be. For me the culture of a football club is absolutely critical because the difference between an elite player and an average player is probably just one per cent. It's just getting that extra small margin that makes the difference between winning and losing.'

The budget at Turf Moor is obviously vastly different to some of the clubs Hoos has worked at before and he spoke of sounding like a 'broken record' at board meetings when he has to push for more finances.

'But what I said at my interview, which is in my opinion the biggest mistake clubs make, are that they try to shave margins off recruitment and sports science. For me, those are the two biggest areas you need to invest in rather than cut expenses. If you have a good, strong sports science department, you can't do anything about some injuries. But, you can do a lot of injury prevention on soft tissue – things like groin strains and hamstring pulls. I'm not saying you can eliminate them, but you can certainly deal with them.'

TOOTHACHES AND PENALTIES:
Burnley 0 West Ham 2

AT the same time as I kept these diaries, another project was on the go and the response to the *Charles Buchan Burnley Gift Book* idea was excellent. All of us of a certain generation loved that magazine.

Graham Threadgill responded from the USA. It was either 1973 or 1974 and he was at Nelson and Colne College having been shipped there from Colne Grammar as part of the shift to Comprehensive Education. He was studying biology, chemistry and maths. Maths, he says, was beyond him, so he always took a *Football Monthly* in with him to read under the desk as the lesson droned on. Alas the maths teacher spotted this one day and quietly suggested that Graham leave the class. He was happy to comply and never returned to a maths lesson. Eventually he ended up with a PhD in biochemistry from King's College, London, and has been in the USA for the last 30 years in Southern California, returning once a year and taking in a game. His success in life of course he now attributes to *Charles Buchan's Football Monthly* and the abandonment of maths.

Responses came from the most unlikely places. Kenneth Blom wrote from Sweden to say that he has followed Burnley since 1962 when he first saw a colour picture of the 1962 Burnley team in a Swedish football magazine, *Rekord Magasinet*. He fell for the club colours and learned they were England's best team. The magazine also featured the Burnley teams of 1957, 1962, 1964 and 1967. He had watched the QPR game on Swedish TV and like the rest of us was crossing his fingers for 'Mr Dyche and the others.'

Kevin Lumb remembered my mother when she was a teacher at Roomfield Junior School in Todmorden. He was in the same class as John Kettley and my mother was always saying 'ooh I used to teach him' every time she saw him on the telly. He said the thing he remembered was carrying her golf clubs out of the boot of the car into school and she talked to him about the great golfer Dai Rees. Any teacher using a pupil to carry golf clubs these days on a school day would probably be had up before a tribunal.

With huge foolishness my own collection was disposed of when we moved house back in 1999. There weren't that many but since then I've kicked myself, especially as I now buy them from eBay at the mere mention of Burnley. There was one colour picture of a crew-cutted Doug Winton that became almost the Holy Grail. I'd seen it somewhere and had to have it, one of those wonderful old black and white photos that were then hand coloured and became works of art. As a kid I'd always loved that crew cut he had but my stern, humourless, Victorian father would never let me have one. An Elvis quiff was OK, but a crew cut, never.

The images of the QPR game were slow to fade. *The Football League Show* didn't do it justice. How could it? I didn't see a Sunday paper that wasn't fulsome in its praise. But all of them featured the moment the coke bottle was thrown at Barton. On the Monday after the game it was a rare occasion when *The Daily Telegraph* condescended to report on a Burnley game. Sadly, over half of it waffled on about the bottle incident rather than eulogising the terrific win.

Yep: it was one of those memorable days; the Bee sent off (the news travelled as far as the press in the USA), a half-time wedding proposal on the big screen and the bonny lass said yes while the crowd shouted 'NO'. One of the great characters of the game was in the opposition dugout. He ducked the press afterwards; his face and jowls throughout the game a picture of helpless frustration. His expensive team from Harrods were impotent, outplayed by the boys from Poundstretcher.

And Ings's first goal; if this had been a Premier League goal, at the Emirates or Old Trafford, if it had been scored by Suarez or Rooney, it would never have been off the screens. Little Joe was down for a sleepover and asked could he see it again. Then he watched the Bertie Bee video on YouTube and was desperate to meet him. He wants an Ings picture for his wall. Thus is the Burnley bond embedded in a new young 'un.

'What a joyous afternoon,' said one message-boarder. 'I can't remember celebrating a goal like that since Robbie Blake against Manchester United.' This same well-read poster, whose father was John Jackson, a former chairman of the club, compared Ben Mee to Horatius Cocles. For a moment I scratched my head at that one until I dredged up from murky memory a poem we used to read at Tod Grammar; 'How Horatius held the Bridge' from the *Lays of Ancient Rome* by Lord Macaulay.

It was one of those heroic stories so beloved by the Victorians of how the one-eyed Horatius led a handful of Romans, including his chums Herminius and Lartius, to defend a key bridge against the invading armies of Lars Porsena, thus saving the city. Eventually even the exhausted Horatius had to jump into the Tiber to escape, given a helping hand and a prod of encouragement when a spear was thrust into his buttocks.

Both Romans and Etruscans thought he would surely drown but he had shown such bravery that all of them cheered when he emerged from the murky waters and rejoined the Romans. Ben Mee as Horatius; this was high praise indeed.

The guy who compared Duff to a fine wine was spot on. Is this player really in his middle-30s? He's lucky. He has one of those lean, wiry bodies that last longer than some of the muscle-bound, heavyweight terminators that masquerade as centre-backs; his speed little less than it was ten years ago. His tackling at key moments is crucial. His reading of the game is based on years of experience. His heading is awesome and his bravery unquestioned.

The Great Storm had abated. The *Daily Express* was stuck for a headline. True, the south was badly affected, but up north we got away lightly. A clothesline was blown down in Horsforth. A garden chair was blown over in Cleckheaton. A survey revealed that three million elderly will struggle to keep warm this winter. Downing Street advised us to wear an extra sweater if we were cold and just heat one room. The words 'f*****g imbeciles' sprang to mind.

After I got an emergency appointment, the dentist whipped out one of my wisdom teeth on the Monday before the West Ham game and solved the toothache problem that had raged over the weekend. Mrs T said losing a wisdom tooth wouldn't make too much difference; I never was too bright to start with.

Next up was West Ham in the Capital One Cup. Here was Sam Allardyce, the second of the 'big names' to grace our stadium with his presence, though I'm not sure 'grace' is exactly the right word. There was contact with him when Brian Laws departed this parish but though he spoke kindly about Burnley, he preferred to wait for a Premier job.

There were changes to the line-ups. In came several squad members to the West Ham team. Carlton Cole, not quite on the dole, but recently unemployed, was now back with the 'Ammers to resume the blowing of bubbles. West Ham fans would love the doorway in Hebden Bridge from which bubbles forever blow and float down the street in quite spectacular fashion so that you could be forgiven for thinking it's a Chinese laundrette. In fact it's a wonderful soap shop, The Yorkshire Soap Company, on Market Street where they make their own soaps. Soap boys Marcus and Warren create soaps in all shapes and designs.

The much-admired multi-coloured heavy overcoat made its first appearance of the season; the one I got years ago from Camden Market and allegedly was made from old horse blankets. It could be true. As soon as I put it on I wanted to break out into a gallop, but boy is it warm and cosy and when the bitter winds blow into the Upper James Hargreaves, strong enough to blow the ears off an elephant, it's like wearing an electric blanket. Todclaret was the first to see it and gasped at its elegance.

In front of a 14,000+ crowd, Burnley had a second-string midfield of Treacy, Stock, Edgar and Stanislas. Long came in for Duff. And despite all that, the first half was mostly Burnley playing neat, tidy stuff and outplaying a timid West Ham. The

West Ham keeper made two stunning saves and was in regular action, while Heaton at the other end might as well have brought out a book to read. And then: presumably Big Sam read his lads the riot act at half-time for out they came, a team transformed, and proceeded to dominate Burnley with a changed formation, putting huge pressure on in the box, although with few shots or end product.

Bit by bit Burnley got back into it. The 'reserve' midfield did a decent job. Edgar and Stock looked good in the first half with Stock pinging balls to all parts of the field. But for Ings, by his own high standards it was an off-night. If he was superb on Saturday, on this occasion he was well held, and had few if any chances to burst through into the box, other than one turn and stinging shot in the first half that was saved and tipped over.

With Burnley back in the game again, Trippier was unlucky with his free kick that hit the bar. Despite West Ham having upped their performance and brought on fresh players, it was still anybody's game until the last ten minutes. Funny how a bit of a thought so often becomes reality; it'll take a penalty or something daft for either side to settle this game, I'd just thought to myself and lo and behold the referee awards a controversial penalty to West Ham when a superb stretching tackle by Shackell was adjudged to have been a foul.

We looked on incredulously. Shackell was disbelieving. In an instant, the referee had handed the game on a plate to West Ham. 'We had a bit of luck,' said Allardyce. Their second penalty in the dying seconds made for an unjust scoreline. Treacy being red-carded was the icing on the cake.

We left for home wondering just how we had lost. You couldn't say any Burnley player had played badly and this was most definitely a makeshift midfield. Even so it outpassed West Ham for long spells and it was Burnley who looked the Premier outfit for the first 45 minutes. But if you don't score you don't win.

I suppose West Ham shaded it in the end and just about deserved the win. But I also suppose the way it was handed to them by a dubious decision was the painful bit. Pain from a dodgy wisdom tooth you can get fixed and it goes away. Pain from a dodgy decision that decides the course of a game is a whole lot worse.

The game marked the anniversary of Dyche's first year at Turf Moor with Burnley's lofty position making him the subject of a plethora of newspaper features. Most of them referred to the 'Ginger Mourinho' tag.

The catering department presented him with a superb claret and blue cake. A win over West Ham would have been the icing on that cake.

Chief executive officer Lee Hoos spoke again with Jamie Smith for the No Nay Never website (www.nonaynever.net) about the club and what was going on in the background, in an article part-reproduced here:

> While the board is open to investment he revealed that, 'They're not looking for any Tom, Dick, or Harry, or Ivan or Abdul who might come in and just want to put money into the club. If they find somebody, it'll have to be the right person.'
>
> He was bullish on the subject of attendances, one of the key topics of debate at the club with just 9,641 for the 3-0 win over Birmingham City. Yet 11,256 attended a top of the table clash with Reading, only 600 more fans than were in for the Charlton Athletic win. But Hoos insisted that crowds were not much lower than in previous seasons.
>
> 'The week before the Birmingham game I told the board that this would be the lowest attended game of the season because we had four home games in 14 days,' Hoos said, adding that Sky screening the Blackburn Rovers match 'killed' the attendance to only 15,699.
>
> 'There's only so far I can go devaluing the season ticket,' he said explaining why the match was a gold category game despite the television coverage. The big thing with that, if you think about Blackburn, their away attendance was a third less than it was last year because last year it was 3,500, this year it was 2,300. That's a huge difference. If it's on TV, it's like,

ah why bother; why go through all the hassle? It's a combination of TV and frankly, the way the fans treat each other. There'll be a lot of fans who say they just don't like the environment and I can't blame them.

'People say why was the Blackburn game so expensive? But, it's like, well, the way the fans treat each other – did you see the number of police that were there? I had to pay for that. Did you see the number of stewards? I had to pay for that. I spent £3,000 just repairing the seats in Block three over here. Our own fans destroying the seats in our own stadium!

'Repairs and maintenance costs after a game like that are pretty damn expensive. It's simply that. I have to pay for the stuff that people do. I have to pay for the police, I have to pay for the stewards and I have to pay for the maintenance and repairs. So next time you see some numpty ripping up a seat next to you you might think about that in terms of pointing out that it doesn't help the club going forward. Forget the rest of the stuff; just in Block three in the lower James Hargreaves Stand. Forgetting the away section; £3,000 just for one section; that's really foolish.'

Hoos was asked about the flexi-ticket scheme, 'Working well and very popular; it's something that we worked on and batted around last year. The idea was passed after talks with one of the club's supporter liaison committees. We're looking at doing something for the second half of this season because we only did it for the first half. But it's gone very well so I'd be looking at doing it for the second.'

Hoos revealed that there would have to be work carried out if the club was promoted this year but he said plans were ongoing, 'There would still have to be a bit of additional work done here to meet Premier League rules; changing rooms, press facilities, hard wiring in terms of the ability to carry TV. There would have to be quite a bit of infrastructure work. We'd have to do a real quick conversion, but first things first, one game at a time. That's all we need to do – concentrate on the game. But let's not get carried away. Of course you have it in the back of your mind but the reality is, it's one game at a time.'

He was asked about plans to redevelop the Bob Lord Stand and the Cricket Field Stand but a lack of bank lending and the ongoing economic climate seems to have put that on the back-burner for now. 'For clubs it's a tough environment out there because so many, even big clubs, like Rangers, you see them go bust so you think no-one's really safe. You just have to watch your Ps and Qs and the financial management of the club, otherwise you can get really stuck.'

However, the chief executive was unsure about whether the new financial fair-play rules would have a positive impact for Burnley. 'It depends on who you talk to. I was talking about this with another chief executive the other day who thinks it has had a negative impact, not because they have a ton of money, but because the way they're structured, their owner from a tax standpoint doesn't want to put things in equity.

'From my standpoint, I think clubs are trying to rationalise their payroll now. This summer there were a lot of players who were out of contract. They were making big noises at the beginning of the summer, but by the end of the summer, they still didn't have a club.

'Sean Dyche thinks FFP is great. It will help identify who can manage and who can't. We don't have a lot of money, but what we've got; we've done really well with. We've recruited well. We've made the relevant investments in the infrastructure for sports science. I'm really pleased with how that's turning out. I know it's tough out there for fans and I know it's a tough environment throughout the country, and we've talked about the economy.

'But the money the fans hand over, we try to stretch as far as we possibly can. It's not like the money is being paid in and we're paying out dividends to the shareholders or anything like that. It goes right on the pitch. That's where we're trying to put the money; on the pitch because ultimately if we can get promoted, that's where the payday is.'

SEAN DYCHE
ONE YEAR ON

OCTOBER 2013 and a year into his Turf Moor reign Sean Dyche was insistent that the Clarets were moving in the right direction. A victory over West Ham in the Capital One Cup on 29 October would have been a fitting end to that first year. But it was not to be, thanks to a poor, poor refereeing decision and the resultant penalty. The programme that night gave a rundown of the year that had passed by, with the article below reproduced thanks to the kind permission of Darren Bentley at Burnley Football Club:

Tomorrow (30 October) marks the first anniversary of the appointment of Sean Dyche as Burnley manager. As he reflects on a year in charge, the Clarets boss believes the foundations are firmly in place to take the club forward. Challenges still remain for a club unable to punch on an equal financial footing with the Championship heavyweights. But as the side sits proudly at the top of the table, the real strength within Turf Moor undoubtedly lies in one of Dyche's greatest challenges and achievements so far, healing a fractured club.

From day one, he has preached a 'one-club mentality' as a priceless asset to counter a growing number of cash-rich Championship rivals. He said, 'The board have come out and told some harsh truths about the club financially but I always felt that this was a value because I felt it calmed everyone down and cleared up one or two grey areas. The fans here had a thirst for information and wanted the club to come out and speak to them. It wasn't deemed as good news by some, but for others there was a reality to it and it gave us a more level playing field mentally.

'Fans immediately realised where we are and that gave us a much better chance of bringing expectations down to a real level. The squad size in terms of injuries and suspensions is a challenge here, as is the financial side of things.

'We are not a superpower financially in the Championship,' said Dyche, 'or as a club, but we're a power because of all the history of the club and what it stands for; a real town club with real people who support it. Right now I think we're back to that, I really do. I think the people of Burnley have really gripped onto the club again and there is a nice open feel about the players and the general communication between the club and its fans and all of that encapsulates into that one-club mentality.'

The journey has not been a smooth one, nor without distractions. Last season, at the business end of one of the tightest Championships in recent times, nerves were jangling among some supporters, not just here at Burnley, but for around half of the concertinaed division.

Dyche insisted, 'Let's not forget there were some question marks last season, but it was only the fifth time in 14 seasons that the club had finished in the top half of the table. I think we've made great strides overall. People forget a year goes by very quickly and it's very difficult to form a team and change from what it was, to what it is. You are often judged in football after just a week, or a month.

'But the reality is that getting things to how you think it should be takes a long time. To get a lot of the key things into a team in a year is, I think, a reasonable time scale. Among all the questions, there was a team that performed on the pitch and now we're looking to just build on that and take it further. I always say it's not a guaranteed process, it's a work in progress but we'll look to continue that good work.'

So just how has Dyche transformed the Clarets into a side so well respected and in some quarters, feared? The answer comes down to a high-performance cocktail of an ultra-dedicated backroom team, meticulous planning, a team willing to go that extra yard, and as you might expect, one of Dyche's favourite sayings; namely that maximum effort is the minimum requirement.

Dyche said, 'Ian Woan, Tony Loughlan, Billy Mercer and myself, along with Mark Howard, who has come in on the sports science side, are all different. That makes for a good process because if everyone gives the same answers, or you have yes-men, then you never get a better outcome. We all give a different opinion and we've all got different ideas, whether it's training, planning, team preparation, or on players. So we all throw them about as wisely as we can then, of course, it's up to me to make the end decision.

'It has to be that way because I'm the manager, but it's nice to have that support system of a staff that is very honest and very open with their opinions, in order to get the best outcome we can.

'I find great value in reflecting on what we hoped to put in place when we came in, and some of the good work we've done so far to put that in place. We are not the finished article but there have been some good things we felt we could improve on, especially stuff behind the scenes. Those include support systems and improved analysis, sports science and the support of the players in terms of dietary requirements, strength and condition and athletic performance.

'The change in culture and environment is there to support the team and improve it and I've been very pleased with how the players have adapted to that, both last season and this. I think there's been a good mixture of players who were already here and took ownership of that, plus the new players who automatically adapted. It's all added up to a really powerful weapon for us.

'The immediate task was always to shore up the team defensively because when I came here we were letting in 2.8 goals a game. That had to change. Then it was to find a balance between having the secure frame to stop goals going in, but still to be attack-minded, which we found spasmodic last season. Then we had the challenge of an awkward run which can happen in the Championship, not aided, it must be said, by some indifferent decisions that were out of our hands.

'But the work that was put in then, irrespective of the fact that you either win or lose, has stood us in good stead going into this season. A lot of the principles and the framework that we believed in, the players already had a feeling for, and in pre-season we really impressed upon the players what we thought was appropriate, what we planned to do, the reasons for doing it, and the information and education in doing it, in order for the team to have clarity to bring in performances. That's exactly what's happened so I've been pleased with that all the way through.'

A year on, the Clarets remain a work in progress. But that progress, in itself, is a testament to a manager that will always demand more.

Opinions are divided on where we would be had Eddie Howe remained at Burnley. Many suspected we'd have remained in mid-table, leaking goals for fun (if you score four then we'll score three), and maybe even we would have eventually headed towards the bottom three. There was never any conviction that he was the right fit at Burnley or that the side he took over from Brian Laws was capable of a top-six finish that season with a more charismatic manager. His signings ranged from the very good to the downright awful waste-of-money variety. It always seemed he was a fish out of water at Burnley.

The reasons for his departure were genuine enough; in fact it wasn't only the death of his mother, there were other personal reasons as well that will remain private. I do know that had I been in the same position, the chance to return to Bournemouth would have been impossible to refuse. He was neither a disaster at Burnley nor inspirational. The parting of the ways was beneficial to everyone.

Sean Dyche, when he came in, was in fact never really the fans' first choice. Few if any had even heard of him other than in association with Watford. The names that fans bandied about were those of Mick McCarthy and Ian Holloway. Perhaps Howe's bland anonymity left people feeling in need of a 'celebrity', someone who could excite and raise interest levels. But Dyche impressed the board and he also impressed most people at Watford, none more so than Frank Smith of the *Watford Observer*.

Smith praised Dyche at Watford and was insistent that his achievements should not be overlooked. He had guided them to their highest position and points total in the last four seasons and a top-half finish with one of the smallest budgets in the division, and all that against a background of the best players being sold.

Smith paid tribute to Dyche's calmness, respect for the supporters and the media, and the way he turned things around. Watford finished 11th with a team to be proud of. It was clear that the group had the hallmarks of a Dyche side – togetherness and a great work ethic. There were poor refereeing decisions, the restrictive budget, in-fighting behind the scenes, and the players sold were attacking players, but Dyche never once made excuses. He was honest with his views, said Smith, never tried to hide and was full of good sense. All in all, Watford were a reflection of their manager.

An article in *The Guardian* in late October was one of several that were written now that Dyche was appearing in the limelight more and more as his Burnley side won game after game.

'I believe in the players,' Dyche told Andy Hunter. 'But to say you will be top of the league at this stage is hard, not so much to imagine, but to actually do. I was absolutely sure that we had a group of players who could compete at this level. To be top and to equal the best ever start in the history of Burnley Football Club; now that's a different thing. I would be a liar if I said that I expected that because you can't expect anything in any business, let alone the football business.'

Burnley's rise, Dyche suggested, stemmed from a freedom that allowed his players' talent to flourish. It was a lesson learned not from Jose Mourinho but from two-time European Cup winning manager Brian Clough. It was under Clough that Dyche learned his first football lessons when he started as a youth at Nottingham Forest before moving on to Chesterfield without making a senior Forest appearance.

'I always remember,' said Dyche, 'how as a youngster the whole club knew the structure of how the team played. The basic requirement for each position was always crystal clear and that provides a nice clarity, so that players went on the pitch knowing exactly what was expected of them. Once they have done the basics, they have the freedom to play.

'They are encouraged to do that and it enhances what they can do as individuals. I think these players can achieve whatever they want to. It's about being open-minded. The biggest thing I have promoted to these players is having no fear, just going out and playing with an open mind. They know they're organised; they know they're fit enough and this allows them the mental clarity to go for the performances.'

Full-back Kieran Trippier added to the picture of Dyche, 'The most important thing was having the gaffer's first pre-season. The spirit this year is unbelievably high. We have no fear of any team in the league and the big difference is our fitness. We ran non-stop for 98 minutes against QPR.'

Dyche's confidence might well have been put to a severe test during a run of 16 league games at Watford in 2011/12 when there were just two wins. But he insisted, 'You have to believe that you are working in the right fashion. I think I do and so do my staff. And the players have mostly done so while I have been here. I sleep well in the evenings. Last season we had an awkward run and it's fair to say there were big question marks but I didn't lose any sleep over it. I knew what our intention was and what we were doing behind the scenes. I knew we had a group that was working hard and it was functioning. Then you build from that.'

Dyche laughs at being compared to Mourinho. He is far quicker to say he received more inspiration from Pep Guardiola, said John Edwards in the *Daily Mail*. Edwards pointed to a Dyche pre-season pep talk as being a key feature that reinvigorated the side.

'I had a chat with each of them individually,' revealed Dyche, 'and made it clear what I wanted. The demands were laid out openly. It was about mentality, fitness levels, how we were going to play as a team and how each individual was going to contribute. Sometimes in football people settle for less.

'I'm not saying that applied to this group but people can get comfortable. When you are a kid you demand things from yourself. You want to win. You want to achieve but for many different reasons some players lose that as they get older. I made it clear I wanted the players to be pushing themselves every week.

'When I started out with Watford's youth team, Barcelona were the best exponents of pressing their opponents to get the ball back. Everyone raved about their passing but I thought it was their pressing game that was unbelievable. When I took over we looked at how they did it and felt that as a group we could do the same. It starts with Sam Vokes and Danny Ings up front, goes through midfield and on to the back four. Everyone has to do his bit to deny the other team space and get the ball back.

'It is just as important that the players know the tactical structure we have put in place and the fitness levels and mentality that are required. Add a bit of talent and you have a chance of performing. Honestly, I'm not reinventing the wheel here. You need the right players as well, and these lads have been brilliant. It's a great feeling when you look into their faces in the tunnel before kick-off and know how hard they are going to go to win. I was promoted four times with four different clubs and that same level of respect and honesty was there each time. I can feel that with these players.'

Referring to Danny Ings he said, 'Danny hasn't exactly come from nowhere. He's had a few injuries prior to this season but don't forget Eddie Howe paid £1m to Bournemouth for him a couple of years ago. I was interested in signing him for Watford but I think we offered a bag of crisps.'

Dyche played a total of 460 league games for Chesterfield (231), Bristol City (18), Millwall (69), Northampton Town (56) and Watford (72) with a loan spell at Luton Town consisting of 14 appearances.

Perhaps the most famous of his matches, when he scored, was a 1997 FA Cup semi-final against Middlesbrough which Middlesbrough won despite a Chesterfield shot clearly going over the line but officials ruling that it didn't.

Dyche scored a penalty to put Chesterfield 2-0 up only for the full-time score to be 3-3 and then the replay was lost 3-0. The goal that 'wasn't' robbed him and Chesterfield of an astonishing FA Cup Final appearance at Wembley.

He won promotion at Chesterfield, Bristol City, Millwall and Northampton.

Dyche was always realistic about the Burnley situation. 'When I got here the club was in transition after coming down from the Premier League in 2010. We had to bring everyone together and settle them down. We've affected the things we could affect, and the things that we can't, we've said we can't. We are a town club, and a club that supports the town and that link has become more authentic with the realities. They're not negative realities, they're just realities.

'The reality of Charlie going was always there and was always hanging over us. There will be that reality about some of our players in the future, not at this moment, but certainly in the future. It's been there for 131 years. There have always been moments when the club has had to sell players. It gives someone a great opportunity. The next one comes in and gets a chance to grip it.'

The winning run in the league was ended at Millwall and then the next game against Bournemouth was drawn. These are the other realities that teams will raise their game against the league leaders and Bournemouth certainly did that. The worst defenders in the division came and for this game defended heroically as if it was what they did every week.

Early days: there was very little talk of the 'p' word around Turf Moor although the players and manager and staff were receiving deserved accolades for their start to the season.

'Just one step at a time,' said Dyche.

November

THE QUEST FOR PIE AND MASH:
Millwall 2 Burnley 2

THIS chapter is dedicated to John Markey. John passed away over the weekend of the Millwall game. We received the news on Saturday lunchtime, not long before we were due to set off for the game. Suddenly the match didn't seem important.

John and Pat, his wife, were regulars on away weekends and he was a supporters' club committee member. He was a lovely man and on away trips on Saturday evenings we'd always eat together. He and Pat were two people who Mrs T and I could sit down with and just pick up where we left off last time, the mark of a real friendship. Along with so many others I just felt a deep sorrow. God bless you John and thank you for your friendship.

A first: a trip to Millwall with the supporters' club for the weekend. Fortunately we weren't staying anywhere near Cold Blow Lane, the site of the old Den.

The stand that faces the away supporters still bears the name, though, a grim reminder that this is still Millwall, once a horrible place to come but now a bit smoother round the edges and not quite so intimidating. What a name though, a name to conjure up the bleakest of images, like the name Bleak House, a Burnley area.

Nothing bleak about Burnley these days though, recognised now as an enterprise zone and featured glowingly in *The Sunday Times* over the weekend as a place for a first-time buyer to get on the property ladder. And Burnley fans are pussy cats – unless Joey Barton turns up.

Millwall were first formed by workers in a jam factory. They'd be turning in their graves if they knew the EU Brussels meddlers are now issuing dictates to regulate the production and quality of our jam. Tip a jar of English jam upside down and it stays in the jar. It's the best in the world. If they get their way, all jam in future will be runny and messy. Marooned on a desert island there are ten things I'd like; ten jars of Frank Cooper thick-cut marmalade.

Simon Inglis describes the old Millwall as 'special', and adds, 'It was rough, tough, proud and prickly, warm and wild all at the same time, and also extremely difficult to find.'

Like the old Ninian Park in Cardiff, too many football supporters have poor memories of the Millwall of old, a place of rioting fans, racism, frequent abuse, and violence where visiting fans rarely felt safe.

Talk on the coach on the way down was about the way Burnley lost the Capital One Cup game, about how well they'd played with a scratch midfield. It was Adrian in the West Ham goal who kept his side in the game in that first 45 minutes when the number of shots piled up and West Ham were comprehensively outplayed.

The memory of the referee's penalty gift was still vivid enough to raise the hackles.

But it was eyebrows that were raised when it transpired that Burnley appeared to have signed 'a one-armed goalkeeper' (barrister John Whitting's words). It was revealed that Alex Cisak was about to sue his former surgeon for the damage done to his wrist, he claimed, by being allowed to return to training too soon when he was a youth player five years earlier. Cisak alleged that he could only train at 75 per cent, took painkillers, had been affected mentally, pulled out of shots and couldn't develop properly because he couldn't fully train. Other than that, he wasn't a bad keeper.

The opposing barrister countered with, 'It's difficult to see how a goalkeeper playing at an extremely high level can get rave reviews if he can only use one arm.' I must admit I found that a quite compelling argument. Within 24 hours of the BBC revealing the story, Cisak had unsurprisingly withdrawn the claim and was ordered to pay the surgeon's costs.

The road to London is well worn by Clarets buses, down the M6 and then across to Banbury. Banbury always was a coaching station. This is a place steeped in history that dates back to Saxon times and where Oliver Cromwell, never the most cheerful of blokes by all accounts, planned one of his key battles in the back room of a pub, Ye Olde Rein Deer Inn.

Banbury used to have many crosses until they were all destroyed by the Puritans, who as general miseries took their lead from the main man – Cromwell. If Cromwell was a miserable bloke, who could blame him; his face was covered in warts. The present and renowned Banbury Cross was built in 1859. Both Garry Glitter and Larry Grayson were born in Banbury. Of that, we will say little.

We always stop there for an hour or so. When departure times used to be later in the afternoon, in days gone by, the supporters' coach always stopped conveniently by another olde pub into which most folk decamped without even having to open their eyes, it was so close. Conversely, the hardened drinkers after several pints could just exit the pub door and fall back into the coach. It all worked rather well. Of late, with morning departures, it's a wander round the shops and in this respect the town centre bears a strong resemblance to most other identikit town centres.

The rain and a dreadful journey meant this time Banbury was given a miss. That was a shame. We were due to meet Banbury Dave and he was due to give me some Banbury cake, a flat, currant-filled, spicy, oval-shaped cake. Instead, he ate it.

It was raining when we set off. It was raining down the M65. It was raining down the M6. The queues of dense nose-to-tail traffic slithered along at a snail's pace. The wheels of the bus went round and round, round and round, all day long, through spray and foam and every so often ground to a halt. Five hours later it was still raining, still slithering and traffic was still stopping and starting. And we were only near Birmingham. Such is the lot of the dedicated football supporter whatever team he follows. What can you do? You just put up with it and say a silent prayer of thanks that you don't drive a coach for a living.

Three hours later we reached London, stiff, numb, and with addled brains unloaded suitcases and headed for the hotel 'pub'. My eyes lit up. There on the menu was pie, chips and gravy. Suddenly, life seemed back on track. Mrs T restored her equilibrium with a G&T. For me it is the pie, man's greatest invention, that puts the smile back on my face. Greenwich was on the Sunday itinerary and in Greenwich lies Goddard's famed pie and mash café. My lips smacked in anticipation.

On the previous London trip we'd abandoned all attempts to fathom out how to buy tickets from the bewildering array of buttons and options for the Docklands railway into town. This time Mrs T cracked it. Research shows that women are good at this sort of thing along with ironing, crosswords and following recipes.

Men are better at putting the right sort of petrol into the car, changing a lightbulb, starting the mower and turning off the central heating.

The end stop was just minutes away from Tower Bridge and the Tower of London. The 15-minute ride takes you through the sprawling mish-mash that is messy London. It always feels like a giant jigsaw puzzle and the dog-eared, shabby parts don't fit. The Tower was heaving, the weather good, huge queues lining up, English faces and voices hard to find. The Thames was chocolate brown and choppy, more queues lining up for the tripper boats. The return journey on the railway gives an eye-level view of the rooftops of tenements, apartment blocks, and old housing with ancient chimney pots of all shapes and sizes all squeezed in as if no one has given a minute's thought to planning.

And so to the game: Millwall were a much improved side after a dodgy start to the season. Some games you can nod off, daydream, wish you were somewhere else. This was not one of them. Leicester had won at lunchtime and were level on points, refusing to be shaken off. When they heard the score was Millwall 2 Burnley 0 after just half an hour they must have thought 'this is our day'.

Burnley were slow to start, lacklustre and leggy. Maybe the seven-hour coach journey the day before had stiffened them up. Maybe it was going to be just one of those days. All good things must come to an end and a defeat looked inevitable when centre-half Shittu scored to make it 2-0 after his shot looped off a Burnley player's foot.

Shittu is a most unlikely-looking footballer; a frame the size and width of a barn door with two speeds – slow and very slow. This looked a day when Ings, he of the nimble feet and quick acceleration, might have had a field day, turning the big defender inside out, but it was not so. The statuesque Shittu somehow got his plodding, massive bulk in front of most shots and headers. If a leg was stuck out and diverted a shot, it was Shittu's. It was, in fact, a Shittu afternoon. Ings left him for dead just once but other than that Shittu was forever in the way. And he had the gall to score. His mates mobbed him. Presumably a Shittu shot that goes in is a rarity.

We groaned. A heavy defeat looked the likeliest outcome. Edgar did nothing wrong but is no substitute for the box-to-box Marney. Millwall fans were over the moon but that was just for one minute when the wind was taken out of their sails by a Burnley goal within a minute of Shittu scoring. Vokes leapt high and in it went; Shittu nowhere in sight, probably having a lie down somewhere after his visit to the far end. Millwall silenced. Burnley fans revived and back in full voice.

From that point on Burnley came to life. We roared and exhorted them. Play became slick. The passing game returned. But Shittu was there all too often, broad of arse, barrel-chested, ambling around at his mono-pace but always in the way. After a game Millwall probably put him on the sofa for a week till the next game comes round. And then the breakthrough; a Kightly run at pace into the box, shot unleashed, maybe going just wide but in off a sliding defender, fortunately not the bus-like Shittu. Jubilation at the Burnley end; this was some fightback.

A superb move ended with Arfield smacking the ball against the post with a thunderous shot. From our faraway end it looked like it was going to cannon in off the other post, but it came back out. Vokes chased for the rebound and was most definitely clipped and down he went. From our end it was unclear but TV showed it to be a clear penalty. Not content with waving play on, the referee booked a protesting Vokes.

At 2-2 and dominating the game, this could so easily have become a win, the Millwall defenders afterwards saying it was just wave after wave coming at them. Millwall is a tough place to come and at the start of the day a draw might have been gratefully accepted. But this is a new Burnley now, resilient, full of fight, committed, determined to the last minute – the 11 musketeers. Still top then by just the one point, Leicester fans must have groaned. Just over 1,000 delighted Burnley fans exited the stadium, although not before having to remain penned in for something like 20 minutes. Such is the lot of the dedicated football supporter.

If I had to live in London I think I'd settle for Greenwich. They've done the Cutty Sark proud, the masts and rigging rising high above the rooftops of what is essentially a bit of Olde London. The views of London across the Thames from the Observatory are magnificent. We headed there on Sunday morning on a day of sunshine and yes there was Goddard's. I looked inside longingly. Truth be told it was too early to tuck in even for me, a confirmed pieromaniac.

And anyway had I broached the idea I'd have got short shrift from my personal dietician and health guru – Mrs T. The last visit we had here was on a cold dank December day when hundreds of folk dressed up in Santa outfits were running up and down the hill to the Observatory. It was a memorable image. This time it was warm and sunny enough to enjoy the male voice choir that sang sea shanties outside the Cutty Sark.

The journey home took us on a mini tour of London, along the Thames, and passed the Houses of Parliament. Half of our esteemed politicians claimed a refund on their gas and electric bills said the morning's *Sunday Mirror*, while us ordinary folk try to make ends meet. One of them claimed nearly £6,000. The words bag and scum sprang to mind.

The papers we bought praised the Burnley fightback. Sean Dyche was pragmatic and realistic. Yes some teams will make it hard. Teams will always raise their game against the league leaders. No way can Burnley win every game. This was a damned good point. At that moment we were flavour of the month.

The esteemed *Daily Telegraph* again featured Burnley as their main report with Ian Ridley full of praise for the whole Burnley set-up. Contrast that with the huge losses posted at Blackburn Rovers. You couldn't help wonder if they would be the next Portsmouth. Who cares, the Burnley fairy story continued.

Dedicated to the memory of John Markey.

PONDERING ON THE NATURE OF THINGS:
Burnley 1 Bournemouth 1

THE club celebrated the return of Eddie Howe by making this a silver category game and Bournemouth laid on ten free coaches for supporters. Was it this special? His stay at Burnley was in no way a disaster but neither was it inspirational. He signed several good players but Sean Dyche was taking them to a whole new level. If Howe had managerial qualities that didn't work at Burnley, they have been more than impressive at Bournemouth where no one can take away the promotion last season when he clearly was inspirational. Horses for courses I guess.

It's reasonable to suppose that neither Howe nor his assistant Jason Tindall were ever happy or comfortable at Burnley. Opinions are divided regarding his time at Turf Moor. For me there are just a couple of questions: if he had stayed would we have been top of the division for this game? Or would we still be letting in goals for fun? Maybe there's a third: does Jason Tindall ever take his hands out of his pockets? I often used to wonder were they superglued in there.

While I'm pondering on the nature of things; why does Halloween get bigger and bigger every year and Bonfire Night dwindle? I can't abide Halloween and all that it has become but I bemoan the passing of bonfires on street corners and penny bangers and jumping jacks. If your garden was big enough you had a bonfire of your own. We'd go round chumping (collecting wood for the bonfire) all over the place; make a Guy and sit him on the top. Our mums would make parkin and toffee and the whole street came out.

In the days leading up to it we'd make the Guy and sit him in a pram and push him round the streets and shout 'penny for the Guy'. That was the money we spent on fireworks. Few of them cost more than tuppence. Now you need a mortgage to buy a selection box.

I went into Sainsbury's to buy some for little Joe and she said, 'That box is £35 sir.' They never call me 'sir' in Wilkinson or Netto. I nearly fell over and needless to say didn't buy it. For that price I can buy a gold ticket at the Turf and still have change.

At school we'd learn what the Gunpowder Plot was all about and it was a history story that always had me hooked. I always used to make a balsa wood aeroplane and fasten a rocket to each wing. When I lit them it usually flew round in circles on the floor or up my granny's leg. She'd get hopping mad, and I'd get a clip round the ear. Yes sirree… those were the days except that some idiot on the Longside would usually lob bangers down into the crowd in front; no stewards or ground safety officer around in those days folks.

With this being the home game nearest to Remembrance Day there were impeccably-respected tributes before the game. My grandfather somehow got through four years of the First World War. He was part of a three-man mortar team. It was something he could never talk about without his eyes filling up with tears at the memory of the things he'd seen. The only thing he ever said was that the parcels sent every month by my grandmother filled with foodstuffs, chocolate and pairs of dry socks kept him going.

My father was in the RAF in Africa for just the last two years of the Second World War. According to him it was the hot desert sun that burned off all his hair. There are fewer now of these guys who fought in the Second World War around to tell the tale. There are none left now from the first. The war started in 1914, the year Burnley won the FA Cup with a Bert Freeman goal – the last carefree summer until the war kicked off at the end of July.

With Blackburn Rovers in such dire straits (a club where prudence is the name of the cat), there were fundraising suggestions on the websites. One poster suggested a 'Chicken in Need Day', or a 'Parson's Nose Day' or 'Chicken Relief'. The general reaction to the huge losses that were posted was one of pleasurable gloating. Burnley had losses to post too, but nothing on this scale. Another poster was rather more analytical in his appraisal:

> An excess of 130 per cent wages to turnover ratio; on crowds of around 11,000. They won't even be able to service the debt at that rate. Even if they got promoted, £30m would be sucked up in fines straightaway. They'd still have massive wages to pay and the losses would still creep up and up and they'd be straight back down again. Come January 2015 at the very latest a transfer embargo awaits (it could start as early as this summer) under FFP rules. Rumours abound that they have defaulted on payments for Rhodes, so a transfer embargo awaits anyway. Given the size of their predicament they won't get the much touted £10m for him, more like £6.5m or so, so no gain there.
>
> Whichever way you look at it I reckon they're f****d flatter than steamrollered dogsh**. Their best option would seem to be to opt for administration, take the ten-point hit and hope to avoid relegation. That would see the back of the Venky's (and can I say a great big THANKS to the comedy chicken farmers). There isn't another sugar daddy out there; so it would probably mean reverting to a supporter-owned model, and a swift decline into League 2 or even lower. I just hope we kick their arses before this happens.

Back on planet Earth (Blackburn haven't lived there for years), Ings was Championship Player of the Month and Sean Dyche was again Manager of the Month. Add to that the call-up for Jay Rodriguez to the England squad, Ings getting his second call-up to the under-21 squad, and Burnley fans were truly proud.

Dyche was now the first Burnley manager to win consecutive monthly awards. Harry Potts won it twice and Brian Miller won it twice. There was unanimous agreement that to win it in consecutive months at a club where there were clear financial constraints, the 'star' player was sold before the season began, and the squad was so small, was a colossal achievement.

There's a genuine affection for local-born Jay Rod. A Twitterer tweeted that she overheard two guys at Euston station talking about his selection. She said it felt like they were talking about one of her family. I guess that's the thing about Burnley. At the moment that's just what it feels like – one big family. There are times when football is so incredibly powerful.

Throughout October I guess before each game most of us kept asking, 'Would the wheels fall off?' But they didn't. Millwall looked like it was going to be a bad day, but it wasn't. And next up was Bournemouth. It had been a while since games approached where we'd felt such anticipation and felt such enjoyment seeing all these exhilarating games that have come one after the other.

In the summer Howe was on record in one newspaper piece saying that he felt he should have stayed at Bournemouth; that the move to a bigger club came too soon. That said, there were no regrets, he added. Most fans agreed that he came in to a difficult situation with an ageing team on high wages. But at the same time it could be said he came to a club that was in a good position to head for the top six even with those same players.

There were some who predicted a goalfest against a Bournemouth team that had leaked goals week in, week out. The glass-half-empty group foresaw a banana skin game, the kind of game where an away side comes and wins because that's just the way things happen when a returning manager or player arrives.

It was neither, although at one stage it looked as if it would be the kind of smash-and-grab raid that leaves you shaking your head in disbelief. Of course it had to be a game when the usually wretched Bournemouth defence looked impregnable; that it had been coached to perfection and drilled meticulously week after week. Centre-back Elliott Ward had a mammoth game. The whole back four looked like a brick wall. Burnley dominated the first half but somehow either they missed good chances, Bournemouth got bodies, heads and legs in the way, or the goalkeeper made good saves, and there was one acrobatic goal-line clearance that was worthy of an Olympic gold medal.

It was 0-0 at half-time and you wondered if this was going to be one of those days.

When Bournemouth took a 1-0 lead early in the second half with a vicious shot from the edge of the box that went in off the bar you really did think that this was going to be their day and Howe et al would return to the south coast chuckling all the way at the sheer cheek of it.

Their ten coaches had departed at 7.30am from the normally tropical south. In the morning the M6 was declared a skating rink after a downpour of hail and sleet. On Twitter the club advised that care was needed because of monsoon conditions. The away fans must have thought they were heading to Siberia. That's what it felt and looked like on the moors above Burnley as we drove over with temperatures just above freezing and the skies blacker than any of my dear departed mother's burnt sausages. Mercifully it was dry for the Remembrance Day ceremony when Chris Gibson played the Last Post like Gabriel himself.

A Bournemouth win would have been a travesty after second-half headers straight at their goalkeeper, a Treacy free kick that was miraculously palmed away, a Vokes header that looked like it would trickle in but shaved the post, two low diagonal balls across the box that were inches away from being converted, plus other shots that went high or wide.

And all that is before any mention of two penalty claims, one an absolute stonewaller when Ings was sent flying three feet up in the air by Ward well inside the box; the second when it looked like Ward again had an arm clearly round Vokes's middle as he powered through, both incidents right in front of where Mrs T and me sit. Yet another referee in need of Specsavers waved play on. Add those to all the first-half chances made and a comprehensive Burnley win would not have been an injustice. But 20 shots in total and only seven on target tells its own story.

At last a deserved Burnley goal arrived with just minutes to go when Ings headed in a ball knocked on by Vokes or Shackell; it was difficult to tell who. It was Ings who was the bravest as he beat Lee Camp from close range.

Reactions to the result were mixed. Some said Burnley looked tired. Some said several players had off-days. Some said Burnley never really got going. But others said it was a storming game and a credit to the Championship. In truth it was just one of those days when in the first half the Bournemouth goal seemed to lead a charmed life.

This was a 'could have won it, should have won it' game, exasperating and frustrating, but again a gripping game that you couldn't take your eyes off for a second. And, this was a result decided by penalties not given. A poor decision gave the cup game to West Ham. A poor decision at Millwall denied Burnley a probable win, and two poor decisions against Bournemouth denied Burnley another win. But the lead at the top was stretched to two points when Leicester surprisingly lost, leaving Burnley in pole position with a goal difference worth an extra point and two weeks to rest some weary bones.

Little Joe, when we told him the score, was disappointed but pleased with his picture of Tom Heaton. His class history topic was the 1960s. I told him about the title win of 1960, the FA Cup Final of 1962 and the World Cup win of 1966. We looked at pictures in the Jimmy Mac scrapbook. Lots of them were in colour.

'Oh,' he said, 'colour pictures. I thought everything was in black and white when you were little.'

DIRECTOR CLIVE HOLT TALKS WITH DAVE THOMAS

IF there is any man at Burnley Football Club who knows at first-hand the history of the Clarets over the last 27 years better than Clive Holt, then I'd be surprised to meet him. A thwarted footballer himself, being a director he says is the next best thing.

I went to see him a couple of days after the 2-2 draw against Millwall. Yes, he was surprised to be top of the division, but at the beginning of the season he thought there might be a top-six place.

I'd arrived to meet Clive at 11am and we spent a good two hours talking about his background and how he came to be involved with Burnley in the first place. Then the conversation turned to the current season.

'Yes, we are prepared for promotion this time having learned from last time,' said Clive when I asked. He and the board were aware of the statistic that teams that were top at this stage of the season usually went up. Yes they had tried to take Connor Wickham on loan but Sunderland wanted him somewhere he'd be getting regular games and with Ings and Vokes in such fine form how could they guarantee that?

He touched on the difficulties of setting prices at a realistic level that were affordable but at the same time high enough to pay the bills. The accounts were soon to be published and would show a considerable loss but they had already been made public in an earlier communications exercise.

Player wages were under control in as much as no player was now on more than £10k a week. But he asked whether the supporters that were critical of prices realised that because of the success of the team and the number of wins so far, the number of player bonus payments had increased dramatically and was now very high?

He had read through much of one of the topics on the Claretsmad message board. It was mostly critical of the Bournemouth game being upgraded to a silver category. Just what was the reasoning behind this, people were asking. Decisions on which games to grade as gold or silver, he explained, were made by the management team not just Lee Hoos.

'I was tempted,' he said, 'to go on the message board myself to say that it was a game that could be attended for just £20 if people bought a flexi-ticket that allows them to pick and choose six games they particularly want to see.'

This was the first of a series of meetings Clive had agreed to, spread out over the coming weeks, so that we could not only look back over his time at the club but also chat about the way things were going this season. It's clear he thinks that one reason for the good things so far is Sean Dyche's organisational skills and the boardroom working well. The financial report wouldn't be good news but things were under control.

The meeting reached its end and I asked was his role that of general fixer and trouble-shooter. He said nothing but just grinned. Next meeting, sometime before Christmas we agreed, and hopefully still top.

SEAN DYCHE, AN OBSCURE POEM AND FAMILY TREES

IN the absence of any proper football and a Saturday afternoon minus the normal nervous anticipation, I went through all the stuff that Mrs T has been finding out about my family tree. She'd set to work on mine getting as far back as 1776, folk who lived in Halifax, and a great, great, great, great grandfather, James Pickles. James might well have been a handloom weaver and if so would have made his way down to the Piece Hall where there were over 300 separate rooms built around a central courtyard; built back then so that the weavers could sell their cloth.

1776: at that time the redcoats were being given a tonking, losing 5-0 in the American War of Independence; James Cook was off to the Pacific again; the first ever St Leger was held at Doncaster. George III was King. He suffered terribly in later life and ultimately starred in a film called *The Madness of King George*. William Pitt was Prime Minister. And if you lived in Halifax then, London for the embryonic Thomases – who would no doubt have doffed their caps to the wealthy Listers, owners of Shibden Hall – was as far away as a journey to the Moon.

The old expression 'From Hell, Hull and Halifax, good Lord deliver us' tells you all you need to know about 18th-century Halifax. There was certainly no Halifax Town FC. For sport and entertainment people made their way to the Halifax Gibbet to see a good hanging. Fortunately, the Thomases were indeed eventually delivered and as far as I know none of the family was connected with the 'Halifax Slasher', although some ancient relative lived at Slicer Lane. Just imagine, being able to say to your prospective mother-in-law, 'Oh hello I'm one of the Slashers from Slicer Lane.'

So far the most exciting things had been a great, great, great somebody or other who was an engine driver for the Lancashire Yorkshire railway in the mid-1800s. I liked that. And then there was somebody else who fell in the River Calder in Todmorden and drowned and his body was found miles away still in the river in Elland. He was presumably drunk when he fell in. The Thomases in general are a pretty sober lot so this chap was obviously the one in the family we don't talk about.

We've never been a wealthy family but the nearest was my great, great grandfather. He had his own cotton manufacturing business in Todmorden with several employees. My grandfather had a bakery and confectioners and in it, actually in the shop (no health and safety in those days), resided a squawking parrot in a large cage that was famed through the town for its bad language and the coarse remarks it made to unsuspecting customers.

There was always the story that my grandfather was a bit of a dab hand at ducking and diving on the black market during the war. When I was a nipper I used to go down into my granny's cellar to see what I could find and there was the parrot's cage, all forlorn and rusting. Memories were heaped up down there; old ornaments, ships in glass bottles, possers, mangles and old tin tubs where she did the washing; she used to do the ironing with one of those ancient black irons that weighed a ton into which you put a hot brick that had been heated in the fire range.

There are a whole bunch of people buried at Blackshawhead Methodist Chapel on the moors above Hebden Bridge. There's another group in the graveyard of the old ruined chapel at Cornholme, on the way to Burnley. On a cold, dank, grey day on the way to a game we spent an hour trudging through the overgrown grass and weeds, picking our way through mud and moss-covered headstones that were leaning over, half fallen down, looking for names of old family members. We made a mental note that next time we'd make sure we did this on a warm, sunny day. We came out blue with cold.

Mrs T has dug up old names of streets and places in and around Todmorden that brought a tear to my eye. They were a part of my youth and are now just receding memories; Summit, Cornholme, Lineholme, Stackhills, Der Street, Ferney Lee Road, Mankinholes, Lumbutts, Wellfield Terrace, Adelaide Street…and Portsmouth. Polish lorry drivers still arrive in Portsmouth having arrived at the wrong one. They look for the sea and the docks and then a local will tell them, 'Na then lad, tha's come ter wrong place. T' Portsmouth thee wants is 300 miles that way.' If it's a Spanish lorry they'll add 'ole' and do a quick flamenco.

With nothing better to do I spent days trawling through old emails making a database of folk who had bought books or made enquiries. This was one from Brian Sellers from way back in 2010:

> I attended the evening with Jimmy Mac at the Turf towards the end of last year. At the end of the evening I recalled to Jimmy a story that my father told me. I asked Jimmy if he ever had a milk round and he remembered that he and Barbara did have one for a couple of years.
>
> One day during his delivery round, he came down the back street of my parents' house on his milk float. My dad spotted Jimmy and said he couldn't believe that here he was in the same back street as his football idol. People of a working background like my father just did not meet their football heroes. They just admired them from the terraces. Yet here he was on the same back street.
>
> I am not sure if any words were exchanged; I suspect my father would have been completely dumbstruck by the occasion. He did say though, that had the float been pulled by a horse and the horse had lifted its tail, he would have scooped up the result and had it framed. When I told this story to Jimmy it brought a smile to his face.

Re-reading it brought a smile to my face too. Jimmy Mac with a milk round – astonishing. Footballers back in the 1950s did all kinds of things to supplement their wage. A bit of painting and decorating on the side was a popular one. One Burnley player continued with his steeplejack job. It is hard to imagine Danny Ings turning up at your house with a paint brush and tin of white gloss, or Sam Vokes rattling the bottles at 5am and delivering two pints of red-top and a carton of cream.

Some while ago I bought a book about Millwall and their promotion under Kenny Jackett. Journalist Michael Calvin spent the season on the inside with full access to everything going on (how I'd love to do that at BFC). In it there's a poem that should probably be pinned up on every team's dressing room wall. Maybe it is.

Calvin attributes it to sprinter Jesse Owens but in fact it was written by an obscure poet called Walter Wintle, about whom little is known; probably American, possibly early 1900s, is the nearest anyone has got. Maybe Jesse Owens had it pinned up over his bed:

If you think you are beaten, you are.
If you think you dare not, you don't.
If you like to win but think you can't,
it's almost a cinch you won't.

If you think you'll lose, you're lost.
For out in the world we find,
success begins with a fellow's will.
It's all in the state of mind.

If you think you're outclassed you are.
You've got to think high to rise.
You've got to be sure of yourself before,
you can ever win the prize.

Life's battles don't always go,
to the stronger or faster man.
But sooner or later, the man who wins,
is the man who thinks he can.

Sean Dyche spoke about state of mind on *The Footballers' Football Show*. It was a fascinating insight into a number of things. It certainly showed again how Dyche is the man of the moment, so much so that he was strongly linked with the vacant Crystal Palace job. He talked huge sense sitting alongside the director of sport research at Liverpool University, Dr Sue Bridgewater, who runs football management courses.

Psychology now plays a huge role in that management, the analysis of individuals and their specific needs, along with self-knowledge. Football now is about getting the best out of individuals within the group and then applying that 'best' to the group. He likened it to 'horse-whispering'. It raised a few smiles. Some quiet players respond to 'a nibble in the ear', others are happy to be spoken to in front of the group.

The key was observation of players at the training ground, standing back, assessing their mental strengths, body language; all the clues that indicate a person's state of mind. Much of it is not rocket science. Continual learning is the key.

Football is so different now to what it was just 20 years ago when he was a player. Clubs and managers can no longer treat the apprentices, or established players for that matter, as they once did. They once did as they were told mindlessly. It was the way things were especially for the young kids, cleaning out latrines, sweeping terraces and painting barriers. Now they are 'scholars' and come from a culture and society today that is so different to what it once was and will not be treated badly. Today is all about embracing change, open communication and inclusiveness. Think of the media and social networking and its impact.

Twenty-five years ago I jumped from a classroom straight into being a headteacher without training or credentials. It was straight in at the deep end without a scrap of preparation. I survived, learning as I went along. If you were a good teacher it was assumed you could be a good headteacher. So it was in football. If you were a top player it was assumed you could be a good manager.

It was a theory applied to Martin Buchan and Chris Waddle at Burnley. Neither lasted more than a year. A good player could move into management overnight on the strength of his name and yet be a fish out of water.

Bobby Charlton was the classic example of that. Today you don't even need to have been even a moderately good player to become a top manager; look at Mourinho, Wenger and Brendan Rodgers. The era of jobs for the boys is over. Now you need a CV, documentation, licences, badges and qualifications. There's a new brand of manager.

Tuesday 12 October was five years to the night that Burnley beat Chelsea in the League Cup. It's as clear in my head now as it was the day after. Some things leave an indelible mark and what I still think of is the sight and sound of 6,000 Burnley fans in the away end. The word awesome is inadequate.

Mrs T and me were sitting with our Chelsea pal Bob, down the Chelsea Longside in among their fans; fortunately a mature, decent lot who didn't kill us when we couldn't help but stand up and scream and shout when Akinbiyi scored. They politely suggested we sit down before we drew too much attention to ourselves and were ejected by stewards.

We'd driven up with our chum Bob from Kent, stopped for sausage sandwiches on the way, drove through a surprisingly quiet London, had a meal in a restaurant on the King's Road and watched for celebs. And then headed for the ground hoping we'd put up a good show and not lose by too many.

I doubt any of us who were there will ever forget what happened. When Jensen saved their last penalty the away end went ballistic. Me and Mrs T had to sit still and just grin. The Chelsea hordes left quickly, quite stunned, but we stayed for several minutes after the game just watching and listening to the away support, it was so magnificent. Fish and chips on the way home never tasted so good.

With the next game against Nottingham Forest, Dyche spoke to the local media and Suzanne Geldard about his time there under the tutelage of Brian Clough, his first boss.

'If I say anything about Brian Clough, as everyone would, deemed a genius for the right reasons in football management, everyone reflects back to that. But I picked up many good things from a lot of good managers I've worked for. Not just the managers, but coaches and psychologists and sports scientists. But he gets the headlines because of being the marvellous manager that he was. It means a lot, he was such a powerful figure, physically how he was and what he demanded from the players and the feeling he gave you, but also what he'd done in the game.

'I was very young, 16 through 19 before I left, so you have maximum respect for these people anyway. I wouldn't say you were scared of him, but he could unnerve you. You would be unnerved, no two ways about it. When he came down the corridor you stood to attention almost, not in the way of an Army but you'd just go "morning boss" and keep it pretty minimal and players would duck and dive out of the way. You normally got a warning sign when his dog Del Boy came down the corridor. As soon as Del Boy came down the corridor you knew the boss wasn't far behind. He always liked to be called "Boss" not "Gaffer".

'To take a club like Nottingham Forest to two European Cups is quite incredible when you look back, especially when you look at what's going on in European football now. They were certainly a side that were bucking the trend at that time and continued to do that for many years. They were good times. Me and Woany reflect on it sometimes and tell a few stories about it. We enjoyed those times.'

Dyche has never thought he has ever copied Clough's style but one thing has stuck with him.

'Playing on the front foot, he used phrases like that. It's very general but everyone in football understands it. It's been around for years but he was always using that "play on the front foot" expression. I think they're quite generic in football now but they were the first time I'd heard things like that. I think here we've played on the front foot from pre-season and a lot of the time, not all of the time, we tried to do that last season. It's one of the mindsets I've had with the players. It's a general term but everyone understands what it means, being positive in the way that you play.'

Links with the vacant Crystal Palace job would not go away with Dyche second favourite at one stage.

'To be honest you can register many links to our players and me recently. I think people are questioning in the right way what is going on at Burnley; not big finance, not big budgets, not a big squad, but we're still looking to go in the right direction and try to build something, so it will attract attention. We've been linked with every striker going so that's a similar thing. A job comes up and I'm part of a group of people who are doing some good work and I think they have a look at that and start making links straight away.

'I'm pleased that people recognise not just me, but the good work that's going on here. There are good things behind the scenes and people do recognise that eventually. People are always intrigued by things that are bucking trends and we're probably bucking the financial trend at the moment.'

The trend he did not mention was the results sequence at Nottingham, just two wins in the last 19 visits. It was a trend we all hoped would be altered.

SEAN DYCHE AND WINTER ARRIVES:
Nottingham Forest 1 Burnley 1

SATURDAY 23 November: winter had arrived and in winter Gawthorpe is better than Switzerland, Harry Potts used to say. The *Daily Express* went into overtime during the week with its doom-filled weather headlines. Dozens of MPs continued to claim expense allowances for gas and electricity. People claiming basic pensions shivered. Mrs T got the hot water bottles out. I stocked up on candles. I stood by the TV. Pictures of a boiling hot, sunny Brisbane and the first Ashes Test warmed me up. England's batting left me cold.

Doing more family tree work, Mrs T had discovered Alice Nutter, one of the supposed Pendle Witches and hanged at Lancaster, was my great (times ten) grandmother.

The uplands around an embryonic Burnley and outlying villages like Newchurch, Sabden, Barley and Roughlee and all the desolate moorlands were wild and lawless places, a 'dark corner of the land' said contemporary historians. How can anyone live in a place like this said Danny Blanchflower when the Tottenham coach pulled up. Theft and begging were commonplace.

In these small villages, filled with superstition, being a 'witch' who could heal people in the absence of any doctors was almost a profession. If you knew a few herby cures, could cackle convincingly and had a wart on the end of your nose you were halfway there. It didn't help that they were Catholics, almost the same as being a terrorist back then after the Guy Fawkes plot to blow up Parliament and the King. Alas, families in these isolated places often fell out with each other and it was two of the pointy-hat families that were the worst. It was James I, when he came to the throne in 1603, who decided it was time to stamp it out. The Pendle Witches et al were on borrowed time.

Chris Boden of the *Burnley Express* interviewed Sean Dyche in an article reproduced below:

> Pressing is the new passing, according to Sean Dyche. And he is delighted at the way his players have taken that mantra on board so far this season. Burnley's organisation, work rate and desire to win the ball back have played a big part in their climb to the top of the Championship, just as much as the number of goals they have scored and their miserly defence.
>
> Dyche is a student of European and world football and he admits he has tried to take some of the best facets of sides like Bayern Munich to fit his and his team's needs.
>
> He said, 'Barcelona started it in a way, subliminally because everyone thinks about the passing. But the Germans have taken it to a new level. Pressing is the new passing. The way the Germans press at the minute, tactically, individually is fantastic. If you look at some of the pass maps, they've changed. Barcelona dominates with beautiful football, Spain as well, heavily linked with the Barcelona connection, and so then everyone decides that's the way forward.
>
> 'I'm not saying it's not, I'm saying "is it?" Because the Germans have come along and said you can have as much possession as you want, as many passes as you want, but we're going to press, get it off you and score.'
>
> Cardiff, under Dyche's good friend Malky Mackay, earned much admiration for their ability to find several ways to win games on their way to the Championship title, whether at their best or not.
>
> Dyche added, 'The best exponents of mixed, clever football for a long time have been Manchester United.

It's nirvana for every manager, a team that can operate and hurt teams in as many ways as they can. Defending and counter-attacking, muck and nettles, fantastic football, set pieces. I think United have done that for a long time and it's no surprise Mourinho does that. I saw his Real Madrid take on Barcelona and they didn't try to outpass them, they stifled them and found a way to win.

'I can only imagine they thought the only way they were going to win was by being tactically sound, organised, pressing, breaking the game up and picking their pocket. We've shown good signs of different ways of winning, but it's still a work in progress and there are loads of challenges to come.

'But, that's a look at what I feel is happening in football, and what we can learn from it as a group and add into it. Because it's always about that, information, tactics, movement patterns, things like that. Your eyes zoom in and out on that and you try and keep up to date with modern trends. A lot of it is perception. What is the right way of playing? It's got to be to win, surely? That's never changed. If there is a better way of winning, but it doesn't make it THE way of winning. There are things to learn from everywhere and I try and pick up whatever I can to help myself and my staff.

'Transition is a word that regularly crops up into modern football terminology, to describe how teams adapt from having the ball to being without it. It is one of the most important things in football now. It's key, having the ball, not having the ball and regaining it. I look for it in my players. I work with them daily on it and there are great signs from them.'

When one poster began a thread on the Claretsmad message board with the title 'The Season Starts Now' he was pretty much derided and shot down in flames. Such is the nature of message boards everywhere, populated by anonymous folk quick to find fault and respond with smart answers.

What the guy meant was: OK, we've had the first 15 games and now it's the break. Burnley had done fabulously well, beyond anyone's hopes. They were top, but from the Forest game it was like a fresh start and they had it all to do again for the next 15 games. And if the points return could be the same or not far off, they could still be top. A tall order but with the two-week break it was indeed like starting all over again with a refreshed and rested squad.

The club's financial report for the year ending 13 June was published. It posted a loss of £7.6m for the year. It raised barely a ripple in the supporters' pond. The news had already been broken weeks earlier by Mike Garlick in a canny bit of fan/board communication. The raised eyebrows that arose back then were now subsided.

The surprises, if there were any, were in the detail. Staff costs and wages were still above £15m but turnover was down to £15.2m with the reduction in parachute payments. With the forthcoming total loss of parachute payments, that level of staff wages was therefore clearly unsustainable.

Loan debts totalled £9.3m of which £6.4m was owed to directors. Much of the remainder was money borrowed from individuals supporting the buy-back of the ground. Interest on that was £1m a year. But the club once again owned Turf Moor and Gawthorpe. Then we all heard what Blackburn Rovers and QPR owed and the FFP rules that would hit them. Burnley's problems seemed almost insignificant.

A huge contingent of Burnley supporters made the journey to Nottingham, and Ings and Vokes returned from international duty unscathed. Ings scored twice against San Marino; Sunderland and Gus Poyet were allegedly sniffing after him and rumoured to be preparing a January bid. Stories continued to link Dyche with Crystal Palace.

Marney was sidelined again so could Burnley do a Robin Hood and take points from the wealthier Nottingham Forest, and bring back some hard-earned plunder to the poor, goode folke of Burnley? Billy Davies, the current Sheriff of Nottingham, had other plans. But Little Billy was thwarted. Burnley did not come back empty-handed, returning with a point.

'It was a travesty,' said the indignant Sheriff who said they were utterly dominant and was astonished they hadn't whupped the interlopers. The 1,700+ away fans who were there were grateful to come back unbeaten. The reports they brought back were filled with relief; in truth the Sheriff's men might well have triumphed.

'A point was a superb result today and kept the long run going'; 'it was a game we could have lost and had no complaints'; 'a point was a good result'; 'thought we did well Forest were rampant'; 'under the cosh for long spells'; 'worst Burnley performance of the season'; 'absolutely battered today'; 'not sure how we came through that'; 'huffed and puffed throughout and didn't look anywhere near a top of the table side'; 'Marney's energy and verve were missed'.

One fan who was there was particularly blunt, 'That was the worst I've seen us play this season. In the second half we were totally outplayed and very lucky to come away with a point. Daylight robbery is the best way I can describe it. The most worrying aspect for me is that we didn't compete with Forest. They just seemed to want it more and we were second best all over the park. Maybe we missed Marney in midfield. Jones and Edgar never got any sort of grip on the game. We'll have to step up on this form though or we can forget about promotion. Forest fans were singing "top of the league you're having a laugh".'

Others were nowhere near as critical as that, suggesting that the defensive display alone was worth the point with the back four outstanding and this was a side that dug in, put the shutters up and showed huge discipline and resilience.

'Resolute – as unmoved as a rock in a raging sea,' said Monday's *Telegraph*. 'Superb battling display,' said another daily newspaper. Steve Claridge on *The Football League Show* was surprisingly generous, stunning all of Burnley with his positive comments that Burnley could well go all the way to automatic promotion and this was the kind of display that was the evidence; a side does not play well but comes away with a point. He did, however, question the penalty that put Burnley in front.

A Trippier cross smacked into the arm of the defender sliding in to make the interception. Ball hit arm, or deliberate arm hit ball? Was it a penalty? Of course it was for one simple reason; the referee said so. I suspect had that been against Burnley we'd have been a bit disgruntled. Nevertheless Vokes hit the penalty home with ease.

For a few minutes Forest were put out of their stride, clearly miffed at the decision and the unjustness. The little Sheriff fumed. The lead, however, did not last long with Forest equalising a few minutes before half-time. A cross and there was Cox to bundle it home unmarked at the far post. Where was the marking and the awareness, Dyche might have asked in the dressing room. It was a rare lapse in what had been weeks of defensive quality.

Despite Forest's dominance of possession and hitting the crossbar, in fact they created few clear-cut openings and at the other end Burnley did have chances of their own that were either saved or blocked.

Meanwhile Dyche was pleased with the point and, acknowledging that Burnley had not been at their best, came out with surely the quote of the season, 'I knew Billy had injury problems. He was down to his last 32 players.'

And my pal Higgy, father of two rumbustious lads and manager of a boys' Sunday football team, reported, 'Balls pumped up, goals cleaned and rebagged, bibs same, paperwork sorted, team and tactics sorted, half-time Jaffa Cakes sorted, game on, hopefully. One player at kick-boxing tournament, another grounded for calling his grandmother "old" so can't play, another lad benched for pretending to be a wolf for a whole training session. My lad on his last chance following a brekkie Coco Pop tantrum… Does the other Mourhino have to put up with this kinda stuff? Kids' footy, it's a different world tha' knows.'

On 22 November 1963 President Kennedy was assassinated. The first ever *Doctor Who* was broadcast on 23 November. The Beatles were top of the charts. On 23 November Burnley beat Aston Villa at Turf Moor 2-0. The crowd was just 13,606.

And 50 years later on 23 November 2013, Burnley, despite Billy Davies's splutterings, were still top of the division.

A LETTER FROM OLD BOB:
Huddersfield 2 Burnley 1

ONLY minutes from Leeds, Huddersfield was a must. Burnley's support there is always phenomenal. Ten years ago it was a 1-0 win in a cup game when Papadopoulos scored the only goal in a contender for one of the most tedious games ever. We roared when he scored with minutes to go, not because we were thrilled at the win, but because we could all go home and would be spared extra time.

I'd heard much about the Cornish pasties on offer in the food kiosks and drove there looking forward to a treat. When I got there they'd run out. I knew then it was going to be a drab, long evening.

The other time was August at the beginning of 2012/13. Hot summer sun this was not. There was a downpour of tropical proportions that soaked us to the skin between parking and the short walk to the stadium. It was another poor performance and a defeat. Chasing the game at 2-0 down, Eddie Howe took off a centre-forward and brought on another centre-half.

'Ah, protecting the 2-0 deficit,' said a wag behind us. To make matters worse there was that bloody drummer hitting the thing all the way through the game. If you didn't arrive in Huddersfield with a migraine, you sure as hell left with one.

Still trawling through old emails, I found one from Robert Nutter. Robert is from the Ribble Valley area but now lives near Windsor; his family owned a clog-making shop in Nelson in the 60s and his parents were season ticket holders until recently.

He wrote, 'I was a member of Burnley Referees' Association 40 years ago and we used to train at either Turf Moor or

Gawthorpe. Brian Miller used to take the sessions but Jimmy Adamson talked to us once. He came over as someone who knew a lot about the game and fitness. Jimmy was slightly aloof, maybe even austere but someone who commanded huge respect.

'Harry Potts lived in Simonstone Avenue a few doors up from us in Lawrence Avenue. I was good friends with his son Ken. Harry was always genial except when he joined in playing football in the park and then became very animated. Bob Lord lived on Whins Lane in Read and I used to deliver his newspapers. He had two big dogs and we were told not to enter if the gates were shut.

'I wrote to him while I was at university, complaining about him falling out with the TV companies and not allowing cameras in. I just thought it was bad publicity for the club. Bob Lord's reply was a classic.'

25 February 1974
R.S. Nutter Esq.
Van Mildert College, Durham

Dear Sir,
I am in receipt of your letter of the 20th instant. I have noted the contents and I do not appreciate your rudeness in any shape or form. I suppose you have dealt with quite a number of business ventures, and you have always made a success of them. But believe me; I have not the slightest intention of taking any notice of any words that you have written. You do not know anything at all about running a football club, and in the attitude you have shown to me in your letter, you never will.

Do you really suggest that football being shown on television has not reduced the attendances at football matches? Do you really suggest that asking the television authorities for £10,000 for one match is as ridiculous as you indicate? What you want to do sir, is get your facts right. Come out of college and roll your sleeves up. Get some hard work done from the sweat of your brow and go home physically tired.
Yours Truly
Bob Lord, Chairman
Burnley Football Club

Old Bob's letter is a true reflection of the man; forthright, blunt, rude, overbearing and quite disdainful. But in his appraisal of the need for an appropriate TV match-fee he was 40 years ahead of his time. TV did get football on the cheap back then. If only Lord had possessed the entrepreneurial, media and interpersonal skills to match his visions for the game, he'd have been the most influential football man of the century.

Over 3,500 Burnley fans were at Huddersfield. Twice they sent batches of extra tickets. Twice they sold out within hours. Huddersfield had Pato and Adam Clayton back. Both had been kicked out of the Terriers because of fighting at the training ground. Pato we believed had been told to clear off permanently.

But football is football and tends to forgive its transgressors on the grounds of expediency. Thus they had both been brought back for the game the week before and both had scored in a win. Manager Mark Robins had muttered something about having standards to adhere to but good players were in short supply, or something like that. When Pato scored against Sheffield Wednesday his goal celebration was pretending to knock Clayton out again. Clayton obligingly fell over like he'd been poleaxed. Footballers – bless 'em.

Meanwhile the loan deadline day approached and Burnley were strongly linked with Craig Davies of Bolton. A story doing the rounds was that one deal had fallen through because Sean Dyche felt the player in question would be a problem in the dressing room. It fitted in with his belief that those who don't fit in with the group must be shipped out. One or two people, as soon as they heard the news that Pato had allegedly been given his P45, felt he should have been invited back to Turf Moor.

The loan window closed without any reinforcements and chief exec Lee Hoos described it as the hardest loan window he had experienced. Dyche intimated his phone bill would be enormous. Targets had been priced out by economics.

But any suggestions that Davies had been a real possibility were brushed aside by Bolton manager Dougie Freedman, 'There was a small enquiry from chairman to chairman. There was no real enquiry from the manager to say we'll take him.'

Conspiracy theories abounded that other deals had fallen through because Championship sides did not wish to help the current leaders.

Those arriving in Huddersfield by train might have been impressed by the station, once described as a stately home with trains in it. This is a Grade I-listed building described by Sir John Betjeman as the most splendid façade in England, second only to St Pancras, London. This is open to debate. I personally think that the second best façade belongs to Carol Vorderman. It cost £4m to renovate and won a grand European award for architecture (the station, not Vorderman).

Huddersfield has been a market town since Saxon times. In the Domesday Book it was known as Oderesfelt. During the Industrial Revolution, the Luddites, a thoroughly discontented lot, began to destroy mills and machinery until a thousand redcoats were brought in.

The football team was once upon a time a power in the land and won championships in the 1920s. Bill Shankly and Denis Law cut their teeth there. More importantly, Andrew Jones was an award-winning pie-maker.

Without a Burnley win in three games the inevitable questions were being asked. 'Have the wheels come off at last?' 'Has the bubble burst?' But the winning run could not possibly continue indefinitely. Only one defeat in 16 league games was a huge achievement. Pundits suggested that Burnley could not possibly keep it up with such a small squad and at Huddersfield the lack of cover for the still-unfit Marney was abundantly clear.

It was a horrible defeat that ended the top-of-the-table run. It was a sour-taste defeat, an aggravating one that left us frustrated and angry by the end. By half-time no one could have grumbled if Burnley had been 3-0 down. It was a poor, poor performance from Burnley, half-hearted, unconvincing, bereft of ideas, running into trouble, second to nearly every ball, overrun in midfield, Ings was ineffective except for one missed chance from a Trippier cross. And yet, it was still 0-0 at half-time, through dogged defending and good fortune.

Despite all that, by the end of the game, we came away angered by diabolical officiating by both referee and one linesman in particular, and one of the worst penalty decisions ever.

The lead that Huddersfield took was well deserved when Norwood struck home from 25 yards following a corner; though the origin of it was again a poor 'corner' decision that Dyche argued should not have been given in the first place. The killer goal came but minutes later when clearly outside the area, Duff was adjudged to have handled the ball when in fact he chested it; his arms well out of the way by his sides. All of us in the away end were incredulous. Goals change games; decisions decide games. When decisions such as this double a side's lead they are totally infuriating. The yellow card that Duff wrongly received would cost him dear much later in the game.

At 2-0 down Burnley at last started to play, Edgar replaced by Stock, and Kightly replaced by Stanislas who introduced some guile and craft into the side. Ings had already squandered one chance, the only one of the first half, electing to try and guide a deep Trippier cross into the net instead of heading the ball.

In the second half, with Burnley dominating and beginning to look like table-toppers at last, Ings again caught the ball beautifully with a full-blooded close-range strike, but it was straight at the keeper who miraculously saved. A foot either side of him and it was a goal, a golden chance wasted.

By now with Burnley stroking the ball around with urgency and class, Stanislas was a real influence and put a superb low ball across that was smacked home by Vokes who came in like lightning. The away end rose and roared. And then deflation: the linesman stood with his flag raised for offside.

Cue more incredulity at this decision. If he was offside it must have been no more than a centimetre. The referee couldn't wait to book him as he threw the ball to the floor. As soft and unwarranted a booking you will ever see bearing in mind the worse things that players do that go unpunished. Vokes might also have had a penalty claim upheld when he was hauled down. We looked in vain as the referee unsurprisingly waved play on.

Yet more Burnley pressure: by now Huddersfield were a shadow of what they had been in the first half with Burnley unrecognisable from a first half where they just chased shadows. Vokes headed on and Ings latched on to it, racing away and sweetly scoring. You'd have bet money on an equaliser but even with six extra minutes it was not to be.

And, as the minutes ticked away, the icing on the cake duly arrived. Duff, already booked by the ineptitude of a referee who could surely do promotion work for Vision Express, was then carded again for bringing down Vaughan, who was about to break away from him.

And so we came away on the one hand deeply dismayed by the total capitulation of the first half, wringing our hands and covering our eyes at the sheer awfulness of it, but simultaneously hugely aggrieved by officials' decisions that cost us a possible draw. I do actually have this crazy picture in my head of the men in black getting together in the pub the night before and discussing what they could do to help Huddersfield win. By the end Huddersfield could have had no grumbles had Burnley levelled the scores, despite that first-half horror show and Huddersfield playing like table-toppers.

Probably most of us watched the replays of the 'penalty' that never was over and again, wondering how on earth any referee/linesman could do something so monumentally crass; Duff not only clearly outside the area, but clearly with his arms by his sides.

Many fans argued that Burnley got what they deserved because of the poor first half. But say what you like, they had weathered the storm and had survived through a mix of good fortune, the Huddersfield finishing and not least some dogged defending. Poor as they were they came out for the second half on an equal footing. But what good is an equal footing when an incompetent referee and inept linesman decide the outcome of a game? No side deserves that.

Leicester won to go three points clear at the top. QPR surprisingly lost at lowly Doncaster. So Burnley stayed second. And the minute's applause in the 13th minute for 13-year-old Clarets fan Henry Tattersall was another of those lump-in-the-throat moments as the whole ground, Huddersfield and Burnley alike, stood as one. We might be aggrieved at this

Burnley defeat, but the grief felt for the young lad outweighed it a hundredfold.

One supporter, David Blackburn, in mid-November, saw the beginnings of something special taking place. All of us had seen some great performances and results but maybe David was ahead of the rest of us when he wrote, 'Tell your friends, tell your family, this is a surprise promotion challenge that isn't going away any time soon.' His blog was quite emphatic and he has kindly given permission for it to be repeated here:

> I was sat watching Borussia Dortmund's dominant first half against Arsenal, in which the Germans completely stifled Arsenal and maintained play almost entirely in the opposition half and my dad turned to me and said, 'Like watching Burnley this.' At first I laughed. Normally in our house this is a joke for when something goes wrong. Defender loses his man and a cheap goal is scored? Like watching Burnley. Devastating last-minute equaliser allowed against the run of play? Like watching Burnley. But then he said 'but seriously' and I realised that he wasn't that far wrong.
>
> Something weird has been happening recently. Almost everyone I know, even people I haven't spoken to in years, is getting in touch to ask me what on earth is going on at Burnley. After an underwhelming response to Premier League relegation since 2010, Burnley are perched atop the Championship having lost just once in the opening 14 games – and that with the aid of a nonsense sending off for goalkeeper Tom Heaton.
>
> So, it's fallen on me, in various degrees of increasing belief that this Burnley side might actually be the real deal, to tell people where this sudden success has come from. Self-deprecation, assurances that it can't last, even outright statements of shock have been my refuge until now. But with my dad's ludicrous comparison, I'm finally ready to explain why this team is so good – and believe me it is good.

As an aid for those more comfortable with the Champions League than the Championship, the nature of Dortmund's pressing is a genuinely good starting point. Burnley manager Sean Dyche's focus on fitness and sports science has allowed Burnley to play the sort of pressing game unheard of at Championship level. Not a second of opposition possession goes by without pressure, and pressure that is incredibly effective. A midfield of Joey Barton and Niko Kranjcar (a Premier midfield) was rendered useless in the face of it. This is 11 players combining to be so much more effective than the sum of their parts.

This Burnley team has the guile of management, the fitness and know-how and the individual talent to reach the Premier League. Tell your friends; tell your family, this is a surprise promotion challenge which isn't going to go away any time soon.

December

CULINARY TREATS AND COMETH THE KIGHTLY:

Burnley 0 Watford 0
Burnley 1 Barnsley 0

THE question we were all asking was whether Burnley could resume their winning ways with two quick home games – one at home to a stuttering Watford, and the second against bottom of the table Barnsley. The lingering effects of the defeat at Huddersfield were still lingering. The irritating memories of the inept officials were still irritating. Wins were badly needed. Including the West Ham match in the League Cup, there had been five games without one. To add to the growing 'we're doomed Captain Mainwaring' movement, there were worries about Ings's fitness as well as Marney's.

What a Monday morning though: three sackings in the Championship. Flitcroft departed Barnsley, Jones ditto Sheffield Wednesday and the most interesting thing for all Burnley fans – Owen Coyle sacked at Wigan. Mutual consent was the story according to the media. It had been four years since Coyle left Burnley in mid-season with most of the backroom staff, but many Burnley fans had neither forgiven nor forgotten although other fans said it was time to move on.

The websites and emails buzzed. The disappointment that came across, however, was that he would not be there at Wigan when Burnley next visited. It was not hard to imagine the messages that would have been hurled at him again when the two teams met.

His story over the last four years really is one of decline and fall. No one will forget the Wembley triumph and promotion of 2008/09, but having departed Bolton Wanderers and now Wigan, it was hard to think of him having any further opportunity of management at a big club.

The man who at one stage, could, as far as Burnley fans were concerned, have walked on the waters of the River Brun, was now sinking faster than a stone, it seemed. Two removals in 12 months; not even Brian Laws achieved that distinction. Where next for him we asked: Auchtermuchty perhaps, once better known as Tannochbrae in the old *Doctor Finlay* TV series?

The Wigan chairman, Dave Whelan, was blunt with him in a face-to-face, reported the media. 'Do you want me to resign?' asked Coyle.

'Yes,' replied Whelan.

Ever eager to share with you our culinary experiences and gourmet travels, this time we dined at the Queen Hotel in Cliviger before the Watford game. Before that we'd called at Blackshawhead Methodist Chapel high up on the hilltops above Hebden Bridge, in search of family graves. The poignant thing there was meeting and chatting with the lady who visits this windswept graveyard every day to see and touch her daughter and husband's graves. That puts football things into some kind of perspective.

I confess to becoming quite obsessed with finding more Nutters in the family. The previous week we had mooched around the graveyard at Heptonstall St Thomas's Church and found what we were looking for just as hypothermia was setting in, although these were Watsons not Nutters. And the origin of the name Nutter was one who gathered nuts in the olden days, chiefly for feeding to the pigs. There have always been professional nutters with nuttering a respected occupation in days gone by.

Shakespeare recognised their importance, 'Come lads and lasses, now raiseth your glasses, with hey hey nonny no, a nuttering we will go.'

The Queen Hotel was warm, inviting and cosy. Fires burned brightly in the two rooms. The minute I walked in I saw someone with a huge plate of gammon, egg, chips, mushy peas and salad. I fell in love with the place immediately and thought 'that's for me', stomach rumbling.

My chum had the award-winning homemade cheese and onion pie. There's an award I give personally to pies of quality and excellence – the Dave T Pie Award. My chum gave me a taste. Trust me, this was the Carol Vorderman of the pie world; mouthwatering and eyecatching, full-bodied and firm with just a hint of don't-keep-me-waiting. The Queen is hosted by Graham and Carol Knott. Carol makes the pies herself. Phone me when you make the pork and apple pie, I asked.

And what has all this got to do with Burnley FC? For anyone on the way to a Tuesday game or on the way back from a Saturday game, this is a fine watering hole at which to stop and fill up with Bury black pudding, or pork loin schnitzel, or sirloin steak or any one of the huge range of sandwiches and then really stuff yourself stupid with a sticky toffee pudding and Mrs Dowson's ice cream for afters.

Ings was definitely out so both Treacy and Stanislas started. Vokes was the lone striker with Arfield in support. Duff was suspended. Three of the young lads sat on the bench. This was getting down to bare bones stuff. The crowd couldn't make the 11,000-mark.

Two home games in a week, Christmas coming up, southern opposition, no wins in November, and money tight; the reasons stacked up. The atmosphere was flat and lifeless throughout, the 12th man factor absent, posing the age-old question: does the team whip up the crowd or does the crowd whip up the team?

Play was generally neat and tidy, though punctuated by misplaced passes. Stanislas was the likeliest hope. Ings's (coveted now by Liverpool, journo Alan Nixon said) impishness and sharpness in the box was visibly missing. Even if he has a quiet game, defenders are pressured by wondering where he is; ey oop he's behind you, oh no he's not, oh yes he is; and what he's up to. Without him, half their job is done.

Vokes battled away as best he could. In the first half, weakened though they were, Burnley dominated play against a poor Watford side filled with Johnny Foreigners, who frequently looked totally disinterested. Burnley on a cold Tuesday night was probably the last place they'd like to be. And therein lay the disappointment. They were there for the taking. But for all their play and control, Burnley summoned few real threats on goal. An Arfield flick, an Arfield header, a Treacy piledriver, a Vokes header over the bar, a few dangerous diagonal balls into the box with no one on the end of them, and that was about it.

The second half was more even. Hey up, thought Watford, we've got a bit of a chance here and only smart saves by Heaton kept them out. Burnley huffed and puffed, Stanislas and Treacy faded. Young Hewitt made a cameo appearance but even to a blind man on a galloping horse it was obvious that a backup striker was needed. Watford repelled any attacks with growing ease so that the game seemed set up for a sneak away goal and win right at the very end.

But no, 0-0 it ended and the crowd drifted away, by far the largest majority sighing and politely applauding, seemingly resigned to the facts of football life at the Turf that bright beginnings inevitably morph into disappointment.

Sean Dyche, after the game, commented on the strange atmosphere and the glass-half-empty mentality. Small pockets of supporters had been impatient and dissatisfied. Individual players had been targeted once or twice. Maybe these people had forgotten that third place, only two defeats, just two points behind the leaders in December, was nothing short of remarkable.

In between games I kept getting up to watch the cricket. Performances reminded me of what it must have been like to watch Burnley in the Fourth Division years. The England football team were drawn in a tough group in Brazil added to which they had to play the first game halfway up the Amazon.

We chuckled all the way home after the 1-0 win over Barnsley. Top again: if there had been a blip, it was over. Relief all round and a goal worthy of winning a cup final. Blackburn held QPR to a draw, Leicester were thumped at Brighton; Burnley went top on goal difference.

The afternoon was wet and drizzly after a real downpour before the game and the news came that Ings was back but Marney was still out. It was an odd kind of first half in as much as Barnsley, with their number 42 Paddy McCourt having a masterful game, played all the delightful football; quick, incisive, nimble, threading passes to feet and finding space superbly, but toothless.

But it was Burnley, second to everything much of the time, making the better openings, getting the headers in, firing shots and twice wasting good chances with inaccurate headers. At half-time you could have been forgiven for thinking this had 0-0 written all over it. But I gave them a bit of a war-cry at half-time, said Dyche after the game. Presumably he meant he gave them a bit of a bollocking.

Second half and a much better display from Burnley; ball on the floor more, better possession, Kightly and Arfield seeing more of the ball and more effective going forward. Jones was now becoming more influential, Vokes working his socks off and Ings at last showing some trickery. Barnsley were more often than not running into brick walls until at last, the deadlock was broken. The ball broke to Kightly; he cut in from the right and unleashed a superb strike into the top-left corner of the net. Butland stood transfixed. This was the first time Burnley had taken a lead in a game since the win over QPR in October.

Of course Barnsley applied some pressure in the last ten minutes but Duff and Shackell stood firm. For all Barnsley's dominance in the first half Heaton had little to do, but when needed he made two smart saves. Burnley wound down the clock. Thanks to Blackberries most folk knew the results of the other key games and that Burnley had gone top again. You could see at the end what the win meant to the players as they lingered and applauded the crowd.

Dyche of course was delighted but again made subtle references to the impatience shown by small sections of the crowd. 'I am getting to learn about our crowd,' he said with tact and diplomacy. Truth is, some of them are a grumpy lot and take it out on individual players far too easily and readily. These folk should be careful. If an offer comes along from a 'better' club, Dyche might have a ready excuse for accepting if he thinks that Turf Moor is unappreciative of what in fact is a minor miracle.

But yours truly and Mrs T left the ground with big smiles on our faces: the win topped off with a meal at the Queen again and there on the menu was the famed pork and apple pie. The story goes that on the seventh day God rested. In fact He sat and invented the pork and apple pie and pronounced it good and in His wisdom decided that He would give the recipe to Carole at the Queen. The cheese and onion will have to wait, I thought.

The pork and apple arrived. What a truly awesome pie, a man's pie; perfectly round, the pastry light and golden, the texture like velvet, the pulled-pork and apple filling a flavoursome taste sensation that spilled with the juices from the casing in mouthwatering slow motion with the first cut of the knife. And all served with perfect chips, veg, and cider gravy.

What a day. The win might well have been hard-earned, maybe even a tad fortuitous, but there we sat at 5pm, little Burnley top of the pile again. Meanwhile at Manchester United things were not so good although the club shop is cashing in with the new merchandise: Manchester United lamps that look good in the middle of the table, and sledges that go downhill really fast.

But at Burnley we rejoiced; the hour cameth, so cameth the Kightly.

YOU KNOW IT'S DECEMBER:
Leicester City 1 Burnley 1

YOU know when it's Christmas, or at least you know it's December, when the first round-robin newsletter arrives. You groan when you see the letter inside the card. You don't want to read it because you know what will be in it. But you have to. It's like a road crash. You just have to look. Just why do people send them? What compels them to write stuff like this? This one came from people we haven't seen for at least ten years:

> We feel truly blessed; darling hubby's hospital admissions continued throughout December so that despite being ill, they decided to reverse his ileostomy to give him a chance of retaining some nutrients. The net result has been his very gradual improvement and becoming an 11.5st porker from 8.5st. He now has a different sort of lymphoma in his small bowel from in his lungs but the good news is that they are both currently behaving themselves and not developing. Meanwhile, I fell and broke a bone in my right foot and tore ankle ligaments in my left ankle but the swelling and pain diminished in November.

After I'd read all that I could barely eat my bacon sandwich.

You know it's December when our neighbour opposite has put up new lights along the front of the house. They drape the whole frontage, miles of them. You can see them from space; brilliant, white, glaring, in your face, dazzling and blinding. Since they went up we've had to keep the curtains drawn and wear sunglasses.

I suppose all that counts as a moan and here am I saying let's stop it. But the moaning that really ought to stop is the stuff that happens on a matchday, especially the last two home games when the atmosphere was strange to say the least bearing in mind that Burnley – on such limited resources – were third in the table, had still only lost two games, had one of the meanest defences in the division, and when they went 1-0 up in the second of those games they went to the top again.

Top of the pile; little Burnley, running up the debts but just about keeping their head above water and striving to succeed, and when the team runs out from the tunnel they have no idea how they will be received, rapturously, or half-heartedly. And one or two of them as individuals must curl up inside at some of the stuff they can hear directed at them.

Sure the actual performances might not have been as crisp and magical as those that took us to the top the first time, but the draw at Millwall could so easily have been a win, the draw at home to Bournemouth on any other day would have seen Burnley score five. And even at Huddersfield when the first 45 minutes were so disappointing, it was only those unbelievable decisions by the officials – who were appalling – that prevented the draw that by the end of the game would have been just about deserved. That penalty still rankles. What monumental incompetence it was by referee and linesman. And that Vokes booking verged on the incomprehensible.

The 0-0 against Watford was maybe about right over the 90 minutes, but there again, it could easily have been a win if Burnley had capitalised on chances created, especially in the first 45 minutes.

So out they came on to the field on the Barnsley matchday. You would hardly have described their appearance as being received with massive acclaim. And they struggled in that first half. They'd be the first to agree. But what help did we give them as a crowd? Sod all as far as I could make out.

This is a dog-eat-dog league. The stakes are huge; £90m at the season's end for the lucky three if the latest figures are correct. Nobody will therefore make it easy for Burnley to succeed and while 'Arry at QPR can nip out and add another classy midfielder to his squad and pay another huge wage, Burnley certainly can't.

And it was certainly correct that one Championship club would not loan a striker to Burnley. Instead they loaned him to a bottom-end club. Burnley offered to pay this particular club £6,000 a week. Nope they said. The club that he is at now agreed to pay just £3,000. This was a striker that we would have found very acceptable. This guy was one of four targets that were either priced out beyond range, or deliberately rebuffed us.

So what could we do? Raise the noise for a start. And then stop visibly and audibly moaning at individual players when they can hear the abuse being shouted at them. It should be opposition players who we make nervous and apprehensive, not our own.

Sean Dyche was tactful in his gentle criticisms. Maybe he would like to have turned round to those behind him in the Bob Lord, for those are the voices that can be heard by anyone in the dugout, and bellowed at them to stop their moaning especially at a young player who had barely figured and was brought on late in the game. If Dyche decided to blood youngsters away from home rather than at Turf Moor, who could blame him?

Sure, players will make a bad pass, some more than others; wingers will not beat the defender every time. If they were perfect they wouldn't be playing for Burnley; they'd be in the Prem. The position at the top wasn't earned by galacticos and world-class players. It was earned by honest pros that have raised their game, doubled the commitment that we have seen from some previous Burnley teams, and developed a team spirit and work ethic that has been second to none. The leadership has been superb.

And yet during the game against Barnsley there were times when the place was not quite like a morgue but almost; certainly flat and lifeless. When the team needed a lift, they didn't get it. Vocal support was fitful and sporadic. At times, the greater support came from just a few hundred Barnsley fans. It was as if, during the Watford and Barnsley games, that folk were waiting for failure, waiting for the slide to commence, waiting for the wheels to fall off. Turf Moor needs to be intimidating; filled with the 'fear-factor' that daunts the away team, unnerves them as a team and as individuals (I can remember years ago seeing Alan Ball reduced to the level of a novice by the Longside). It needs to be the kind of place that opposing teams and their supporters hate to come.

In the second of the meetings with Clive Holt, he confessed to being baffled by it, saying that it was particularly bad from the Bob Lord, especially during a lull or a quiet passage of play when everything was clearly audible to Sean Dyche and the bench right in front of them – some of it downright hurtful.

All of them want, in fact need, the crowd to be supportive, vocal, loud and passionate. Think back to that night against Spurs in the League Cup. The deafening roars never stopped, wave after incredible wave. If they know the crowd is on their side that's when a team steps up a gear, when it creates an extra energy and the players' adrenalin flows. Then, in effect, you've got a real and potent 12th man.

During that chat, we also talked about the refereeing display at Huddersfield. The day after we talked, the papers were full of the revelations about Obama's 'deaf' signer used during one of his big glossy speeches in South Africa. It was reported that the guy was a total fake and was making the signs up as he went along. Monty Python couldn't have bettered it. Rightly or wrongly my sense of humour is pretty basic. I'm the kind of bloke who laughs out loud if there's a loud fart (fartissimo) during a quiet passage (pianissimo) in a posh classical piano recital. In fact just thinking about it creases me up.

And thus it was with the signer. The president of the world all dressed up and behind him a guy having a whale of a time just waving his hands about. You couldn't make it up. But, it did make me think about that Huddersfield referee. Was he too a fake making up decisions and rules as he went along? Was it just possible that he was an interloper who somehow bamboozled his way into the ground and fooled everybody? Or was he a schizophrenic listening to the angels as the signer claimed? It made you think.

The Leicester game was on TV with Andy D'Urso the referee. Mrs T and me settled down to watch. Why is it that seeing your team on TV is more stressful than seeing them playing live? When you see them for real, you're close up. You can shout and roar and support and feel that you make a contribution. It's not quite the same shouting at the telly. Make no mistake, this was a big game, although far too early in the season to describe as a six-pointer, or a 'decider'. But for sure it was a game neither side wanted to lose.

If there was a perfect example of a game between the Haves and the Have Nots then there it was at Leicester; the latter where the jar on the mantelpiece is forever empty and the former bankrolled by a Thai consortium in which people play polo, have second homes in London and own strings of duty free shops. Where's the level playing field in that? For the first 30 minutes it was the Haves in total control.

With Burnley rarely in contention it was Leicester with all the shots and possession for the first 30 minutes or so. And yet, after Shackell had uncharacteristically given the ball away, it was another soft penalty decision that gave them the 1-0 lead; this time not quite as outrageous as that at Huddersfield but nevertheless a decision where D'Urso fell for the age-old trick of a player falling in between two defenders converging either side of him to give it the appearance of a foul.

Contact was minimal from Shackell; contact from Mee came as the player was already falling. A far more blatant shove in the back on Kightly was later ignored. All that plus a horrible tackle from Nugent on Mee that went uncarded gave Dyche and Burnley fans just cause for dissatisfaction. However an ever-resilient Burnley slowly edged their way back into it with a header hitting the post and an Ings shot going narrowly wide. But the omens were poor. Watching on TV, the squirm factor was stuck on high.

But how can you write off this Burnley side? Within minutes of the second-half restart, Trippier put a wicked low cross over that went between two defenders to find Ings in oodles of space.

He threaded it through like my granny used to thread a needle. Ings took his time, controlled the ball and placed it home from inside the six-yard box.

It gave Burnley all the confidence they needed and much of the second half almost belonged to them until Leicester went all-out in the last ten minutes. Vokes incredibly might even have given them a 2-1 lead when he latched on to a dreadful back pass but Kasper Schmeichel made a brilliant save from the angled shot. From that point on it was a fine game with Burnley's football, passing and moving, improving all the time.

D'Urso alas missed another nasty challenge by Nugent when he went for the tackle on Trippier and left his foot in. This should have been a second yellow and then the red. The pundits too questioned the penalty and then picked Trippier as their man of the match. For me it was Vokes who had a terrific game. By the end it was a tremendous point. Alas QPR won to go top. Derby won yet again to close the gap.

On the day of the game, the esteemed Henry Winter in *The Daily Telegraph* wrote a superb feature about Sean Dyche. If Henry writes about someone, they've arrived. They're a 'name'. He doesn't write about the small-fry. The more Dyche is featured like this, the greater the possibility he will be 'poached' as his profile increases. Perhaps the Burnley crowd is in need of a Dyche 'straightener', that is to say some basic plain speaking that gets your feet back on the ground. If he wants to better himself he won't want to do it at the club if the old 'Grumpytown' label is still evident.

It was Tommy Hutchison who invented the name and the only thing I can offer to Sean is that even back in the glorious 1950s and 60s the Burnley crowd always let their feelings be known. Clearly by the time Hutchison arrived in the 80s it was even worse. By the 90s it was fearsome with demonstrations and regular protests.

The moans and grumpiness may still be there on occasions but maybe today the consolation is that it is a fraction of what it used to be. But sadly, so too are the tidal roars from the once-feared, all-standing Longside when even the greatest players were reduced to gibbering wrecks.

December

CLIVE HOLT CHATS

THIS time we met in the Harry Potts Room at Turf Moor, a room furnished with fine armchairs and solid tables and chairs. The walls are filled with framed memorabilia of Harry at Burnley. The Bob Lord Stand may not be that old but inside this room you feel transported back to an era that is long gone, the glory years when Burnley were kings.

In front of him on the tables, set out in a committee meeting-type square, were heaps of ring binders filled with the minutes of old board meetings. Clive is responsible for minute-taking and the upkeep of these books.

Once again Clive and I spoke at length for some time, covering a wide range of subjects including Colne Dynamoes wanting to use Turf Moor to aid their dream of reaching the Football League in the 1990s; previous promotions and relegations; the Chris Waddle era and the development of Turf Moor as a stadium.

Conversation then turned to the club at the moment. Of course everyone was delighted to be back in the top spot (at the time of writing). Everybody was cautious but the view was expressed that if the club did indeed go up, how much better it would be as an 'automatic' from the point of view of having the extra few weeks to plan for the new season. Having been there once, the club now knows what would hit them.

'We had so little time back in 2009 and so much to do. Much of what we did then in terms of refurbishment would stand us in good stead but there are yet more new regulations regarding

Premier League dressing rooms so that more work would be needed there. But the planning permission we obtained for a new purpose-built block in the empty corner between the Hargreaves and the McIlroy stands is still active.

'However, that's something that couldn't be completed overnight and would not be cheap. We might also need an indoor training arena at Gawthorpe that could cost up to £2m, new extra dressing rooms and new pitches.'

While we chatted, extensive roof repairs were going on at the Cricket Field Stand end. Clive said, 'The stand is a quandary. The current roof repairs are costing £100,000-plus. That's a big chunk of money but it just has to be done. There are health and safety wind strength limits that come into play if it stays unrepaired. This is currently 63mph and that reduces by ten per cent each year unless it is fixed so then you are into game postponements which then creates catering wastages and corporate losses.

'Because of water ingress there is damage to rooms below and in particular to the electrics room so there are further repair costs there. And then, what do we do if there is promotion to the Premier League?

'There's a decision to be made about leaving it solely as an away stand that will sell out with the visits of the big local teams like City, United, Liverpool and the other well supported teams from further away. Or do we do what we did last time and allocate a section to home supporters? Yes, there's the extra income but because segregation becomes an issue then there's more to pay for police and stewards so you lose some of the gains.

'With 18,000 seats in the three sides for home fans it might be best to use CFS for the away fans. It might not suit some but it is safest and gives the club the best return and income to put back into the team.'

And then came what was almost an appeal about the dissatisfaction and frustrations that are being heard in the ground on a matchday. These were sentiments felt right through the club.

'The Bob Lord is particularly bad because it's so close to the manager and the bench. Everything is audible to Sean Dyche and his players. Can people not get off the team's back and help them? We're top of the league for goodness sake; what good does it do to moan and groan? How on earth does it help?

'If there is a lull in play then you can hear every word clearly and some of it is hurtful. It takes guts to go out there and play especially if you know you are not a "crowd darling" and your every mistake is going to be picked on. How can you go out there and perform? How can the manager blood youngsters in this kind of atmosphere? If you're a youngster it's downright daunting. Sometimes you just have to accept a poor pass or a mishit shot.'

This second get-together lasted a couple of hours again and at the end we touched on Danny Ings and the loan situation.

There had been no direct enquiries about him from anybody. But we all know how it works. A manager has a tame journalist who writes stuff geared to unsettling a player. And loans: on the very last day of the loan window, there were four strikers that the club targeted. But young, up-and-coming players from the top Prem clubs wanted guaranteed playing time. There was also a clear concrete example of the frustrations.

Yes, there was a class striker Burnley wanted and offered to pay his club £6,000 a week for the loan. But, his manager did not want him to go to a rival team at the top end of the division and vetoed the deal. So, that same player was loaned to a bottom-half club for £3,000 a week.

The agreement was that I would not name the player or club but suffice it to say we would have been well pleased. It didn't happen. How frustrated do we the fans become? Magnify that 100 times for the directors and Sean Dyche. Huge efforts were made to strengthen but obstacles were met at every turn. Such is football.

WE DON'T NEED GAVISCON AND HENRY WINTER ON SEAN DYCHE:
Burnley 2 Blackpool 1

BLACK Monday: Steve Clarke went at West Brom. Dyche was immediately linked. Gianfranco Zola went at Watford. Dyche was immediately linked. AVB went at Spurs. Dyche never got a mention. What he did do was assure the board and the fans that he would not be demanding big money for big-money signings. 'Football meets reality,' he said. He was the custodian of the club and would not want to put it in jeopardy. There was alignment between him and the directors and he would not spend above the club's means.

The FA Youth Cup tie between Burnley and Manchester United served to show there is some superb talent at under-18 level. Before I lost the internet stream at half-time I was quite blown away by their pace and passing. They were unlucky to lose and only two superb goals from United were the difference with Burnley dominating for long spells thanks to some blistering football and their own top-class efforts on goal.

With Marney back, Brian Stock was once more on the bench. On his day Stock is up there with the truly gifted passers of the ball; short and neat or long and visionary out to the wings. He was always impressive when he came with Doncaster. By all accounts he was a bit of a hellraiser when he was a young lad and revealed that he was always getting into scrapes, making headlines in the press for nightclub altercations, was banned from driving and on occasions even came into training still the worse for wear with drink.

He was given a last-chance ultimatum at Bournemouth by Sean O'Driscoll, someone looked after his money and he was put in supervised digs. He went out once a week playing bingo with his landlord and heeded the warnings. He lived like a monk, he says, for months and with the help of a lot of people rescued his career.

And so from the capital of tat came Blackpool; minus Ricardo Fuller of course because he was one of five Blackpool players red-carded in the space of just a few days. Manager Paul Ince too, had been in trouble for an altercation. It would have been nice if they'd managed to beat QPR in their previous game. Despite QPR's win we were still second.

For the Blackpool game I dug out my Santa hat. The club shop had them on sale years ago. It wasn't quite an antique, but almost. By now the Thomas household was well into the Christmas spirit, cream sherry and sloe gin in particular. Cards filled the mantelpiece and window ledges. E-cards clogged the computer, the best of them a rendition of 'We Wish You a Merry Christmas' accompanied by an accomplished fartist.

It could well be the increased intake of sherry and sloe gin but Mrs T had been suffering from strange tummy rumblings of late. One night it was so bad I thought it was the central heating. The doc was very nice. We are lucky to have a surgery within walking distance where you can get an appointment within 24 hours. Mrs T returned all smiles. Nothing to worry about, said the lady doctor, you probably just need Gaviscon.

Mrs T, who knows her football, replied that we were OK, we already had Duff and Shackell and didn't need any useless Frenchmen. Nevertheless the doc said she recommended Lansoprozole for a couple of weeks. I was over the moon and thought it was somewhere in Tenerife.

Ince had Burnley sussed before Blackpool arrived. He announced that Burnley were just a long-ball team who played it up to Vokes and Ings. The first 20 minutes of the game must therefore have come as a bit of a shock. Burnley were out of the blocks, not quite like Usain Bolt, but impressive nevertheless with smooth football, ball to feet, patterns, smart moves, and determination.

Ince must have been even more gobsmacked at the style and technique of the first goal. It was the well-rehearsed corner routine where someone runs over the ball played diagonally across the back of the area, and someone comes steaming in and smacks it home. This time it was Duff who let the ball run through his legs so that Ings could score from 12 yards or so.

Unfortunately Blackpool came back. Burnley then went off the boil, lost concentration and first and second balls eluded them. Ince Junior began to cause mayhem down the right, going past Mee as if he wasn't there. A series of corners ended in the inevitable, a Blackpool equaliser from the ensuing header. Immediately prior to it there had been all the usual argy bargy you expect now before a corner is taken; pushing, shoving, holding, wrestling, shirt pulling so that in the blink of an eye suddenly a Burnley player was bundled into the back of the net flat on his back. Free kick? Seemingly not as players seem able to do what they like to each other until the moment the corner ball is kicked and is in play, a sort of *Come Dancing* with boots on.

At half-time it was 1-1 and it had been Blackpool dominant and us lot thinking this looked like another desperately dodgy afternoon. But no, just minutes into the new half Arfield scored a peach of a goal, curling the ball into the far corner of the net from the side of the area. We sat directly behind it. Surely it was going beyond the goal, we thought, but no it curled and dipped and in it went. What a start to the half and the right tonic for everyone, team and fans.

From that moment on Burnley clicked into gear. The crowd's support had been terrific all first half. Now it was even better, they were up for it, almost on a par with Last Night of the Proms. Leicester had beaten QPR in the lunchtime game and all of us knew that a win would take us back to the top above the pair of them.

Heaton made two great saves but so did Gilks from Ings in the first half when his header looked certain to go into the bottom corner. Ings could have had four on another day. Another header agonisingly went inches wide when he was unmarked on the six-yard line.

Arfield hit the crossbar. And then right at the death when Marney, back to his best, played him the perfect little pass and he had only the goalkeeper to beat, he took a moment extra to control the ball giving time for the block and the ball went over. What could have been a convincing win by the end remained a tense 2-1, but within seconds of that last chance, the ref blew for full time.

On Christmas Day 2013, Burnley were not just top of the heap but an impressive ten points clear of seventh spot. We've kept on saying it; that this is beyond all expectations. We've kept on saying it ad infinitum; a small squad, no money, small crowds, little old Burnley.

Statistics show that the side that is top on Christmas Day more often than not goes up automatically. But the last time this happened at Turf Moor, Burnley top on Christmas Day, was way back in Stan's day when in 2001 Burnley were four points clear after 25 games. Wolves were second. Alas that season Burnley fell away and even slipped out of the play-offs, sliding down to seventh and missing out on goal difference. Remembering things like that keeps Burnley's feet on the ground, generating that disbelieving glass-half-empty feeling that this is just too good to be true. 'Wait until Christmas before we raise our hopes,' we said. The folk behind us modified this. 'Wait until Easter.'

But they won. They went top again. They'd be top on Christmas Day. The stairs and exits afterwards were filled with beaming faces, a few Santa suits and white beards. Maybe by the season's end we'll all have white hair, or grey at the very least. All that and the buzz of good cheer and best wishes for a merry Christmas to one and all.

On the day of the Leicester game Henry Winter paid tribute to Sean Dyche in an article kindly reproduced here:

Sean Dyche strides from Burnley's training pitch
on the banks of the River Calder, having taken his

Championship-leading players through a detailed and energetic session in advance of Saturday's trip to third-placed Leicester City, and marches into a modest building that resembles a Lancashire village hall on the outside but Nasa on the inside.

It's all sports science, mission statements on the wall and borrowed hi-tech running machines. It is clear there is far more to Dyche, the 42-year-old former centre-half, than the general perception. His shaven-headed, physically imposing presence belies a sophisticated approach to the game, a hunger for knowledge and a determination to change critical views of English coaches.

'I've always thought I was invincible,' Dyche reflects. 'When you are a short ginger kid from Kettering, been the brunt of school ridicule, you learn to survive. I was lairy at school. I gave it back but I was self-deprecating too. I was a midget growing up. When I got to Nottingham Forest, I was 5ft 7in and weighed 10st. A year later, I was 6ft and 12st. Archie Gemmill said, "What's happened there?"

'I broke my leg, still got a bend in my leg, and that inhibited my career early on but also taught me about hardship. I know how to treat injured players. I don't go in and say, "Are you fit yet?" That's acid. You don't want to hear that from a manager. I just say, "How are you feeling, keep going."

'I learned good moral values from Cloughie at Forest, from my parents too, manners, being polite, respectful. Our players don't walk off the coach with their cans (headphones) around their neck. They are smart in and out of the building.

'I'm a humble lad with good morals from my parents. Work hard. If you have to clean the floor, make it the cleanest floor ever.

'My dad was a management consultant for British Steel, working in Egypt and India as well as Corby. He had to go into houses paying the wages. Certain workers would get the pay packet, do their money in 24 hours, so dad would give the wife the pay packet and give the man a "straightener", some advice.

'He used to tell us these stories around the dinner table, which families unfortunately don't do so much now. It taught us brilliant values. I talk to players like that: "Are you all right? Do you need anything, any support?"

'A friend of mine is a partner at KPMG. I speak to him a lot about psychology within the unit.

'Sir Alex Ferguson gave me some brilliant advice. He said that over the years he was easing down from the actual physical hands-on coaching; he looked more at players' body language. Are they up or down? Are they ready? He monitored players and staff. You have to know players as people, know their quirks.

'I can almost smell their mood. I call it horse-whispering. I watch them, then pop round after training; ask them if they're OK. I tell them, "Well done Saturday, different class." I read *The Horse Whisperer*. If that can apply to a horse, with all due respect to a horse, it must apply to humans. Treat them correctly, respectfully. I ask their thoughts. They open up.

'I was talking to Kieran Trippier who came from Manchester City. He didn't know about the Hacienda. I had to educate him. When I was playing at Chesterfield I used to go across sometimes to the Hacienda. I was a massive indie fan. I love The Smiths, Morrissey. I jumped into the rave era, not the drugs I'm pleased to say. Madchester, I loved that, my period.

'I tell the players I've had my time as a player but I now have the chance of making you better. My job is to guide them. For my Pro Licence, I went and studied the Oxford University Boat Race crew in 2010 and I use snippets from there to inspire my players. I got down to the boat house at 5.45am and the lads were there. They have these ergo rowing machines set up facing a wall with a blackboard. Written in chalk is "Boat Race" the start time and date. They all face that. I loved that. It's like walking into a Rocky film. "That's where we are going." As a player, I had four promotions with four different clubs and I'd look down the tunnel and see a group of people motivated to give everything.

'I told my players, "Lads, it's a powerful thing when you want to make history." Those rowers want to be part of history. They don't get money. In the Oxford boat house, there's this meeting room with massive boards all the way round containing the names of all the people who have been in the boat. They are desperate to get there.

'The Winklevoss brothers, Cameron and Tyler, were there. They were unbelievably talented, powerfully-minded people, top students doing their PhDs. They are single-handicap golfers, top tennis players, American footballers, and sprinters, from a multi-millionaire background with more millions coming in from the Facebook settlement. They'd done the Olympics, were flying back and forwards for the lawsuit, and there they were for three hours rowing their rears off every morning.'

For Dyche, it's about winning, about creating a legacy.

'My nirvana wouldn't be buying a Bentley. My nirvana would be building a sports centre where I live and not even having my name on it. That's my idea of success. I made it clear to the players here, "Whatever your key motivation is, I have no problem with it. If it's money, go for it.

'If it's winning, go for it. My drug was winning. Glory, fame, nice lady, big car, go for it. That's all fuel that can drive you. If you understand the fuel and use it for the betterment of yourself and others, I'm happy."

'But it can demotivate you. Some of our players here are wealthy enough. I don't slaughter them. I give them a nudge now and then, a straightener, a message but I always do it respectfully. I look at statistics and tell some players, "You're not running as hard and fast as six months ago."'

Dyche trusts his players but worries about youngsters elsewhere.

'These young ones are living in a world of madness. There was a player on loan at a Championship club last season on £3,000 a week and now he's on £36,000 and not playing. Can't they come up with a system where they put this money in a trust for these kids, calm their world down and keep them focused on what the real goal is?

'That goal is to be a brilliant footballer. Some naturally have that desire. You could pay Alan Shearer, Frank Lampard and Steven Gerrard £1m a day and it wouldn't matter. They want to play hard and win. I know Stuart Pearce well; he's earned a lot of money and yet had always had that real desire. Teddy Sheringham has that desire; it's not about the money but the glory of winning.'

Dyche loves winning, loves management but has concerns. 'I had dinner with Brendan Rodgers, who I worked with at Watford. I said, "Brendan, it's really important for me that you do well. You're a young manager, if you don't do well what chance have I got in the future? If you don't do well, will boardrooms say we need an older manager? It's really important that you do well, that Malky Mackay does well." Then people will say: "The big ginger fella at Burnley is a bit more than just running players around a pitch."

'Coaching is evolving in England but the media can be slightly down on us. There are a lot of really good English coaches out there. When I was at Watford, I went with the under-21s to Valencia. It was a draw, a brilliant game. I saw the Valencia first-team players running round the pitch. The Valencia coaches said, "It's the Cooper run, cones out, 12 minutes."

'Now, imagine you walk down here and you saw a 6ft 1in ginger skinhead running some players round a football pitch, would you think that modern or outdated? And yet if you went to Valencia would you say "old school" or "look at the scientific approach"? The Cooper run was 30 years ago in England.

'I'm not a fashion item. There are lots of managers out there branding themselves up to the eyeballs, coming out with fancy words, new sayings. I'm sick of hearing about "philosophy". It's a posh word for gameplan. Everyone now says, "If you haven't got a philosophy you haven't got a brain." I find that bizarre.

'Sir Alex Ferguson said the hardest thing for young managers now is that past chairmen said, "Can you make this team win? But now it's can you make this team win and by the way we want 500 passes, win 7-0 every week and play the beautiful game."

'When I was at Watford, we had no funds. Danny Graham, Will Buckley, and Don Cowie left so 54 per cent of the season's goals left the building. I took over as manager and spent £1m on ten new players. Do the maths, not exactly highbrow players. They were a fantastic group of people, all blood, guts and determination, but not as technical as the players here, so my philosophy has to be different.

'At Watford we couldn't play 4-3-3, roll the ball out from the back, and play 400 passes before we score. I operate in a different way here. We play through the units, fast attacking football, we pass, we move, move it quickly, counter, cross, finish.

'I focus on the myth that if you've not played at the top you can't manage at the top. Look at Rafa Benitez, Gerard Houllier, Arsene Wenger, Jose Mourinho, Sir Alex, David Moyes and Roberto Martinez.'

Dyche was perhaps destined to be a manager. Aged 12, a friend told Dyche he would make a manager. 'Maybe he thought I was a leader-type, gobby! As a player I began looking at things tactically. I was obsessed with yardages. When Watford were attacking

I used to scream at fellow defender Lloyd Doyley to mark the centre-forward. He'd shout at me why was I screaming, it was only two yards. But those two yards might have saved us a goal.

'I've had some really good influences like John Duncan at Chesterfield and Ray Harford at Millwall. Ray designed a session to get the outcome without stopping it. I don't want to be in there all the time pontificating to players. They might switch off. When we're working on getting in behind a defence, we make a narrow, long pitch, no space wide, so you have to play between the units and get in behind the back four.'

Doing well on minimal resources, Dyche laughed at the recent 'mini-slump' criticism of his team. 'Mini-slump, Burnley Football Club, spent nothing, got the smallest squad in the division. I wouldn't describe going from first to third and back as a slump; in Real Madrid's or Barcelona's world, possibly, but not at Burnley.

'Come on people, let's be as one; our town, our Turf. There are older groups of fans who remember the glory days (of the 1960s); that's good in the sense that it gives some identity. It's bad in the sense of why aren't we top of the Premier? Times have changed radically and financially of course. There are clubs in this division with five times our playing staff budget. Saturday is one at Leicester. Forest, Reading, Bolton, Wigan are others.

'There are challenges here that make it a lot tougher than if you are at Leicester, Forest or Reading because resources do help. We sold Charlie Austin. It was a necessity. As custodian of this football club I don't want to see Burnley get into trouble. I hope to do really well here. That might last ten years, might not, but there'll be a football club beyond me.'

As a town, Burnley has been hard hit economically and endured occasional social strife.

'The hardest thing here is that there are lots of fans, real Burnley fans, who want to come and watch, but because of awkward economics they just can't afford it. I think we are very reasonable to come in and watch but people just can't muster up the money.

'Community is a big part of this club. We want to break down some of the social boundaries. We know there's been all sorts of unrest here. If we can play a tiny part in helping, then brilliant. It's about doing the right thing.'

That's Dyche's ethos. He is passionate about football but keeps it in perspective. 'Without our family, work means nothing. After I left Watford, my son's friends at school said, "Your dad's been sacked." Well, I'm not going to cry. It's family first. It's my little girl's nativity on Wednesday and I have to be there. My son trains at Northampton's academy and plays on Sunday and I try to get there.

'My brother works in the building trade and you know how hard that's been over the past five years. My other brother works at Weetabix. I don't need to go far before someone gives me a straightener.'

TWAS THE NIGHT BEFORE CHRISTMAS:

Middlesbrough 1 Burnley 0
Wigan Athletic 0 Burnley 0

TWAS the night before Christmas and Burnley were top. There was carol singing around the cash registers at Marks and Spencer. No matter how many times you say that's the last bit of shopping, you end up at the supermarket again. There's always one card arrives at the very last minute from someone you haven't sent one to. No matter how much Blu Tack you use there's always one card that keeps falling down.

Mrs T was back in the swing of things after her enforced lay-off a year ago with her arm in a sling. It was down to me a year ago to save the day. I offered to cook again this Christmas but the offer was rejected. Little Joe was thrilled to bits when his package arrived from the Junior Clarets with his certificate.

Twas the day before Christmas, the weather outside was frightful; and the fire indoors delightful… let it snow, let it snow, let it snow, the song goes, but it was rain that lashed down and gales that caused mayhem.

The day before Christmas Eve: Granny Thomas was in the kitchen in food preparation mode. The blender was out. The mixer was out. The robot-chef was blasting away. Everywhere you looked – debris, food, splatter, spills, wreckage, not a surface uncovered, frustration rising, washing-up heaped in the sink, stuffing half made, bread sauce half made, steam everywhere… and a little voice pipes up from the doorway.

'Granny can I help?'

Never got in this mess last year when I did it, I mentioned casually…steam came out of her ears. I heard words that you'd never expect from a granny. I had to cover little Joe's ears.

Twas the day before Christmas, Christmas Eve, and there was Joe's wooden castle to put together before he came to the house. I got caught out a couple of years ago when we bought him a PlayMobil School. The box was gigantic and I assumed the school was in one piece inside, so it never occurred to me that it would be in a thousand bits and pieces you had to fix together with the most infernally infuriating little fixing things. I have never sworn so much in such a short space of time as realisation dawned that there was a mammoth project in front of me. It took three days to do it.

So this time, out came the castle in plenty of time, and the Phillips screwdriver. Woodwork was never my strong point but it went together like a dream. Asda, highly recommended.

Twas the season of bad jokes. 'How do you make an idiot laugh on Christmas Day? Tell him a joke on Christmas Eve.' 'Who says oh, oh, oh? Santa walking backwards.' 'What do you call a brothel at the North Pole? A workshop.' 'How does a Yorkshireman make a few quid at Christmas? He puts parking meters outside his house.' 'Saint Peter meets three blokes at the gates of Heaven. "If you want to get in show me something that represents Christmas," he says. The first bloke pulls out a lighter and says it's a candle. The second guy pulls out a set of keys and jingles them and says, "These are bells." The third guy pulls out a pair of panties and says, "These are Carol's."'

Christmas Day, and what a great idea it was of the club to do little Christmas video messages for deserving fans. Mrs T and me are big softies at heart and at some of them we had a little tear in the eye…especially when Danny Ings sent his message to little Joe and we played it on YouTube.

Joe's eating habits revolve round M&S sausage rolls. Greggs are quite acceptable too. There's a little café near us so we'll nip in there as well. Danny told him if he wanted to be a top footballer he'd have to start eating proper dinners. Joe's best Christmas present…a Danny Ings shirt. Danny meanwhile had Christmas dinner at Nino's in Rawtenstall.

Twas the day after Christmas…and exactly 50 years ago Burnley beat Manchester United 6-1 on an amazing Boxing Day afternoon when a record number of goals were scored. Fulham got ten, Blackburn eight, Liverpool six, Chelsea five. Another game was a 4-4 draw.

I was just 19, home from college for Christmas, standing on a packed Longside in that section lower down where you paid a bit extra to go in. The air was filled with the buzz of Christmas, the smoke from cigarettes, the smell of cigars and blokes took a tot of whisky from their little flasks. Willie Morgan, only 18, had given a dazzling display and scored twice. Andy Lochhead scored four.

Morgan today has a place in Tenerife and when they bump into each other out there, Lochhead still asks how Morgan was man of the match that day and not him. Two days later at Old Trafford United won 5-1 and this time it was George Best who was the star.

Morgan remembers there were few if any tactics. There were no coaches, just the manager. At Burnley it was Harry Potts. According to Morgan he might tell his players to watch out for a couple of names in the opposition team but by and large they were simply told to go out and score as many goals as they could. He might say that the opposition weren't a bad side; but that Burnley were better.

He remembers that it was a joy to play back then; his only regret the state of the pitches. The emphasis was on attack and most teams had several players who were good on the ball, plus a centre-forward who could score plenty.

Twas the day after Christmas, Boxing Day 2013: 1,300+ Burnley fans made the journey to Middlesbrough, not the best of hunting grounds for the Clarets.

That's how it stayed with a 1-0 defeat, Boro scoring with a 25-yarder that swerved, dipped, wobbled, bounced and deceived Heaton.

Shay Given made a couple of decent saves in their goal, one in particular from Ings. According to the stats Burnley had by far the greater possession, but Dyche in the aftermath described them as lacking a cutting edge.

Pre-season against Sparta Rotterdam. Richard Scherpenzeel with the away fans.

Rocky and Rockette on the pre-season tour of Ireland.

On tour in Ireland and a trip to Dingle in the heatwave.

Clarets all over the world, Alex Ross finds a surprise somewhere in the desert, Western Australia.

Who is this? It's Bradley Gray with Danny Ings in Asda Rawtenstall.

Director Clive Holt welcomes new director Brian Nelson to the Board.

Rainbow over Turf Moor and somewhere there is the pot of gold, picture by Chris Gibson.

Scott Arfield in the Padiham hardware store.

Jimmy Adamson book launch with Sean Dyche early in the season.

With former director Chris Duckworth and current director Barry Kilby before the Blackburn Rovers game.

Away with the Supporters' Club weekend, Millwall warm-up and then a Sunday stroll to the pie shop.

At Huddersfield Town by David Ashley.

Turf Moor nestles in the town by Rob Slade.

Joe Riddell waits to be mascot, picture by Harriet Thomas and then leads out the teams, by Rob Slade.

James and Louis Morley.

The Golden Girls at Bournemouth.

Mid-February goals table.

Look who Mrs T found in the hotel away at Yeovil.

Above, Sam and Ben Sutcliffe ready for training.

The main man Sean Dyche after the Millwall win, picture courtesy BFC.

Dave T enjoys a healthy pre-match breakfast.

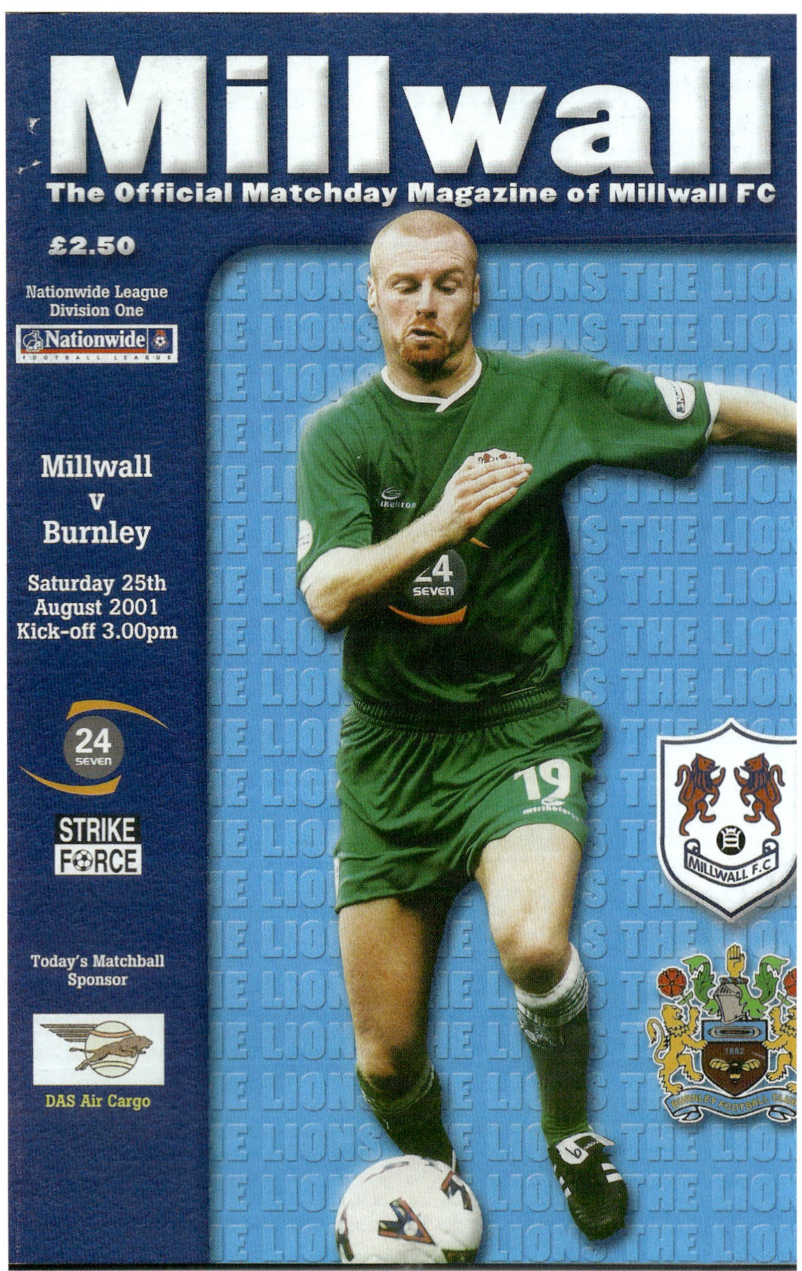

Guess who? Fancy meeting this man on a muddy day at The Den. Courtesy of Millwall Football Club.

Danny Joe's lucky day with Danny Ings, picture by Claire Taylor.

Victoria Thomas and Joe Riddell wait for the game against Nottingham Forest; a resounding win for the Clarets and a blistering first half performance that had us all enthralled as they left the field with a 3-0 lead, picture by Harriet Thomas.

Floods at Upton on Severn on the way to Yeovil with the Supporters Club.

The joy of a win: Ged Burnley Mac over the moon after the win against Nottingham Forest.

The roars from the Longside before Burnley's masterful destruction of Nottingham Forest.

Sam Vokes and Danny Ings being interviewed for BBC Football Focus at Gawthorpe in the February afternoon sun.

The band of brothers 2013/14, courtesy Burnley Football Club.

Granddad, why are they all shouting? Picture courtesy of Gerry O Gorman.

From the Jones corner Burnley go 2-0 up against Derby, picture courtesy James Coldman.

Interview time at Gawthorpe for Football Focus, *no expense spared.*

Badge Girl on matchday. Picture by Joe Vaiders.

Away support at Bournemouth.

Return of HMS Daring *at Portsmouth, courtesy* Burnley Express.

Sam Vokes is Sky February Player of the Month, courtesy Burnley Football Club.

Boundary Clarets before the Blackburn game, picture courtesy Emma Leeming.

Get your Blackburn buses here and mind 'ow you go, picture by Bill Holden.

On the way to a little bit of history as the 35-year hoodoo is ended, Blackburn 1 Burnley 2.

Clarets all over the world (and an intruder) in Perth, Western Australia, courtesy of Andy Pickering.

Peter Shirtcliffe of Burnley Memorabilia, picture by Kelly Travers.

Scott Arfield in the limelight after the match winning-goal against Leeds United, picture courtesy of Burnley Football Club.

Left: *Awards evening, Danny Ings, and deserved halo, the Football League Championship player of the season, with Mike Evans, General Manager Football League Trust.* Right: *Mascot Millie at Blackburn with Kieran Trippier and Danny.*

Legends Roger Eli left, Peter Shirtcliffe modelling, and John Deary right, promote the Vintage Clarets retro shirt available from Peter's memorabilia stall in Burnley market, picture by Vintage Clarets.

A proud Bobby Atkinson visits Charlton, his 50th league ground.

Well worth the visit.

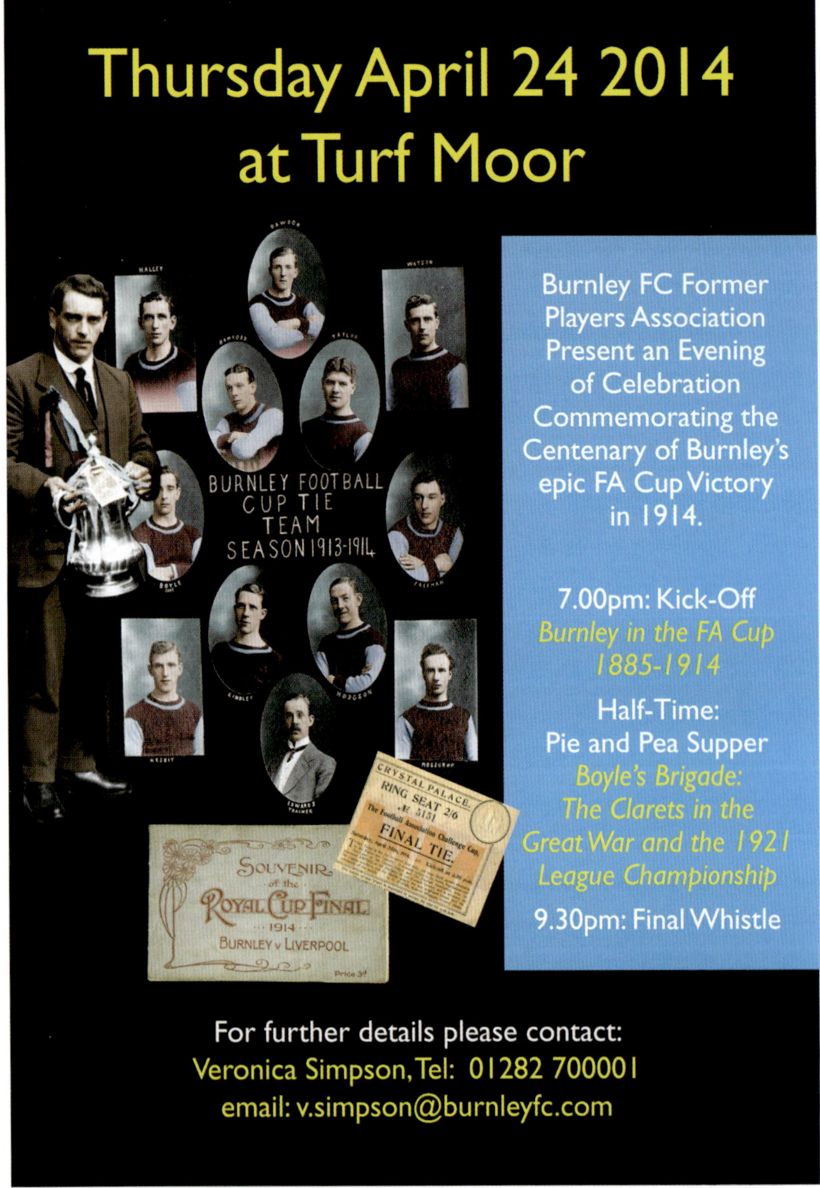

The 100th anniversary of the 1914 FA Cup win at Crystal Palace, Burnley 1 Liverpool 0 with the goal scored by Bert Freeman and the subject of Mike Smith's splendid book The Road to Glory. *Poster courtesy of Mike Smith*

*Hannah Graham at the Towneley Hall 1914 FA Cup exhibition with
the replica FA Cup, picture by Warren Graham and FA Cup courtesy
of Peter Briggs. The 1914 FA Cup was the first major honour won
by Burnley Football Club and exactly 100 years later Burnley won
promotion to the Premier League.*

The Fans Forum with left to right at the table Mike Garlick, Sean Dyche, John B and Lee Hoos with an audience of 300 fans, picture by Chris Gibson.

Ready for the 3-0 win at Charlton.

A Saturday in Watford and a 1-1 draw – pre match.

The Golden Girls with Harry Hornet.

4,000 at Barnsley, picture Burnley FC.

The team celebrate promotion to the Premiership by Dan Black.

After the Wigan game, DONE IT, by Richard Sutcliffe.

Mike Garlick and John B.

All smiles at the end of the season for Sean Dyche. Picture courtesy of Joe Vaiders.

Premier League here we come. Picture courtesy of Dan Black.

The picture that emerged from those who were there was that it was a poor-ish display with some well below average individual performances. Despite just two wins in nine games and just nine goals in those games, astonishingly they remained second, but promotion form this was not.

Leicester won to go top but QPR lost at Nottingham Forest and Derby could only draw. Form at the moment is fitful; the points come in dribs and drabs, goals have been hard to come by but there they were still hanging on to a top-two place. Burnley had Martin Paterson to thank for the points that Derby dropped at Huddersfield because of an equaliser with just minutes to go.

The foul weather with gales, storms, floods and lashing rain returned after Boxing Day. My sister-in-law had been one of the thousands without power for 24 hours down south. It was restored in the nick of time for Christmas Day. England had Australia on the ropes in Melbourne but it didn't last long. Billions were spent in the Boxing Day sales by the haves, the have-nots traipsed to food banks in greater numbers than ever. Malky Mackay was sacked at Cardiff by fashionista Vincent Tan. Phil Brown was hot favourite to take over on account of he loved a good tan.

Twas a few days after Christmas: gluttony and over-indulgence over, leftovers in the fridge dwindling, unwanted presents flooding eBay, another birthday gone by, Claretsmad back on air. We fancied a nice day out and had seats on the BFC Supporters' Club Wigan Express. A staggering 4,600 Clarets made their way to the pie-eating centre of the universe; the world championships are usually held at Harry's Bar on Wallgate. It was a Wigan dancing troupe that gave Charlie Chaplin his showbiz debut.

The coach was filled to the brim. So was the away end with the latecomers standing and filling the aisles to overflowing. A sit-anywhere policy for 4,600 fans did not work. Stewards (what few there were) just ignored it. The stadium is at the edge of the most soulless out-of-town shopping area I have ever seen, Chappy's fish and chips right by the ground the only redeeming feature. We wandered round in the sunshine. Was this really December?

It was a thoroughly engaging game; the first half belonging to Burnley who produced three fingertip saves from the Wigan keeper, whose arms were a very unfair five feet long, and Jones hit the crossbar with the ball bouncing down and some claiming it was over the line, then to be miraculously cleared away by last-ditch defending. Half-time and things looked promising.

But then in the second half the limitations of such a small squad unable to maintain the pace became plain to see, plus the lack of any forward able to get to the byline and send an accurate cross over. The lack of anyone among the substitutes able to take some weight off Ings and Vokes was blatant. Both looked shattered because for them there was no respite. The bruising punishment they take is relentless. Stanislas, as frustrating as Treacy, but the one forward who can take a man on and the most accurate crosser of a ball at the club, remained firmly stuck to the bench.

With Burnley pinned back by Wigan for most of the second half, with no outlets or penetration in wide positions, by the end it seemed like a well-earned point as defenders repelled the repeated Wigan forays. But in truth it was frustrating. Wigan created little in the box. Heaton was busy but this was just the routine collection of crosses and tidying up. He had no real saves to make except for one in the first half.

So there were frustrations. These came from seeing the club in such a fantastic position at exactly the halfway mark, still joint second and with just three defeats, but simultaneously the strong possibility that it would all come to naught without fresh legs to bring variety to tactics and impact from the bench if a game was at the stalemate stage.

Without pace on the flanks, and so much play through the middle, so much relies on the interplay between Ings and Vokes. Both at Wigan were more and more off the pace the longer the game progressed. As one bloke put it, 'This was like seeing two tired horses being flogged to death.' And there were no replacements.

Talk after the game walking back to the car park and then on the coach was of the club and board being at a crossroads.

It could stick or twist. The team was in a totally unexpected position. It had done so well. In truth it had amazed us.

So the board could find a couple of million to bring quality players in, it could make determined efforts to secure signings; or it could play safe with the finances and hope this tired squad could hang on in there. On the evidence of the Wigan and Middlesbrough games, the same squad achieving the impossible seemed unlikely.

There was a new director in the boardroom. Brendan Flood was in the directors' box at Wigan. The board had already said there was money available. Only the intransigence of Billy Davies prevented the loan signing of one of his players in the last window. Andy Keogh wasn't allowed to sign from Millwall; yet more frustrations. To secure even a play-off place, probably ten more wins would be needed but at Middlesbrough and Wigan that seemed a tall order.

It had been a brilliant ride so far. Stick or twist…the crossroads beckoned.

January

GOODBYE 2013:
Burnley 3 Huddersfield Town 2

THE penultimate bend, halfway, the strongest usually start to pull ahead. And such is football and the long Championship slog to the finishing line. The stronger teams emerge and rise to the top, the weaker fall away.

Some, running on adrenalin and sheer guts, hang on in there. It was clear that the latter was Burnley's group. For the last ten games they'd stuttered and stumbled and it was also sod's law that as New Year approached, the two most recent games had been against teams on the up under new managers.

Years ago Bobby Charlton, who scored more than his fair share of 20-yarders in an age when pitches were a mudbath and the ball weighed a ton, said that all he ever did was let fly without aiming for any particular spot on the assumption that if he had four attempts one would go in. Not for him the modern method of deliberately curling it, bending it, swerving or dipping it with boots the colour of a rainbow.

Vincent Tan, the well-known Cardiff stylista owner, advised his players they should shoot more often and quoted an ancient Malaysian proverb, 'If you ask ten girls to go out with you, no matter how ugly you are, I bet one will say yes.'

The most rejuvenated manager of the year must have been Steve McClaren for his work at Derby County. Let us not forget he was once referred to as the Wally with the Brolly for his forgettable performances as England manager, and that while managing in Holland he was much mocked for the Dutch accent he picked up while speaking English. On Boxing Day, Derby overtook Burnley.

The most monumental event of the year in football must surely have been Alex Ferguson's retirement. David Moyes's appointment as replacement was perhaps a bit of a surprise but in hindsight was maybe the obvious one, one dour Scotsman following another.

The most impressive reformation might well be Luis Suarez, he of the cannibalistic urges and with gnashers to rival Dracula's, but after his lengthy ban he knuckled down so that by Christmas he was on course to be Player of the Year and the bloke you'd most like to live next door to.

Non-surprise of the year was probably the news that Bolton Wanderers were £163m in debt. Next year's big surprise will be if they haven't folded.

Burnley hero and legend Andy Lochhead was in the spotlight. This time it was *The Sun* featuring the 6-1 demolition of Manchester United on Boxing Day 1963. Willie Irvine once said old strikers never forget any of their goals.

Andy remembered the four he scored that day, 'Scoring and beating Manchester United was always an achievement. But to bag four goals was something special. I am so glad I played in the 60s, an era I still regard as the greatest the game has seen.

'We started brightly and had the impetus of an early lead after just six minutes when I scored following good work by John Angus. I got my second just after half-time, a speculative shot from 20 yards which went in off the angle of the bar and post. From the start of the second half we ran riot with Willie Morgan hitting his first two goals for the Clarets and my own second-half brace bringing the total for me to four and the team a whopping six.'

Morgan was in the side because John Connelly was injured. His display convinced Bob Lord that Connelly could be sold to United and in Morgan there was a dazzling replacement. It was Jock Stein who suggested to Lochhead that he should sign for Burnley, then a fantastic nursery for young players.

He still lives in Burnley today but had spells at Leicester, Aston Villa and Oldham. At Villa he remains a cult figure. Manchester City and Joe Mercer were keen to sign him but old Bob Lord would have none of it. Later in the 1960s coach Jimmy Adamson wanted him to remain at Burnley and play as a centre-half.

The death of former player Paul Comstive came as a huge shock. He was only 52. Following the near-disastrous 1986/87 season he was one of the new players drafted in to reshape the ailing team. He left in 1989 after 103 games and 23 goals for Burnley.

He was a member of the team that reached the Wembley final of the Sherpa Van Trophy against Wolves. After the horrors of the previous season it was a marvellous achievement, almost fairytale, to progress to the final and two of his goals were crucial in that campaign; one was the winner at Bury, and the other was the final goal in the second leg against Preston.

Twice he hit the woodwork with headers in the Wembley game but Wolves were the victors in front of 80,000 spectators, a quite amazing attendance for two sides in the Fourth Division.

New Year's Day: Huddersfield had been on the up since beating Burnley 2-1 at the John Smith's Stadium. In the first half they'd looked a class outfit. In their most recent game they'd clattered Yeovil 5-1. Paterson was once again banging goals in for them like he used to at Turf Moor. Huddersfield therefore represented a stern challenge and with Burnley's form resting on a knife-edge there was certainly no confidence that a win was a certainty.

There's always something flat and lifeless about a New Year's Day morning. The weather outside the window was grey, dull, uninspiring. It's always fun putting up the decorations. It's always a drag taking them down. It's a symbol that the enjoyment and escapism of Christmas is over. Reality beckons.

The rain began to lash down. This was an afternoon to sit in front of the fire, watch a film, drink sloe gin, eat the last mince pies, read a bit more of Harry Redknapp, above all stay warm and cosy. But the Turf beckoned. How did that old WW1 recruiting poster go? 'Your Team Needs You'.

Some 1,800 Yorkshiremen headed over the hills to Burnley on roads awash with water and spray; all ee by gums and na' then and 'ecky thumps. Yorkshirefolk generally were thrilled to see they could save a quid or two by reusing 1986 calendars. Simultaneously, Bulgarians and Romanians were allegedly heading across the channel by plane, coach, bus, ferry, horse and cart, and submarine to Eldorado and the land of opportunity, according to news reports. They'd all learned to say, 'I go for work not for benefeets.' Yeh right Dave. I'd half expected to see Nigel Farage at Dover shooing them away.

If we thought Huddersfield would play like they did at their own ground we were totally wrong. Other than the last few minutes after they scored their second this was a terrific Burnley performance. By then they should have been dead and buried, the game out of sight, Burnley cruising and relaxing.

What a start: an amazing thing happened. Burnley scored after just six minutes when Ings broke through and smacked it home. There was a brief moment's hush and surprise as if we were thinking, 'Hang on a minute, we don't do this, this isn't the way we do things, we don't score early goals.' Then it sank in and the roar grew.

Huddersfield were neat and tidy but unthreatening. Only a defensive lapse and poor marking from a corner in the swirling wind gave them an equaliser. We groaned. But back Burnley came; urgent, confident, inventive, and it was no surprise when Ings got his second with a crisp shot. Jones hit the bar with a superb effort, the keeper made a cracking save from another shot from Jones that was arrowing in. Another baffling referee gave Huddersfield every advantage and soft free kicks at every opportunity.

Ings was back to his best, Marney and Jones dominant, Trippier magnificent going forward. It brought him Burnley's third goal. I missed it, downstairs having a barney with a pimple-faced steward who looked about 18. Turned out he was 20.

He'd been up to warn me about my language earlier. I was puzzled; I'd stood up and yelled 'absolute cr*p' at one of this infuriating ref's crap decisions and 'absolute rubbish' at another. He told me he'd heard me twice using foul language. Downstairs

I asked him what two words had I used. He told me I'd used the word sh*t at the referee.

'And the two ladies with you as well, they used it as well.'

That was the clincher. I was livid and bellowed at him in full ex-headmaster whole-school assembly mode, 'GET ME THE SUPERVISOR.' I swear his knees buckled. He went a whiter shade of pale. Three of his pimples burst. Off he went. I waited, fuming. I can understand now how easy it must be to succumb to rage and blind fury and take a swing at somebody.

He returned with his supervisor and FOUR more stewards. Is this where I get dragged away to the cage under the Cricket Field Stand, I wondered. Will there be a picture of me behind bars on Twitter and Facebook and then in *The Mirror*?

I let him and his supervisor have it, both barrels. 'Now come and meet the two ladies,' I invited the supervisor. Up he came. The saintly Mrs T and daughter were gobsmacked at the accusation, nobody around us had heard the word. Lots of apologies were duly offered. The pimple-faced one was removed.

And the most annoying thing: I missed Tripps's wonder-goal. 'A champagne moment,' Sean Dyche called it. So: just sometimes we do get champagne with beer money.

The last few minutes were nerve-wracking, the wind blowing stronger, seagulls flying backwards, the rain swirling, the pigeons wearing wellies. We knew Derby were losing and second spot was there ready and waiting.

Burnley weathered the storm. It was Paterson who scored both their goals, his celebrations deliberately muted. He was warmly applauded on to the field in contrast to McCann at Wigan who was soundly booed at every opportunity. Paterson didn't want to leave, he would have been happy to stay, but wasn't guaranteed the central role he craved in the forward line. Oh to have him here still, I thought, to take the weight off Ings and Vokes, as he slammed in his second.

McCann revealed he wanted a new challenge, code-speak for having had enough of Burnley. By and large, many Burnley fans had had enough of him as well. Football is funny. Some players are likeable. Some players are not. They find out when they leave just where they are in the popularity stakes.

The piece about new director Brian Nelson in the programme was a nice one. I've known Brian for ten years and chuckled at the quote that many years ago in the days of the Venerable Stan, Brian had offered to pay for the hotel on a trip but ended up paying for five plane flights for the team. That's Brian. Over the years he's always coughed up funds when asked, quietly, without fuss, publicity or fanfare. I was on one of those flights to Norwich and that's how we first met. All Burnley directors are fans to the core either born and bred or been here 30 years. It's a comforting thought whenever I see Vincent Tan or Venky's.

Goodbye 2013; but here came 2014 filled with hopes, expectations, resolutions (to do my best not to punch a steward) and the dream of Burnley hanging on in there. A pile of books ready to read, Ferguson, Redknapp, Mike Tyson and John Grisham and *The Railway Man* by Eric Lomax. Then there were more Simon Scarrow Roman legion books on the pile. Love 'em.

Alas there was a rather chilling thought. I'd be 70 in 2014. Now that was frightening and far too old an age to be getting into rages with stewards and shouting at referees.

INTO 2014 CUPS AND RE-UNIONS:
Southampton 4 Burnley 3

DECORATIONS down, lights packed away into boxes, mince pies finished, first week of January over, time for a think. Resolution number one, to eat less. Number two, stop shouting at referees.

On a Sky website Sean Dyche provided a sort of review of the first half of the season and spoke about the way things were going, the mixture of traits, the sound tactical framework, the work ethic, the clarity of thought.

The testing spell had seen the winning run come to an end in November and the sequence of draws begin. But by the time of the FA Cup third round on 4 January, the previous six games had seen three wins, two draws and just one defeat.

The victory against Huddersfield looked closer than it really was. Watching Ings's second goal and Trippier's swashbuckling third on replays only served to emphasise what class goals they were; the team build-up followed by individual brilliance, Trippier's hug with the ecstatic lad in the wheelchair a supreme football moment.

Bolton had impressed him in the very first game and yet since then faded. The power of the division could never be underestimated. There are no such things as easy games. The run of draws simply showed the reality of the division. Even top side Leicester had lost two back-to-back. Nottingham Forest were good on their home patch. QPR were and will be a good side. Wigan had certainly impressed him over Christmas.

Challenges come thick and fast. Of course the players like to be at Turf Moor but are motivated to set out to win wherever they are. No game is pivotal at this stage of the season. It's too early for that kind of thinking. The run of draws had no one worrying.

When the mix of the team is right, they are a really good side; the main thing is consistency. That is a key focus. If you get consistency of quality performances you get the outcome you want.

Dyche and his staff chatted with the players at the beginning of the season to clarify the focus. The group did fine pre-season work. Danny and Sam learned to play together and learned to use each other wisely. They get all the plaudits but there is a great support network behind them. The back four have been solid, the keeper too behind them. The midfield unit have played progressive football and intelligent football that is full of energy and full of running. Dyche likes to think that the whole unit has delivered and has been topped off by the lads at the front scoring.

When Charlie Austin left, Dyche wanted someone to find that clarity in their play to be the next version of the striker. He promoted this to the players and worked quite a lot with that. The club made it clear he had to cut his cloth and shop accordingly. It was made clear to the fans that the books must balance and that the club should be in a healthy position. Now there may be some finance available. It's not going to be massive, but if the right player comes along he will look to affect the situation.

Unfortunately when you are doing well other clubs will certainly look at your players. You are always going to attract attention. But the board have made it clear that the club is in a stable position. There are no major resources but it would need to be a very large offer for the board to consider any sale. At the moment the focus is on the players staying at the club.

Managing expectations: the target is only the next game. Everything is one step at a time. No one is getting carried away.

Player of the year so far: no one in particular. Everyone looks at strikers but there are defending principles as well to look at that often go unnoticed. There have been so many good performers so far. The focus is to make sure they stay motivated.

Best character: they are all characters on the coaching staff. The players are a nice mixture, a number of different characters, some quiet ones, some who enjoy the banter. There's a nice collective feel. One of the strengths of having a small group is that there are no egos. There's an attachment to each other, and a demand from them all to perform for each other.

Philosophy: a big word that doesn't mean a lot to Dyche. A philosophy needs to be flexible. He looks at what he's got and then plans accordingly. There is no set philosophy. Everything depends on circumstances.

The circumstances at Southampton for the cup game were that no one expected to win it. A draw would be a bonus and then get them back to Turf Moor for a bit of extra income. The other school of thought was that it would be no bad thing for Burnley to be eliminated and have a free weekend in January to rest tired limbs and recharge batteries, because the promotion target was so much more important.

Having booked to go to Yeovil, Mrs T and me gave the cup game a miss. Mind you the worry was that the Yeovil match would be postponed if the floods, gales and rain continued. When the clubs were in the same division we always went to Southampton, Mrs T having sisters living nearby, one almost within walking distance at Netley Abbey where Danny Ings was brought up. The last time we went was when we had the Scottie.

He distinguished himself on that trip by sneaking out under the garden gate and into Netley. We searched high and low when we realised he was missing. From the garden he'd disappeared across the busy High Street and dodged the traffic. We went into several shops asking if anyone had seen him trotting by. The answer was a 'yes' in the bakery. In fact he'd done more than walk past, he'd trotted in and gone round the back of the counter and helped himself to a loaf from the bottom shelf.

From there, we were told, he had made his way to the door of the working men's club nearby. In we went to see if anyone knew anything. They sure did. Someone had taken him in and he was sat up on a high stool by the bar being fed crisps.

A real character was the old Scottie, a little bugger in fact. He once walked into the house with a dead hen in his mouth. The lady next door kept a few in her yard. This one must have hopped over into ours. It sure didn't do it again. His hobby was rolling in fox or goose droppings he found along the canal. They don't make dogs like that anymore. His first owners called him Scamper but I never saw him scamper once in any sort of energetic way. At best he plodded quickly.

The media was well into the game, it being a reunion for Burnley and Rodriguez. Plus Ings and Vokes were once Saints fans. Sam Vokes's father Tim, a lifelong Saints supporter, was in a real quandary. The best result for him, he said, would be a 4-3 win for Southampton with son Sam scoring a hat-trick. The scoreline was correct but Vokes Junior only got one.

It was a game that had all the feel of a nice day out and not much chance of a win. In the morning we headed over the Pennines and the M62 to Newton-le-Willows for the day to visit relatives, leaving the drizzle and murk of Leeds behind. Betfair meanwhile had Saints v Burnley high on their list of banana-skin games worth a punt on the underdog, the idea being that should Burnley manage to take the lead, then the defence was capable of holding out. We listened to Sky Sports News and the reports. The relatives were delighted that Everton were winning; the Southampton relatives no doubt chuffed at their own scoreline.

We headed back home at half-time with Southampton winning 2-0 and the prospect of a bit of a tonking for Burnley. There was no urgency to switch on the car radio so when we did it was a real surprise to hear of a 2-1 scoreline and Burnley being right back in it. Funny how you have hunches sometimes and this one felt like 2-2 was on the cards.

Within minutes the radio guy was beside himself when he reported that it was indeed 2-2 at St Mary's and Burnley were on fire. A replay at Turf Moor now seemed a distinct possibility until hunch number two. 'You just watch. Rodriguez will score for Saints,' I said as we sped along the M62 skirting Manchester.

And he did. Game over was the next thought. They're not gonna come back again. Disappointment grew. Feelings of indifference at the prospect of a routine defeat when the game started were now replaced by a tinge of what-might-have-been especially when the next report said it was 4-2. All that hard work to make it 2-2 and the elation they must have felt when the equaliser went in counted for nothing.

With Rochdale on our left and the slopes of the Pennines ahead, by now there was only the consolation of the scoreline at Spotland: Rochdale 2 Leeds United 0 and the hammering QPR were receiving at Goodison. Except the radio guy was on again…now it was 4-3 at Southampton with time still for the impossible to happen.

By now snippets were coming through that Ings had hit the post; that goalkeeper Kelvin Davis had made a superb save from Vokes to stop Burnley going 3-2 up. If only…if only one of them had gone in. Football success comes down to such fine margins.

Ings had hit the post immediately prior to Saints' fourth. It would have been 3-3 had it gone in. And what a mess the Rodriguez goal was. On film afterwards the Burnley defenders seemed to stop in total confusion as if they expected the whistle to blow. The pundits too were baffled by it. Was it a free kick, but a free kick to whom? The ball came out to an almost apologetic Rodriguez who showed no joy at all when he scored from ten yards.

Even at the death Burnley battled away and a lightning raid gave Vokes a final chance. But it was not to be. What a second half it had been. Supporters who had been there were proud; so close to a remarkable scoreline that would have meant a replay at Turf Moor against all expectations. It was a game that could have been 8-8 said a grinning Gordon Strachan on ITV, quite blown away by the quality and excitement of what he had seen.

Vokes and Ings bagged a goal each and that would surely have delighted their friends and families who had turned out. Both had shown the Premier side and their fans that even against a classy top-flight outfit they and Burnley could turn it on and compete.

Three of the Southampton goals were long-range blockbusters that gave Heaton no chance; the first was world-class. Three unstoppable shots from 25 yards in one game is just sod's law. It had to be against Burnley. Rodriguez's goal was one of those things written in the stars beforehand. You could have put money on it. Such is football.

It was a unique game. Rodriguez has so many ties, family and friends back in Burnley. Burnley made him, the classic, modest, local-boy-done-good that the town is proud of. Then there are Vokes and Ings with their Southampton connections. Vokes saw his first Saints game when he was just three. He was a Junior Saint. He had a six-week trial but was told he was too tall and lanky. All that plus Jack Cork, formerly with Burnley, and a player fans would love to have stayed, was now in the Saints team.

Dyche was understandably proud. 'At the end of the day it's taken three goals from three England players to win it for them, but a scratch of luck and we could have won that. In the second half we were outstanding and but for a great save at 2-2 who knows. The harshness of the business is that you don't always get what you deserve. It's a strange one to lose a game and have such a feeling of pride.'

The Independent summed things up succinctly, 'Courageous Burnley go down fighting.' It left Southampton fans mighty relieved at the outcome and as the car headed up the drive to the house, me feeling thoroughly miffed we'd lost this epic game.

BREAKFAST WITH THE GALACTICOS:
Yeovil 1 Burnley 2

THIS report is dedicated to Victor Collinge. Victor ran the Border Bookshop in Todmorden for as long as I can remember. I lost count a long time ago of the number of times I called in when I was passing through Tod, browsed through the hundreds of football books, and bought books when I needed reference material for anything I was working on.

What a beautifully organised bookshop; rooms and rooms of books all sorted into sections and subjects and topics. Magazines, comics, annuals, you name it, they'd be there somewhere. But for me it was the rows and rows of football books that were the attraction.

Someone I know said it wasn't so much a bookshop but a Tardis, filled with rooms, nooks, crannies and passageways and just after you thought you'd been in the last one, you found another one; and all of them immaculately set out and presented, never a book out of place. Victor had followed Burnley for over 50 years. He died on New Year's Day.

⌗ ⌗ ⌗

Storms, tempests, monsoons and gales had lashed the country day after day. The *Daily Express* headlined continuously with doomsday warnings. Floods of biblical proportions covered vast swathes of the countryside. Streams became rivers, rivers became lakes; the land for miles and miles fast disappearing beneath brown swirling water. Whole towns awash, small villages completely cut off, power-lines down, thousands of homes ruined.

People canoed down the streets. Twenty-five-foot waves battered the shorelines, beaches disappeared, promenades crumbled, landmarks disappeared; cliffs tumbled into the sea, Aberystwyth almost vanished.

In the south and south-west of Wales there was no respite. And that, for the Yeovil game, was where we headed on the Friday beforehand. The football supporter is a hardy specimen. Nigh-on 1,700 of us wrapped up, wellied up, hatted up, all determined to get there and follow the lads; a quite astonishing turnout for such a distant game. The day before we departed, the *Daily Express* changed headlines. Floods and rain would be replaced by Arctic conditions that would last for weeks.

There were no new players as yet, the January window only a few days old. But Joseph Mills had returned from Oldham and Luke O'Neill from York. Ross Wallace, back from a long injury, had played half a game. Vokes had signed a contract extension.

With the transfer window being open various names were touted as Burnley possibles; Ashley Barnes stories would not go away. Luciano Becchio turned up from out of nowhere, Nahki Wells was a target, but the one I liked was Billy McKay from Scotland. Now there's a proper name, a no-nonsense name, a footballer's name, a name that sounds like it belongs to a striker; none of this Johnny Foreigner stuff for me. And, befittingly, one of Burnley's most prolific strikers was called McKay back in the 50s and Jimmy Mac rated him the best goal-poacher he had ever played with rattling goals from all angles, at any height, from left or right.

For most of the game he'd read the newspaper, contemplate the meaning of life, or just stroll around with seeming disinterest leaving any hard work to his team-mates. Work-rate, tracking back, covering; what were they? But when he and ball met in the penalty area he was lethal. He didn't stay long, no one quite sure whether he fell foul of Alan Brown on account of his on-pitch 'laziness', or a verbal set-to with Bob Lord when legend says McKay told him if he wanted a drink, 'och the noo' he'd bloody well have one.

Coach departure at 10am from the Turf; all the same familiar faces plus several new ones, most with a brolly or plastic mac tucked away somewhere. On Twitter a couple of days earlier the Yeovil plod had advised people at the away end to wrap up in suitable weatherproof clothing. This was an exposed, open end, they warned, standing only, just like football used to be.

Huish Park holds just under 10,000 and was only built in 1990 when Yeovil were in the Conference. The old ground had the infamous slope upon which giants were slain in the FA Cup like Sunderland in days of olde. If you put a coconut at the top end it would roll all the way down to the other, although there is no evidence to suggest that anyone ever actually did take a coconut in.

On the way to Burnley from Leeds, trotting happily along the pavement, without a care in the world as the morning traffic whizzed by, was a little black sheep. I've seen some funny things in my time on pavements, but this was a first. We took this as a good luck sign.

Arriving at the hotel, the notice board in reception said 'Welcome Burnley FC'. Surely it couldn't, wouldn't be the lads. Surely it was a welcome for us. But no: the team were staying there as well. The last time this happened was five years ago in Plymouth and that was the promotion year. I mentioned this to Sean Dyche later; I'm sure he was impressed.

On the way down we heard the news that Ashley Barnes had signed. We stopped at Upton on Severn. There was every chance it was about to be renamed Upton under Severn as the raging river swirled just a foot below the flood defences. Even the ducks were in canoes.

It's a nice little village and has the kind of tiny shops where if you have a mind you can buy spare parts for your church organ. The rain mercifully had stopped. Oliver Cromwell made the place famous when he crossed the bridge at Upton on his way to Wetherspoon's at Taunton.

I can report to you that we breakfasted with the team and mingled, Mrs T quite beside herself surrounded by so many young fellas glowing with health and positively radiant with fitness. They reminded me of me years ago. They didn't ask us for our autographs because Sean must have told them not to bother us at breakfast.

The previous night we sat and watched Leicester take Derby apart while we were sitting with Trippier and Ings. Mrs T chatted away to Danny about being brought up in Netley Abbey. Funny to think that we probably walked by him playing footie in the schoolyard when he was just a little nipper in the school there, as we walked to the shops. Her sister's house was just over the road.

Of course what they all had for breakfast is confidential. It would be wrong of me to reveal the names of the three players who had to be shown how to use the toasting machine. Our friend Anne was toastmeister and is now available for training days. I wouldn't dream of telling you which player ate the most, which player had a plate of scrambled eggs and then buried it with an inch-deep layer of tomato sauce, or who had the full English, or who just had a banana.

Mind you, there's nowt wrong with tomato sauce. It's one of your five fruit and veg and has contents that help fight cancer. I will report though that as hotel breakfasts go, of all the ones we've had on our travels with the supporters' club, this one at the Holiday Inn, Taunton, was one of the best.

On game-day, we'd all planned for one of two eventualities, more rain or bitter cold. None of us were prepared for the warm sunny day and the blue skies. I sat at this match dressed like Scott of the Antarctic as the sun shone from a cloudless sky. Before we went to the ground there was a most pleasant stroll round the streets of Taunton. I was impressed by the food stalls; the Italian Hot Sausage Co, the roast pork baguette stall, the West Country Pasty Company.

Huish Park was heaving with Burnley folk, the standing area a reminder that there needn't be any problems with standing at football grounds. It's ace going to games like this where you meet and greet faces you haven't seen for a while, people from all parts of the country, people who have come because it was another new ground to visit.

The stewards were a good bunch. Those of us at York in the pre-season can remember the utterly pathetic, miserable sods there who confiscated the inflatable dolphins that everyone had fun batting around. Here at Huish Park the stewards returned the inflatable footballs with a smile.

And the game: a win was imperative. Leicester were now seven points clear, QPR only a point behind. And Burnley hadn't won away for some time. They did win but despite Yeovil's lowly position this was no easy pushover. The last ten minutes were nailbiting.

On 80 minutes and two goals to the good, Burnley were coasting and in control. But this is Burnley and somehow a hopeful low cross from the left gently made its way into the far corner of the goal with defenders either mesmerised by its serene passage into the area, or all of them leaving it to each other.

One message board poster summed it all up nicely, 'As relaxed and assured as an evening with the Pasadena Roof Orchestra until we decided to let someone skip past three or four defenders with ten minutes to go…leading to the mandatory period of angst before the final whistle.'

From that point on, Yeovil, average height something like 6ft 3in, pumped, pummelled, and pushed ever more threateningly at the Burnley goal. On 80 minutes there we were, relaxed, calm, at ease, enjoying the moment, admiring the setting sun, and then suddenly it was worryingly tense. Until that soft goal went in, there was only one team in contention and looking likely to add to the tally. Vokes had hit the post minutes earlier. The Yeovil keeper had made a couple of excellent saves.

By this time news that QPR were winning was filtering through. The giants of Yeovil continued to hammer away, every ball lobbed into the area giving us the heebie-jeebies. Shackell was whacked, the injury minutes mounted up, five of them in all, and they wound down with agonising slowness.

The last three wins have all come by the odd goal; tickets should now carry a health warning. Before Yeovil scored, the game should have been dead and buried, totally beyond their reach. Three or four goals wouldn't have flattered Burnley despite this being a difficult pitch and not quite being at their fluent best.

Ings and Vokes scored the goals, our very own Little and Large; Ings's an absolute beauty when he picked up the ball maybe 30 yards out and let fly and it went like a rocket into the far corner. It was so stunning; blink and you missed it. Vokes's was the result of quick thinking by Marney when he picked up on a Yeovil error and the resultant ball across the box was neatly converted by the big man about ten seconds later. Ings's strike must surely be a contender for one of the goals of the season. Alas speculation mounts regarding his future in direct relation to every goal he scores.

Meanwhile Billy McKay scored again for Inverness. The game ended with something we hadn't seen all season. Ings was taken off and replaced. On came the new man Ashley Barnes for a few minutes.

The win saw the 50-point landmark reached. 'Staying up, staying up, staying up,' the Burnley fans sang. People were now looking at permutations and how many points would be needed for second place.

Winning half the remaining games would guarantee 80 points, while 82 and above usually means an automatic place. Which would be the team to crack first, with it looking now that Leicester, Burnley and QPR would be the three that looked likeliest to pull away from the pack?

We came away from Yeovil impressed with the players in the hotel. They seemed at ease with each other. They had a nice manner about them. Look for wild hairstyles or these headphones that the galacticos wear round their ears, and you don't see them at Burnley. They seemed so relaxed and comfortable. In the morning it was the little things that impressed like the way they greeted each other with a smile. The night before, Sean Dyche had spent time with a group of supporters in the lounge area chatting away.

A message board poster listed all the positives of the season so far: the hard part is behind us, the games played, the points tally, the lack of injuries, the two games a week period all done and dusted, 12 points clear of seventh-placed Reading, 21 games left and a leisurely 16 weeks to play them, no major suspension worries, a new signing at last.

This was all real glass-half-full stuff. It made you want to break out into a quick song and dance. And then he asked, 'What can possibly go wrong?' This is Burnley, we thought. There's an awful lot can go wrong.

CALM, PRAGMATIC AND DOWN TO EARTH:
Burnley 1 Sheffield Wednesday 1

SHEFFIELD Wednesday were in town fresh from the 6-0 drubbing they'd given to Leeds United and a four-goal cup win. Burnley's record against them at Turf Moor was abysmal with not one win since 2001. It was therefore a game we approached with some trepidation even though we were up there in second spot, only one defeat in eight, and with praise from Harry Redknapp.

'People keep writing Burnley off. I don't think Burnley are going to fade away,' said Redknapp. 'From what I've seen Burnley are a very good team. Their two front men are excellent, they score goals and both scored at the weekend. They are solid. The right-back is an outstanding young player. They're a good side and I think they will be bang there at the end.'

Sean Dyche was calm, pragmatic and down to earth, 'We look at what we have and what we can do, rather than what we don't have and can't do. Our main focus is what we think about ourselves and everyone else can come across for the ride. It's about dealing with our own expectations and setting them where we feel it's appropriate. I know what we are about and what we are trying to challenge ourselves to do, individually and as a group. We've been very strong at home and we look to continue that.'

I hate teams that play in all black. Small teams look big. Big teams look like giants. Whatever their size, teams in black look mean and cussed and Neanderthal. Sheffield Wednesday were in black instead of their usual blue, bananas in pyjamas strip. They looked big and strong and menacing.

The omens had been good. Mrs T had news of a windfall in the morning. Then we learned of a mascot cancellation so that we could book grandson Joe to do the honours at the Millwall game. It made we wonder. It's quite a lucrative little sideline for the club. So: if kids can be a Junior Claret and become a mascot, why not the Pensioner Clarets and we too could pay to be a mascot and limp out on our Zimmer frames or be pushed out on a trolley.

There seemed to be conflicting views of the game. Dyche waxed lyrical about the performance and said it was one of the best. Second half maybe, but much of the first half was dour, attritional, ball in the air too much, much of the play matching the dull and leaden skies above. Even so, with Treacy in scintillating form, Burnley carved out chances that had us with our heads in our hands. Treacy, in the local press, had just confessed to feeling lower than a snake's belly during the Howe reign but said Dyche's man-management had rekindled his love for the game.

Ings thundered a shot from 25 yards that Kirkland tipped over, the goalkeeper destined to become man of the match by the end so that it would be Ings with his head in his hands more than once. Treacy's goalbound shot was kneed away, and Marney spurned a glorious chance when played through, electing to cunningly slip the ball wide of the goalkeeper, but in so doing cunningly slipped it wide of the right-hand post with the other side of the goal at his mercy.

At last Burnley did score, Vokes tucking home a through ball from Marney in style. Not much before half-time we perhaps felt a bit too cocky. So too did the team maybe because just 60 seconds later a sloppy equaliser was conceded, the result of lax defending of a free kick given for a needless foul. How many times had Wednesday been in the Burnley area in the first 45 minutes, five or six at the most? Where was the Wednesday team that had scored ten in their last two games? They weren't at Turf Moor, that's for sure. It made the equaliser all the more annoying and frustrating.

It was in the second half that Burnley's play became brighter, more inventive and dominant especially when the ball was on the floor, Vokes by now giving a masterclass in leading the line and winning the headers. But would the ball go in? No it would not.

Notwithstanding a ten-minute spell of Sheffield attacking, the number of efforts on goal piled up. At last a tolerant referee booked a couple of Wednesday players. The defender going through the back of Treacy was ignored in the first half. The theatrical fall-over in the box by one of their forwards, as blatant a dive as you will see, was ignored. Both sides had legitimate penalty claims ignored.

How did we not win this game? Duff powered a free header over the bar. Jones had a cannonball shot headed off the line. Ings fluffed the chance, with his legs in a tangle, of converting a Trippier cross. Arfield wildly shot across the goal with Ings begging for the pass to come across. The stats say there were 23 attempts on goal. The stats say there were ten Burnley corners. Alas they were all too similar, lacking in imagination, guile or variety.

The game now was more open, more end to end, Burnley still the more dominant. Into the last 20 minutes and this had become a cracking game. Wednesday's raucous hordes from the wilds of Yorkshire had the atmosphere bubbling. Burnley's support, the longer the game went on, became more and more vocal as it began to seem they must score with all the mounting pressure.

New signing Barnes came on with just ten minutes to go and Treacy was the man to leave. It could just as easily have been Arfield. Now it was three up front and the pace hell for leather, with Trippier breaking from the back more and more. Barnes reached an impossible ball by the goal line and pulled it back. The chance went.

How did Ings not win this game? Into the last five minutes and his cracking shot hit the post. Then a terrific Ings shot was superbly saved by Kirkland. And then he fired in again in the final minute, another stupendous shot that once again produced another dazzling save. We groaned. The whistle went and Ings lay on the turf on his back contemplating the nature of things and undoubtedly reaching the conclusion that this was just not his day. It clearly wasn't Burnley's.

At least with the Worsthorne pipeline replacement roadworks completed and traffic lights gone, we didn't have to grind our way back home up Todmorden Road at a snail's pace as we'd had to do for several weeks.

Of course we stopped for food at the Queen Hotel again in Cliviger.

Behind us we left a Wednesday fan with a stab wound in the leg and the Miners' Club not quite trashed but almost, according to reports when things kicked off in there with a brawl between the different sets of fans. Outside, gangs of lads wandered the area looking for trouble. A dozen police congregated outside the Queen, presumably to stop Wednesday fans going in and to keep the minibuses of fans moving. There were fewer than 2,000 of them at the game. Gawd 'elp us when Leeds arrive, we said as we went in.

At lunchtime Leicester had beaten Leeds 1-0 at Elland Road. Nugent, with just three minutes to go, scored as sloppy a goal as is imaginable when a soft cross came over, the defenders dillied, the goalkeeper dallied, and Nugent nipped in to slip the ball home, giggling at his good fortune.

QPR beat Huddersfield and Burnley's stay in second spot was over as they slipped to third. How could you be gloomy though? It was just one of those days at Turf Moor. While the ball ran kindly for Leicester it didn't for Burnley. The images that remain are the two world-class saves that Kirkland made in the dying minutes and the ball slamming against the post just seconds before them.

The Sauvignon Blanc (just the one glass mind) and the hunter's chicken pie with chips and mushy peas at the Queen was the deserved consolation for the two lost points, while the team prepared to jet off to Alicante for a few days in the Spanish sun and the Levante versus Barcelona game.

While rival fans smacked lumps out of each other in the Miners, and played pin the knife in the supporter's leg, we sat back and smacked our lips with the hunter's chicken pie and the luxury fish pie. Luxury here simply means it is generously bigger than your average fish pie and packed with extra-flavourful, fishy goodness.

The hunter's chicken pie is made not with just any old chicken but a delicious blend of silky pastry and the tenderest local chicken and stock and cream sauce, with a layer of cheddar, whole grain mustard, barbecue relish (the secret ingredient) with a lid on top to keep the flavours in until that first forkful that quite honestly, and you have to trust me on this, is almost better than sex.

If the Queen's steak and ale pie is the Carol Vorderman, then the hunter's chicken is the Charlize Theron; alluring and sensual perfection, enticing, totally pleasing on the eye and something made in Heaven so desirable you just can't wait to get hold of it. Sex on a plate; there, I've said it. The chunks of chicken, bathed in relish, melt in the mouth. The pastry smoothly slithers, you groan with pleasure; the rough puff pastry enriched with layers of extra butter in the mix.

Rough puff (ruffe puffe in Shakespeare, rough pough in Islington) is a much richer pastry than mere ordinary pastry. I'll back Carole at the Queen against Paul Hollywood any day. It was coffee and home-made fruit and cherry cake for afters, while the team were probably by now passing through customs and the lad who'd headed Jones's thunderbolt probably still wondering what day it was.

Sell Ings for £4m this month and there'll be riots in the streets, I said to Clive Holt in midweek when the subject came up. Sunday morning with the papers and Fulham were planning a £4m bid for him, giving the club a choice: sell him for £4m now, or maybe, just maybe, collect £90m next season with an improbable promotion, if they kept him?

Co-chairman John B had personally been phoning people to persuade them to buy shares and get some cash into the club coffers so that bills could be paid and Ings bids could be rejected. The guy needs support, I decided, as he works his socks off to find more cash. He'd had the odd chuckle when people thought he was selling insurance until he explained who he was. In a way he was selling insurance – insurance against having to sell Ings, or anybody else for that matter.

At start of play Burnley were a marvellous second. This was a Lancashire–Yorkshire derby game. And yet still the gate was under 14,000. If there's a chairman prepared to work his socks off raising money with personal phonecalls, he needs help. Back at home I remembered how I used to try and raise funds, but in a much smaller way, in my other life, head of a small village school. Sometimes I felt like I was the only one that bothered. Sometimes I wondered if I was wasting my time.

We urged each other; spread the word and bring a friend to the Brighton game. Raise the roof. If it could maintain the pace and retain Ings, this homely, hard-up club was on the brink of something extraordinary.

ORMSKIRK WITH CHUMS:
Burnley 0 Brighton 0
QPR 3 Burnley 3

THERE had been no game on FA Cup fourth round Saturday and the squad had been away in Spain. So now it was two matches in a week, essential that the first was a win to keep in touch with leaders Leicester and vital to get at least a draw at QPR to prevent them also pulling away.

The blank Saturday was therefore a day devoted to some TV catch-up. The taped *Three Musketeers* was a gem. Swash at its best; swords that really swished and lots of heaving bosoms. Buckle at its most buckling. Imagine big Sam Vokes in one of those terrific musketeer costumes, girls. Your knees would turn to jelly. Those leather coats and wide-brimmed hats – fantastic. I want one.

Before the Brighton game we received the news that Arthur Bellamy had passed away at the age of 71. 'There was no hint of stardust, rather the blond wryly humorous north-easterner cut a salt-of-the-earth figure.' News of our heroes passing away seems to come with unfortunate regularity these days.

Although he played many games for Chesterfield he was Burnley through and through, player, coach, assistant manager and groundsman. Arthur was always a Harry Potts disciple and never forgot a game at Tottenham in his very early days when the legendary hardman Dave Mackay was kicking him all over the field. Harry wasn't having that and at half-time got hold of Mackay and pinned him against the tunnel wall and told him to lay off the young lad.

Arthur helped enormously with the Harry Potts book with no end of memories and stories and when Margaret Potts said she had never visited Gawthorpe, husband Harry's spiritual home, it was Arthur who arranged her first trip when I mentioned it.

Describing him as a gentleman is an understatement. People he coached and worked with thought the world of him.

How he got the groundsman's job is one of those possibly apocryphal stories that abound in football. John Bond had arrived and had begun his cull of the staff. Arthur happened to be passing by one day and Bond asked him if he knew how to drive the tractor and operate the lawnmower. It may or may not be true, but Arthur realised if he said no he'd be out of a job and nodded yes. And thus, that is how he became the groundsman, allegedly. True or not, it's a lovely story befitting of a lovely man.

For 48 hours before the Brighton game there had been speculation in the media that West Brom were about to offer £7m for Ings. With the Baggies having lost Shane Long to Hull City, and being desperate to offload Nicolas Anelka, Ings was reported as being the obvious replacement. Sean Dyche meanwhile had said that there had been no offers for any of his players.

With the Sky News transfer-window-ometer ticking down towards the final evening when presenter Jim White would froth at the mouth, we did our best to convince ourselves that the directors would see a possible £90m at the end of the season as an inducement to rebuff any offer. As we took our seats, thankfully there was Danny. Surely they wouldn't sell the lad while he was doing his stretching exercises and playing piggy in the middle or when he'd gone back inside to the dressing rooms. They didn't, and out he came for the game.

Not that it did much good; this was as disappointing a night as we've seen this season. It just didn't click. The ball just didn't run kindly. We seemed to be out of luck again as well as being out of sorts and so predictable. The first half was, in a word, dreary. Mrs T said dismal. The sum total of first-half excitement lasted maybe a minute in a spell when Kightly drilled a shot/ cross at 100mph that either smacked into the post or the keeper shoved out (we couldn't tell) and then the cannonball return was blocked away miraculously on the line. At the other end Heaton saved a certain goal when faced with a one on one. Glum faces all round at half-time.

And then just as glum at full time, even though the performance picked up in the second half. But still it lacked all the features that brought the run of games that took us to the top. The sizzling, sexy, samba football was now mainly a sort of slow, tea-dance shuffle, Flavia was now Anne Widdecombe.

Nevertheless, bit by bit Burnley became more dominant, Trippier surged, Jones prodded, Marney scuttled, Ings twinkled. Vokes had a point-blank header saved; Duff hit the post with a header. Jones hit a screamer just an inch too high. A hopeful lob trundled wide. And yet Brighton could have nicked it so easily in the final minutes when somehow one of them was clear in the box but there again was Heaton to save the one on one as we had our hands over our eyes.

All of us in our little enclave were agreed; with Kightly and Arfield offering much running but little threat, both Stanislas and Barnes could have come on to freshen things up after half-time. And those corners: how many more did we have to add to the ten in the last game? And not one delivered a goal. The game cried out for the quality corners and crosses that Stanislas can deliver.

The eagle-eyed spotted that Brighton midfielder Keith Andrews had a simple role – supporting the back four making their formation almost 5-4-1. You could see the thinking – get past that, Ings and Vokes, if you can. They couldn't. It cried out for someone to beat a man and cross from the byline. We didn't have a forward who could do that. Thus the hopeful long ball was humped, pumped and lumped forwards where Vokes jumped but to no avail.

Brighton were good, organised for the draw and a breakaway, skilful and difficult, but irritatingly the ghost of Gus Poyet still lingers as they auditioned for RADA, fell, rolled, clutched heads, knees and did all the things that made them such an unpleasant team a year ago. Not quite as bad 'tis true, but enough to annoy us all intensely. Dyche thought they'd come to park the bus. 'Gerraway,' the Brighton assistant replied. But Poyet we missed. His touchline dramas and hysterics used to be worth the entrance money alone.

Burnley stayed in third place and were three points behind QPR, who won, and 11 behind Leicester, who won. The dream of a top-two place seemed to be slipping after this game. The QPR fixture was thus set up to be the match of the season so far. A win for them would leave Burnley six points adrift. A win for Burnley would put Dyche's men back to second. Austin had damaged his shoulder against Bolton and had been subbed. He'd scored most of their goals so far. The less sympathetic of us hoped it was bad enough to keep him out of the game.

We were in Ormskirk with chums for the QPR weekend. So here's the restaurant bit. On the Friday night we ate in Burscough at the Hop Vine, built in 1874 and once a stopping-off point on the old turnpike road. There's a microbrewery in the back garden. The food is outstanding. It was my treat (took some doing as a Yorkshireman I can tell you) as a thank you to our friends for the way they looked after us a year ago after the accident we had over there.

Any Burnley fans in the area or passing through, it's worth a visit. I had the pulled pork, marinated in a Tennessee-style rub, steamed over apple cider overnight and loaded on to a sourdough bun with chips and spicy coleslaw. Mrs T and our chums had the small fish and chips. Small… it hung over the plate. The large fish overhangs the table.

Harry Redknapp previewed the game saying that his squad was down to the bare bones – yeah, right Harry. And then as the window closed he went out and signed five players. One of them was Kevin Doyle; we grimaced at that and with good reason when he scored after just six minutes. Burnley were slow out of the blocks.

When Ings equalised from a Trippier cross it was about all they had done in the half. At half-time we could be forgiven for thinking that this was going to be a bad day at the office as QPR went in 2-1 up when Dunne was left all alone to volley the ball home when it came out to him following a clearance from a corner. Burnley just weren't in it, the millionaires stroking the ball around, Harry looking relaxed, Barton pulling all the strings; the referee allowing QPR to dump Burnley players on their backsides as and when they chose, while Kightly was booked for merely brushing against a QPR player.

We were watching in La Cantina; stone floors, low ceilings, furnishings from old churches, schools and libraries – a rustic little wine bar in Ormskirk that specialises in imported red wines from Sicily, venison pies from Wrexham and cakes from next door.

Seven of us made it into the temporary Burnley bar. Half-time pies, bacon sandwiches and toasties cheered us up. Must have put fresh energy into Burnley as well; they came out a different team and had a superb second 45 minutes. Dyche must have worked his magic in the dressing room. This was terrific stuff they played.

If QPR were deservedly ahead at half-time a Burnley win would have been deserved by full time. Vokes scored two classy goals; the second after an Ings run and cross after he had robbed Benoit Assou-Ekotto. The first after a passing move that involved several players, then a Kightly cross and in Vokes raced to place it home.

Ings fashioned his own chance to make it 4-2 with a moment of magic but missed the top corner by inches. It would have been game over and at that point QPR chairman Tony Fernandes must have been worried that he would lose the side-bet with Burnley co-chairman John B. A Burnley win and Fernandes would have had to paint the tail of one of his Air Asia planes claret and blue. A QPR win and John B would have had to run around the pitch in a QPR shirt.

John B was the canny one. A QPR shirt would have cost about 40 quid. Painting an aeroplane costs a small fortune. It was John B who netted the newest board member Terry Crabb and the word was that Terry isn't short of a bob or two.

La Cantina was rocking with optimism. But this is Burnley is it not. Instead of 4-2 to Burnley it became 3-3 as a mix-up between Mee and Kightly allowed Hoilett to dance through and cross for the equaliser. La Cantina fell silent. The minutes ticked by, no side wanting to lose, Hoilett the danger man. But again Assou-Ekotto goofed, he with the lavatory-brush hairstyle, does he not know what a twit he looks, and this time let Stanislas in.

Stan, buffeted by the toilet brush and off balance, some say having his shirt held, lobbed. Green was out of the area. The ball arced high. We gawped with mouths open. This was the very last minute. It peaked. The trajectory turned downwards. Was it going in? Down it came in slow motion, bloody hell this would be 4-3 and a wonderful win. Fernandes must have been thinking where to get the paint from.

But no, it bounced agonisingly inches wide. Sean Dyche talked about rub of the green. There hadn't been any for several games. If we'd been having Leicester's luck we'd have been having results like theirs and it would be us ten points clear at the top. Had that gone in I suspect we'd have drunk La Cantina dry.

We were drained. It must have been worse if you'd been there. Leicester then went on to win with another contentious goal, Bournemouth players hollering it hadn't crossed over the line. But Derby, on track to go above Burnley, succumbed to an injury-time equaliser at Birmingham so the Clarets stayed third.

Dyche was understandably proud of the team. He knew they'd come within a whisker of a deserved win. Ings had apologised to the lads for missing the chance he created. Dyche told him he had no need to.

Crunch time then, came and went. Just the two points from the two games but by the end we were still hanging in there. Meanwhile, if you're ever in Burscough do try the Hop Vine. If you're in Ormskirk do try La Cantina – the venison pies are ace – and tell John you're a Burnley fan.

February

A SEVEN-YEAR-OLD'S BIG DAY:
Burnley 3 Millwall 1

LIVING in Leeds you couldn't avoid the current shenanigans down there at Elland Road; the latest story doing the rounds being that the newest bidders wanting to take over were Wacky Warehouse. Ownership was about to change if a Miami-based Italian by the name of Massimo Cellino took over from Leeds's Bahraini owners, Gulf House Finance; the club thought to be losing £1m a month, and living on loans and handouts to pay the wages.

Miami, Italy, Bahrain, all a long way from homely names like Bacup, Ramsbottom and Dole House. And Massimo – I think I prefer homebred names like Barry, Mike, John and Terry, not forgetting Brian and Clive. Massimo sounds like one of those villains from *The Borgias*.

Outside Elland Road fans massed to vent their spleen at the latest comedy of errors when Massimo jumped the gun and sacked manager Brian McDermott after thinking he had completed the takeover. They even chased away the taxi that had come to collect him, making it drive round and round in circles with the driver radioing in that he was running out of petrol.

The takeover was christened the Elland Road Hustle mainly on account of the speed at which Cellino, with previous convictions for fraud and false accounting, was already shoving Gianluca Festa into the Elland Road dugout and had even signed an Italian player before the takeover was completed.

'Where's he from?' said a nonplussed McDermott, by Sunday reinstated and popular because he buys drinks for fans and pays for the staff Christmas dinner among other things. Cagliari was the best bet, where Massimo had reportedly sacked 35 managers in 21 years.

Henry Winter called it a farcical, sorry saga, and *The Independent* said it made Leeds look like a laughing stock. The root cause of course was Leeds's dire financial state and the owners' desperation to sell. And then if Massimo did win the day, he had a son called Ercole; not Poirot surely?

I sat back at my computer screen, headphones on, listening to piano jazz; Twitter on, watching for news from the under-21 game at Exeter (postponed at the very last minute because of yet another West Country downpour), and thinking what a damned good job our men in the boardroom do at Turf Moor Towers.

I still chuckle at something Barry Kilby said a few years back at the time of the Wembley game when he said that Sheffield United had links and contacts and scouts that spread even as far as China, then adding in that quiet understated way of his that Burnley's just about extended as far as Skipton.

And that still just about summed things up for me. We're a homely local lot. Our feet are firmly secured to the solid ground of Lancashire, where we eat hot-pots and pies. You can look out from the stands at the ground and still see row upon row of terraces and chimney pots.

And while Carson Yeung at Birmingham stepped down as chairman and awaited the verdict from a Hong Kong court for money laundering, and the Egyptian guy at Hull wanted to change the name of the club, our directors speak with broad, local, earthy accents, rather than Russian, Arabic, or Malaysian. And while other clubs around us sank into the Venky's and Gartside lake of incurable massive debt and faced such an uncertain future, little old Burnley paddled along, keeping its head above the water, counting the pennies, and switching the lights off in empty rooms; and even then managing to jostle for promotion. And that's how we like it.

It was a special day for grandson Joe at the Millwall game. He was the mascot. Should he wear his Danny Ings shirt, the Tom Heaton outfit, or the brand-new gear he got as part of the day? What's the weather forecast, he asked every day the week before. He stunned me when he mentioned Eagles, Elliott and Thompson as we played football in the hall. Where on earth had he picked up those names from? He's only seven. He looks in the atlas and finds all the names of the Championship sides.

Dyche said he'd be proud if the club at this game set the new record for post-war home matches without defeat. Ian Holloway said he was due some luck at Turf Moor. He'd never won a game there. The weather forecast was grim and pictures of people abandoning their homes in Somerset, and animals being shipped out of the sinking farms put football in perspective. The win was deserved, the football splendid, the conditions atrocious as we expected them to be.

The wind swirled and gusted; players leapt to head the ball and it wasn't there – it had been blown somewhere else. Goalkeepers took goal kicks and the ball was blown back into their own half. Passes heading for the stands were blown back into the field of play. And the rain sheeted down; sideways, diagonally, great clouds of it, horizontally, behind you, in front of you. In these conditions Burnley put on a master show that saw Holloway describe them as the best team he'd seen this season. This was the football that the team had played during the first months of the season and in conditions where you'd have understood if they'd all worn fishermen's oilskins and John West hats, and had wellies instead of boots.

Ings scored two sublime goals, the first an opportunistic swivel and shot from just inside the box. But Millwall had scored first. Visions of banana skins began to dance in front of me, a reminder of why I don't like bananas. A Millwall goal! The impudence of it.

Burnley raised the tempo and proceeded to punish them for their impertinence. Marney scored a peach from distance and then the third was just such an audacious piece of skill and control from Master Ings that you could only shake your head at its brilliance when he beautifully controlled a long pass that came high over his shoulder in the box, and then caressed it home under the hapless goalkeeper's body.

Had this been Messi the football world would have drooled. Make no mistake; it has been a privilege to watch this little magician this season. He's like Robbie Blake. He doesn't score ordinary goals or scruffy goals. He only scores gems. In years to come we'll say Danny Ings once played for Burnley, a player lightly sprinkled with that rare quality – stardust.

So the win was comfortable; the passes to feet, the little passing triangles, the incision, the movement, were all back on show. And yet astonishingly it was all played in monsoon conditions. Dyche talked afterwards about the belief that was growing and how proud he was that this group had set a new post-war record of undefeated home games. The win took them back to second place with the media giving it scant attention. This is a team that just does the job unobtrusively, never much in the limelight, usually given two minutes or less on *The Football League Show*, rarely mentioned in the media, just quietly carrying on being the surprise package and sneaking in under the radar.

But if this was Ings's day on the field (or Marney, or Trippier, or Kightly; any one of them could have been MOTM), it was grandson Joe's day off it, his special day, his mascot day. Can we comprehend how a seven-year-old sees the world? I know I can't, I've forgotten. For me it was 62 years ago. His face was watching from the window when I went to collect him in the morning. All his shirts were laid out in the bedroom he has chez nous. He chose the one that had JOE on the back and his orange striped trainers. Just like a real footballer he had a slice of toast pre-match.

What do you see then through the eyes of a seven-year-old?

You wait at home in the morning by the window watching for Pop Pop's car to come. You see a world of grown-ups that's all exciting and unknown, a football ground and stands that look enormous and reach up to the sky. You know you are going in the dressing room to meet the players because you've been told and you've read the timetable sheet that Granny and Pop Pop keep looking at and they fuss you and ask will you be warm enough, hope it doesn't pour down, ask will you be nervous and you just wish they'd stop worrying and nagging.

When you've changed at their friends' house in Burnley they get out the cameras and start fussing again. Sasha the cat rubs up against your legs so they want more bloomin' photographs. You just wish they'd get you into the car and then down to the ground. They've given the car park pass to their friends who are coming and Pop Pop moans because he has to park streets away. He's always moaning.

A nice lady called Adele meets you and takes you upstairs to a big room they call the Foundation Lounge. Pop Pop met someone he knew, a bloke called Dave Timberlake. I heard him telling Pop Pop that one day he'd come home and his wife said, 'I want to leave you.' 'Why?' said Mr Timberlake. 'Because I'm fed up,' she said. 'I think you love Burnley more than me.' 'Darling,' said Mr Timberlake. 'I love Blackburn more than you.' They both laughed a lot but I'm only seven so I didn't understand what they were laughing about.

Adele takes you all the way round to the dressing rooms. It's a long walk but it wasn't raining. Granny and Pop Pop kept waving until I was all the way round to the tunnel and went in and up to the dressing room door. You go in and all the players are there, talking and reading the programmes. I wasn't nervous but I didn't know what to say but they were friendly and Danny signed my programme on the middle page and everybody signed it on the back. Danny put a smiley face and a kiss. I like Danny. Granny says she likes Danny. Pop Pop likes Danny unless he misses a goal and then he swears.

You have to walk all the way back along the pitch back to the Jimmy Mac end. Pop Pop sometimes goes to see Jimmy Mac. When we got back up there everybody was eating pies and chips. Pop Pop said he wanted a pie but Granny told Pop Pop he couldn't have a pie because he'd already had bacon sandwiches. Granny is always telling him he can't have a pie but she says it's for his own good and if he ate too many he'd begin to look like one.

You have to go over to the gym next to do some practising and training. It was massive with a sort of green carpet on the floor to make it look like grass. I practised slides and celebrations. We jumped up and down, ran round and you have to play a game called traffic lights like we do at school when the man whistles and you have to stop if he holds a red cone up. Traffic lights always make Pop Pop swear if they turn red.

Then we had a game with goal posts at each end. We don't play a lot at my school so it was all new so the man said I'd done very good if it was my first time. Well it was my first time and it was great. Granny and Pop Pop watched and took loads of pictures. Pop Pop's camera was messing about so I heard him swear again. He thinks no one can hear him but I can.

They had a claret jumper for me to put on under my shirt when we went back out on to the pitch. Adele said it would be cold so I should put it on. I liked Adele so I did. You have to walk back up to the players' tunnel again and I walked out with Jason Shackell. He talked to me as we came out. There were lines of other boys waving flags and we shook hands with all the Millwall players.

I'm glad I had the warm sweater on under my shirt. I thought we'd finished but you have to go back to the middle and have your picture taken. And then I ran as fast as I could back off the pitch.

The man with the microphone shouted my name out. I think he said 'just look at the mascot Joe running fast'. I like running and we run at school. I don't think I've ever seen Pop Pop running ever. Granny and Pop Pop were waiting for me in the corner of the pitch. I heard Pop Pop say something about the bloody camera. He doesn't know I heard him.

When I had my chicken nuggets and chips after the game the waiter in the pub looked at me and grinned. Granny told him I'd been mascot. 'Ey are you that lad that ran reyt fast ont pitch?' he said. He said I'd be famous in Burnley.

I think I slept all the way back to Leeds in the car. Pop Pop says some things you remember all your life. He says I'll remember this when he and Granny aren't here anymore and I'll remember them as well. When I woke up the next morning my programme signed by Danny was under my pillow. Who put it there? I bet it was Granny.

Pop Pop said it cost a lot of money and said he was only a pensioner. He's always saying that. But he didn't swear. He just smiled and said I was worth it.

233

THE HISTORY BOYS:
Bolton 0 Burnley 1
Bournemouth 1 Burnley 1

THE games now fast and furious, the final run-in not far away. We'd hardly recovered from Millwall and setting a new post-war record for unbeaten home matches; little Joe still on cloud nine after his mascot day. The press were full of praise for Burnley and Ings. Talk on the coach to Bolton was of Danny's missed penalty; that it should have been retaken because the keeper was way off his line and so many players were running into the box before he kicked it. And then there was the atrocious weather the game was played in and the open conditions that the disabled supporters must sit in when the weather is so bad.

We talked too of the hard-as-nails Gordon Harris, another Burnley hero who passed away. The young folk had no idea who he was.

Those of us who watched Burnley in the 1960s remember him well and with huge respect. He played 313 games, plus one for England, and scored 81 goals. I remember him for his wonderful mid-60s partnership with Brian O'Neil in midfield. Before that he was a truly menacing outside-left with a cannonball shot. It was his cross from the left from which Jimmy Robson scored in the 1962 FA Cup Final.

His altercations with opponents were legendary. In today's game for softies he would have rarely lasted the 90 minutes. He laid John Bond out at West Ham. He laid team-mate Jimmy Adamson out in the gym at Turf Moor during a five-a-side game, something graphically described in the Willie Irvine book.

He and O'Neil, plus the likes of Willie Morgan, Ralphie Coates, Willie Irvine and Andy Lochhead, formed a superb team in 1965/66 that came so close to winning the title until it faded towards the end. It was a team that came to be sold off one by one, some to pay the bills and some because their face no longer fitted. He was only 73 but had been plagued by ill-health for several years.

Sir Tom Finney, too, passed away aged 91. The scenes outside and inside Deepdale were deeply moving. Jimmy McIlroy rated him the best player he had ever seen or played against; a man who could play in any forward position and was at Preston North End for the whole of his career.

In *Prince of Inside Forwards* Jimmy said, 'Tom Finney was the greatest all-round player I have ever seen. He had more talent and skills than anyone I've known. He had tremendous speed and could score goals. He had speed off the mark, an exceptional ability to cross the ball at speed, wonderful ball control and a calm, unruffled demeanour. He scored goals slipping the ball past the goalkeeper as if he was just posting a letter.'

No other player has played at outside-right, outside-left and centre-forward for England with the ability to switch from one to the other. He was two-footed, nimble, had superb balance, and was razor sharp. His acceleration and timing of when to make a sprint, and then shoot with either foot, was superb. He was totally unflappable even against the most brutal treatment and on top of all this was the perfect team man.

Comparisons were inevitably made with the players of today like Cristiano Ronaldo and Lionel Messi. Those who saw him play insist that he could do all the things that they could do but the difference was he did them in an age when there was absolutely no protection from referees; if you were injured you simply played on and, on mudbath pitches. A few years ago he unexpectedly turned up at a book launch and the room was in awe of this modest man. Anyone who managed to get his and Jimmy Mac's autograph that night, on the same menu or picture, acquired something unique.

Meanwhile at Gawthorpe talk of promotion was banned at training. The 'p' word they call it. It was the same in Coyle's time. Enter his room and use the word and you'd see the door slammed in your face, said former CEO Paul Fletcher. Danny Ings said there was no fine if they used it but they did get told off. They don't look at the league table and just don't want to talk about it. His two goals were numbers 23 and 24 for the season. The lofted pass from Trippier for his second was the full-back's 12th assist of the season.

On Sky, Burnley were mentioned in the same sentence as Barcelona. High praise indeed except it was only to say that the conditions that Barcelona were playing in were as bad as those at Burnley against Millwall.

It's ten years on since the first book, *It's Burnley Not Barcelona*. That was the season of defeats with scores like 6-5, 7-4 and 7-2 and a lot of water has passed under the bridge since then. We went through near-insolvency more than once, flirting with the top six with Stan, flirting with the bottom three after that; then that marvellous 2008/09 season and promotion at Wembley. We've had Cotterill, Coyle, Laws, Howe and now Sean Dyche plus a change of chairman when Barry Kilby stepped down after his ten-year stint.

By now it wasn't just Somerset slowly disappearing, it was the Thames Valley. The party leaders donned their wellies and splashed through the streets issuing soundbites and having photographs taken, Wallys in wellies all of them; the deluge we experienced during the Millwall game a taster of what they've had for weeks in the south.

Bolton manager Dougie Freedman had been spouting how he had tried to sign Danny Ings from Burnley in the transfer window. He said it was the fourth time he'd tried to sign him. He mentioned an offer of £1m he'd made but the talks broke down. We discussed on the coach what planet he might be from. In his pre-match ramble he spoke of knowing everything about Danny, had a gameplan to contain him and they would squeeze the areas he operated in.

We remembered Vinnie Jones who made an art out of squeezing opponents.

The yellow-jacket brigade was out in force to frisk and search us all as we arrived. The unsmiling guy who searched me was about 6ft 6in and built like a brick you-know-what. They were looking for flares and I attempted a little humour and told him he wouldn't find any on me as I hadn't worn any since the early 1970s. He remained stony-faced so while his plate-sized hands moved menacingly up my trouser leg I said, 'I think you call them flurs in Bolton.'

'Do you want to go in or not?' he growled with the kind of stare that Clint Eastwood used when he said 'make my day punk'. At this point I thought silence was the better part of valour, I didn't fancy a night in A&E and wimpishly nodded and said, 'Yes please Officer Dibble.' Once past him I blasted him with the invisible death ray I keep up my sleeve.

Freedman's plan seemed basic enough: smack Danny around. He was whacked and dumped in the fifth minute and after that, by his standards, had a fairly quiet game, every now and then rubbing and holding his chest as if he'd been left in some discomfort.

But Freedman's approach didn't seem to include Vokes. He was left to finish off some intricate passing on the right, the ball coming to Kightly (ha ha Dougie you forgot about him) then Arfield who then skipped along with it, and fed Vokes who scored from inside the six-yard box. It was the deciding goal and left us all in a state of euphoria at the end, but how much more at ease we might have felt if Arfield had put away the best chance of the first half when he was clear on goal, but sliced the ball wide.

When the final whistle went the massed ranks of jubilant Clarets roaring and dancing was a sight to behold. So too was Trippier's face and instant reaction; elation, joy, achievement, pride all rolled up in one small chunky bundle of beaming football talent.

Freedman lamented afterwards, citing they'd hit the crossbar and a ball had flashed across the goal. Wow: in Dougieworld this meant he thought they should have had at least a draw. To be fair Eagles and Chung-Yong Lee in the first half put Burnley under pressure on several occasions. But in the second half Lee vanished and Eagles demonstrated the art of how many ways you can fire a shot up into the stands and hit a different spectator each time. His hilarious shooting should carry a Government health warning.

Bit by bit Burnley got a stranglehold on the game. The defending was superb, the midfield immaculate, the full-backs adopting the Freedman master-plan of squeezing the wingers in the areas in which they operated (the brick wall that was Burnley, said one unhappy Bolton website). From our front row seats it was close up and personal – the grit, resolve, bravery, the headers and blocks and the immense camaraderie.

Dyche thought his team was outstanding. The longer the game went on it was hard to disagree. He'd talked with the team about being relentless and limitless; the strikers instructed not to put limits on their scoring targets. And while Dyche seems to possess the wisdom of Nelson Mandela, the competitiveness of Attila the Hun, the motivation of Dale Carnegie, the insights of an industrial psychologist, and the rhetoric of Winston Churchill, when looking at Freedman, it was hard not to come to the conclusion that he seemed a bit of a Wally.

The supporters' club ran a weekend trip to Bournemouth. Alas we had to give it a miss because of a bit of a family 'do' on the Sunday. Every single away ticket had been sold. The weather forecast for the Friday journey was horrendous yet again; the south of England slowly sinking beneath the waves. The word was that on Friday morning it had been pouring down for several hours over Bournemouth. In Burnley it was hail. Every hour our chums Anne and Pete sent a text and others were on Twitter and Facebook:

> 'Coach left at ten past ten'; '40 of us'; 'we can hear the clink of wine bottles'; 'how nice'; '12.30 bar now open'; 'on toll road weather atrocious'; 'Banbury cake in Banbury'; 'weather still awful'; 'stuck in traffic'; 'pitch inspection at 7.30am'; 'not looking good'; 'the most horrendous conditions imaginable'; 'trains stopped between Southampton and Bournemouth'; '10 to 7'; 'weather horrendous'; 'just seen sign 10 miles to

Bournemouth'; 'here at 6.30 and straight into dinner'; 'not good news about tomorrow'; '80mph gusts of wind all along south coast'; 'absolutely shocking weather and no signs of that changing'; 'absolute nightmare down here at the moment'; 'a wild night'; 'some people have changed rooms because of rain coming in'; 'tree blown down behind the hotel'. Come midnight, 'Here in Poole gusting wind is now very mild and very drying.'

At 7.30am the game was declared ON. In the hotel at breakfast there was relief that the night was over and a buzz that the game would go ahead after several hours of doubt and thoughts of a wasted journey. Burnley to Bournemouth: that's a long, long way and an awful lot of people, down for the weekend, were already there. Anne's texts resumed:

'Met team walking round Durley Park'; 'on coach just setting off windy but sunny'; 'in the ground only got Pukka pies'; 'been in club shop'; 'makes Burnley's look poor'; 'impeccable minute's silence for Tom Finney, at kick-off clouds came over and we sat soaked on second row'; 'just as wet and grey on pitch'; 'we are terrible, don't think we had a shot yet. Can see blue sky so hope it gets better'; 'Stewart next to us eating large pasty'.

I've seen Stewart eating pies before. It's a homely sight. On what Sean Dyche described as one of the worst pitches he'd seen, Burnley fashioned a 1-1 draw and a point. On Sky, the match summariser was Paul Merson. If he was clearly unimpressed and probably nodding off watching it on TV, he made damned sure we nodded off listening to his drab, dull, mournful words of wisdom. In truth it was a poor game said most people who were there, comments ranging from uninspiring to stinker. Dyche was more tactful, commenting that even with half the team below par they had still taken the point.

The most satisfied person on the pitch must surely have been Keith Treacy when he scored the equalising goal. During Eddie Howe's reign he had been banished for his sins to the Siberian outer edges of Gawthorpe, with Howe having washed his hands of him and his problems. Funny how football sometimes works out; Dyche has slowly rehabilitated him and drawn him back into the fold. Dyche sees handling footballers as similar to being a horse-whisperer; no two footballers can be handled the same.

While most other folk were probably relieved to get back up north, Treacy was no doubt singing 'oh I do like to be beside the seaside' all the way home.

IT'S TOUGH BEING A MAN:
Burnley 3 Nottingham Forest 1

IT was a traumatic week. First there was the article Mrs T found about men doing nothing much around the house other than putting the bins out. And then there was the wrestling match with the flatpack IKEA step/stool.

I love Mrs T dearly but I took exception to the magazine article she plonked in front of me the other day while I was relaxing and reading a feature about Ings and Vokes in one of the sports papers. I'd just put the bins out which is always a bit strenuous.

Anyway, this article was one of those things written by a woman where they complain that husbands do so little in the house while they run round in circles seeing to things. I read it while she made lunch and unpacked the shopping. Later in the afternoon after she'd finished the ironing I decided to retaliate and while I was watching TV I made a list of all the things I do. I read it to her while she was making dinner.

'I put the rubbish in the bins. I put the wheelie bins out every week. I empty the dishwasher. I am forever wiping the sink. I wash all the pans after dinner. You get a cup of tea every morning in bed. I keep the window ledge in the office tidy. Granted I don't do any dusting. Dust is only layers of history. And I like history.

'I bring the washing up from the basement. I am not allowed to hang it in the garden because I peg it out wrong. I am not allowed to put the washing in the machine because I get coloureds mixed up with whites. To my dying day I will never understand why some coloureds are whites.

'It is me that feeds the cat. I hoover and keep my bedroom tidy and put away all my toys. I make all the beds. I drive you to the games at Burnley and don't forget this is 80 miles there and back.

'Last year when you had your arm in a sling I cooked Christmas dinner from start to finish. I take the cars to the car wash once a year. I organise the servicing of the cars, the gas boiler and the alarm system. I do all the packing at supermarket checkouts. In fact I am so bloody good I have been asked to do training days. I assemble IKEA flatpacks.'

The IKEA step/stool: there were only eight pieces to bolt together. There were only the 11 bolts. But it took two hours. It took that long because for a start the pictures in the instruction book were in Swedish. Some of the bolts were different sizes. Some of the holes in the different pieces of wood that needed to match up didn't. Certain holes needed certain size bolts. Certain holes needed to be on the inside. When we figured that out we had the thing half-made.

We dismantled it and the air was blue. Once a bolt was half into a hole the thing got harder and harder since these cunning Swedes had drilled the holes just that fraction too narrow. IKEA, by now I had figured, was Sweden's joke gift to Europe. Somewhere in Europe, I imagined, someone else would be having just the same problems as me, be it with a cupboard, a wardrobe or a stool.

At the end of the two hours the thing was complete except for the last bolt that fixed the step to the frame. Now then: the step is the important bit. Loose, and it will slip and whoever is climbing up will fall flat on their arse. 'The last bolt,' I muttered. 'And then it's done.'

Twenty minutes I wasted turning the bolt round and round wondering why it wouldn't go in with what can only be loosely described as the fixing tool. Even this tool came in two parts that had to be fixed together.

What do you do then? You get the biggest hammer in the garage and you look at the bolt and you hit it. You pretend it's Nick Clegg and hit it again. And it worked. In it went and the step was firm and the whole thing was finished.

I therefore looked forward to the game against Nottingham Forest. In midweek Derby had beaten Sheffield Wednesday and snuck up to within two points, thus overtaking QPR and shoving them down to fourth place. Forest had just got the one point against Leicester. Leicester got another penalty; funny that. There was a QPR fan who had been interviewed on TV and had wailed and bemoaned that with their money and their players they should be leading the division by 20 points. Doesn't quite work like that does it, I thought.

BFC had undertaken a huge and vigorous campaign to promote the Forest game and its importance. Co-chairman John B had written an impassioned plea for fans to attend. It was widely featured on Facebook and Twitter and in the press.

Sean Dyche had waxed lyrical about the away support, especially on long-distance trips; 1,705 to Yeovil, 1,447 to QPR, 1,300 to Bournemouth. The tickets for the away game at Blackburn were sold out, despite the atrocious, compulsory bus travel and it being on TV. 'The away fans have been phenomenal,' he acknowledged. The fan and player connection at Bolton had been particularly noticeable. He was aware of the costs involved. But, as a 12th man, the away-support effect should never be underestimated. Good home support that is non-critical helps the players relax. Then they play better.

Saturday 22 February, Burnley in second place, the first of two home crucial games; win them and the finishing line we all wanted would be that much closer. Forest unbeaten in 14 league games and Burnley in nine and aiming too for a 20th home match unbeaten; Forest the team that spent £5.5m in the summer and bankrolled by Dubai billionaires.

I truly thought that we wouldn't make it to the game by 3pm. Roadworks in Mytholmroyd caused a huge tailback halfway back to Halifax. Traffic inched its way forwards. Never mind, there's the quick route over the tops we can do immediately after Hebden Bridge to make up time. This is the infamous Mytholm Steeps, one of the top ten UK gradients as it snakes for nearly two miles, almost vertically in some places. It's the last place on earth you want to do a three-point turn.

Halfway up, a red sign announced ROAD CLOSED. It's Saturday I decided, it won't be closed, they won't be working, so up I went. Wrong, they were working and a gang of blokes was resurfacing the road resulting in a three-point turn at just about the steepest part of the hill with a calamitous drop on one side.

By now it was after 2pm so back all the way down the hill we went and joined the traffic again as it queued agonisingly slowly through Todmorden. We did make it in time but I'm a born pessimist and decided that with luck like I'd had all week a Burnley defeat was on the cards.

I couldn't have been more wrong.

The first-half display that Burnley put on against Forest was acknowledged by everyone as being one of the best performances for years. Comparisons were even made with the great team of the early 1970s that passed the ball around for fun and opposition teams hated to play against because as Bobby Moore once said, they were, 'Chasing leather and could never get the ball off Burnley.'

Within 37 minutes they were three goals to the good as Forest were ripped apart; shredded, mangled, and made to chase shadows. Manager Davies's explanation was simple; his team didn't follow his instructions, and Burnley caught them on a good day, he had so many players out injured.

Truth is, they were simply woeful in that first period and made to look woeful because of Burnley's superb approach play, accuracy, passing and movement. It was one of those halves that you wanted to go on and on because you knew that Davies would give his team a rocket, and they might be a different proposition in the second half. And so it proved.

Forest came out bullish, no longer the donkeys. This was no longer one side clinically dismantling the other, it was now two evenly-matched teams with Forest making chances and nearly scoring twice before a soft penalty was awarded against Duff for allegedly tripping the Forest forward. Those in line with the incident said Duff made no contact as Cox dropped to his knees theatrically.

The score was 3-1 but had Danny Ings been more accurate two of his chances might well have gone in. Duff's teasing shot went narrowly wide. In the first half his header was disallowed for a narrow offside. Treacy's piledriver was well saved. Penalty apart, Burnley never really looked in danger of losing the points so admirably won in the first 45 minutes with football that sizzled and scintillated; football that was so slick and sophisticated it would have ripped apart any team that Billy Davies had put out.

One by one you could go through the team and drool over each performance. Heaton actually saved the penalty but the Forest player ran in to head home. Trippier was sensational, Vokes unplayable, despite his misses Ings dragged players all over the place and Jones was simply magnificent, Kightly and Arfield terrorised their respective full-backs. Duff came forward imperiously including a marauding raid down the wing, Shackell was calm elegance personified. Mee was a rock and Marney covered every blade of grass.

The best of the goals: the second, following some dancefloor footwork from Trippier on the byline before he slung a vicious cross over at perfect heading height so that Vokes could bullet home the header, almost a carbon copy of a Connelly cross and Ray Pointer header way back in 1959/60 against Spurs. Trippier's stepovers and the final split-second sleight of foot that left the defender for dead probably had the full-back needing a trip to Specsavers to untangle his eyes.

The old codger we met in the pub afterwards had also been to the game and ironically he too saw something that harked back to that golden team that won the title. 'Vokes is like the great Jimmy Robson,' he said. 'Unsung, underrated, just such a great team man, a big man with delicate skills, but always on the spot to score goals.'

The crowd was a disappointment however. Despite all the efforts to drum up a better attendance, it failed to top 15,000 and maybe 2,500 of those were from Forest. The Burnley folk who stayed at home missed a treat.

This was vintage claret or a Noel Wilde Rhapsody in Claret and Blue. Dyche purred with satisfaction and pride and like the rest of us talked of that first 45 minutes with awe and admiration.

Second place was retained although Derby still remained within two points. But poor old millionaires QPR lost again away at Charlton. The chicken and ham pie at the Queen in Cliviger on the way home, the buzz in the pub, and the memory of that mesmerising first 45 minutes banished all thoughts of nightmare drives and IKEA flatpack stools. Trauma gave way to equilibrium.

By coincidence, Colin Waldron was in the Queen Hotel. I never thought that one day I'd tell him that I'd seen a display as good as the Team of the Seventies.

March

A BARGAIN AT THE CROOKED BILLET:
Burnley 2 Derby County 0

INJECTIONS: that was one of the reasons for their defeat expressed by Forest fans following their demolition by Burnley. The other was there was a football university at Turf Moor so that lots of the players 'were doing sports science'.

Meanwhile it was being suggested in *The Times* that QPR were ready to replace Harry Redknapp with Michael Laudrup; that Harry was ready to quit anyway after their third consecutive defeat. On *The Football League Show* after the Forest game (the usual two minutes of coverage) Steve Claridge still seemed bemused that Burnley could still be up there. There seemed to be this universal view that at some stage it would all implode and Burnley would fade away.

One Forest blogger however, Steve Wright, was worth reading on the Seat Pitch site. He clearly loves all things Burnley:

> The drive from Nottinghamshire is a pleasure. I have a soft spot for the Calder Valley which bristles with subversive creativity, and the dramatic geography as you wind through Mytholmroyd, Hebden Bridge and Todmorden is a beautiful distraction from the pressure of a promotion-seeking campaign in the Championship.

Our hosts whisked us up to the Crooked Billet pub in nearby Worsthorne. The Billet is a free house and Burnley's CAMRA Pub of the Year in 2013, serving an excellent range of ales including those from the nearby Worsthorne Brewery from whom Billet Gold is a tasty session beer. They also provide impressive value with their matchday offer of pie, mushy peas and a taxi to the ground for £5. No wonder landlords Alison Leigh and Paul Miller have turned the pub's fortunes round since buying it from Punch Taverns.

An away trip to Burnley has a lot going for it and if you haven't made the trip before I do recommend it.

Sometimes you pick up a good bargain on eBay. Just such a one was the August 1973 *Observer Sunday Supplement* I snaffled up for next to nothing. It surprised me that I was the only bidder. Other avid Burnley collectors must have been snoozing. This is the supplement that has the big feature on the 1973 team that had just won promotion back to the top division.

One page out of the four was devoted to the irascible Bob Lord. There were the usual paragraphs about Burnley the town and the cobbled streets, plus honourable mentions for several players but the best and longest was devoted to Leighton James. But the two things that provided the most intrigue were the mentions for non-players.

One was Carol Sparks, a leggy beauty who besported herself on the old terrace steps in one photograph in a claret and blue bikini. It clearly wasn't just London that had the hot babes of the day. Claret and blue bikinis were on sale in the club shop. Did Hilda Lord wear one?

I set to thinking about this fascinating look at yesteryear. Who was Carol Sparks? Who is she today? Where is she today? Does she still live in the town? Today she will be in her late 50s or very early 60s. Does anyone remember Carol Sparks or know her today? Could we manage to trace her? The quest got a smattering of publicity, but we never did.

Derby arrived at Burnley with just one win against any of the top six sides. Burnley hadn't lost any of the previous nine games against them. Opta statistics showed that Burnley had the highest proportion of goals scored in open play in the Championship. You could interpret that in two ways: one, that they were brilliant at moving the ball around sweetly and then smacking it home; or two, they just weren't very successful at set-pieces and corners. There is some truth in both of them.

Over 3,000 Derby fans descended on Turf Moor, creating a true big-game feel. *Football Focus* had turned up in the week to feature the build-up and the game was the main feature on *The Football League Show*. At last there was an attendance of over 17,000.

Meanwhile, a number of Championship clubs were involved in a legal challenge to the Financial Fair Play rules; no surprise there then, especially when they were thought to be Leicester City, QPR and Blackburn Rovers.

Vince Cable had been in town speaking and said that if the rest of the country was on the up as much as Burnley, there'd be no recession. In the pubs, clubs and message boards the consensus was Burnley needed four points from the upcoming Derby and Blackburn games.

There was apprehension amongst fans in the build-up. Win it and a five-point gap would open up. For the sixth game in a row, very unusual in today's football world, Burnley fielded the same team with senior-citizen Duff at centre back but playing like a 20-year-old. It was good to see *The Mirror* featuring him in a special article. The Duffs of the football world receive little publicity, like Arthur Bellamy; salt-of-the-earth rather than stardust. They've been around the block a hundred times but they are at the non-glamour end of the game.

Solid, reliable, loyal, dependable, professional, well-spoken with the wisdom of 20 years in the game at his beck and call, nobody would merit another crack at the big-time more than Duffo. A £30,000 snip from Cheltenham Town ten years ago, he's been one of the best investments of the decade. It's thought that he is the only player ever to move up through EIGHT divisions of football in the correct ascending order, starting with non-league and then up to the Premier League.

They were still digging the road up in Luddenden Foot. I'd driven through on Thursday as well and that time there was a double whammy. They were lopping trees AND digging holes. The queue went back almost to Halifax. On Derby day it was just the one hole. This is a stretch of road that for ten years has been the most dug-up stretch of road in the universe. When the team is doing well nobody minds. It was 1 March and a beautiful spring-like day with stretches of the grass verges along the roads filled with crocuses.

Outside the ground the fans walking in were vibrant and excited, albeit nervous too. Inside when the teams came out Derby looked ominously good in their white shirts and black shorts. Burnley too have always looked good in a black and white away kit.

And Derby were indeed ominous in the first 20 minutes or so of the game; crisp, full of movement, neat with their passing. They looked a good side. But admiration and respect slowly turned to dislike and annoyance at their petulant and sly tactics. Over and again a Burnley player would find himself on the floor, more often than not clutching his head. Three or four times crafty elbows went in. And Chris Martin, their centre-forward, displayed a petulance and niggliness that would cost him and Derby dear.

Slowly but surely Burnley weathered the pressure and got themselves into the game once their passing game emerged. Jones and Marney became the fulcrum, Jones's display in particular that of a master craftsman. Who knows if Derby had been told to rough Burnley up, shove them out of their neat stride, give them a few bruises and a few banged heads. But that's what they proceeded to do, though to no avail as Burnley dominated.

The Burnley opening goal was out of the Barcelona manual. Forget the old book title *It's Burnley Not Barcelona*, this was Burnley just about Barcelona. There was the same pressing game, the same high-tempo hustling and hassling, the forcing back of opposition with pressure exerted on any opposition player with the ball, and all of them as fit as a butcher's dog. Then the strike of a cobra, blink and you miss it.

Kightly fed Ings, Ings inside the box flicks the ball up in the air to Jones who controls it on his knee and then as the ball comes down volleys it, and it loops in a perfect parabola into the roof of the net leaving Lee Grant clutching at thin air. The ground erupted. The noise was heard in Bacup. An abiding memory was the guy in a wheelchair below us, a big guy with grey hair and in a yellow jacket, doing wheelies and spins in his electric wheelchair; the smile on his face ecstatic.

By this time Derby's Martin had been booked, and could have been booked several times over for other petty incidents. Maybe the ref had had enough of him but when he fell in the penalty area he was carded again and then given the red. It was contentious. Film showed he slipped.

Was there contact with Trippier? But he had appealed for the penalty. So did the referee card him thinking the slip was a dive? Or did he know full well it was just a genuine slip, so he carded him for appealing for the penalty? Or had he just had enough of his unacceptable antics? Whatever the reason, Martin got his just comeuppance. On such turns of events promotions can be won and lost.

In for half-time 1-0 up and Derby one man down; Easy Street we might have thought in the second half but Easy Street it was not. With nothing to lose Derby came out all guns blazing. McClaren sat up in the Bob Lord with a large file opened on his knee. Whatever he had said to them they were better with ten men than they had been with 11. That's how it goes sometimes.

Heaton made three smart saves, one of them pouncing on the ball just six inches away from the line. But then Burnley got the clincher and again it was Ings who made the goal with a sweet shot from the edge of the box from the corner that Duff the decoy let run by him. The shot was heading in but somehow bounced back, then back again to Marney lurking just inside the six-yard box. He slotted home. Delirium and delight in equal measure round three sides of the ground. Deflation at the other, the Rams now put out to grass, tails between their legs and bleating about all the perceived injustices.

McClaren must have got to the page in his ring binder that had the picture of Conor Sammon and the caption, 'Don't forget

Steve, this is a striker.' He brought him on at half-time in a move that put real pressure on Duff and Shackell. More than a few of us decided that had he been on from the start instead of the irksome Martin, then things might have been a lot different. From the stifling 4-5-1 employed in the first half it became four at the back and the rest of them swarming all over Burnley.

Derby fans were by now thoroughly miffed with the referee. 'Burnley's a sh*t hole, I wanna go home' they sang. They duly did at the end of the game, venting their spleen at the referee for ruining their afternoon.

Neither Ings nor Vokes scored but they were magnificent again. Ings was a thorn in their side all afternoon with darting runs and made the two goals. Vokes gave a peerless performance, leading the line and covering the width of the pitch. Arfield and Kightly each had another gigantic game. The whistle went. Grinning Burnley folk exited the stands. QPR were held to a draw, Forest were thumped. Redknapp's post-match quote was, 'Name me a team that wouldn't miss Charlie Austin and his goals?' Well, erm, Burnley for starters I suppose.

The pie on offer in the Queen Hotel at Cliviger was sausage in cider and potato pie, a new-to-me taste sensation. The pastry might be the same, light, golden and with a crispy rim to the lid, but this was a new inside. This was the Vanessa Feltz of the pie world – big, brassy, a real mouthful – with the body bursting to get out. Then: the chips to die for, mushy peas and extra gravy and for an added treat Frank Casper to chat to at the bar.

What a day; and it had started well. Cheques had started coming in early for the Charles Buchan book, jumping the gun. One was from Mick Carswell, born in Cliviger, now in Stockport, but once of Tod Grammar School in the year below me. I phoned him up and we reminisced about headmaster Albert Greenough (less than affectionately known as Crun after one of the characters from *The Goon Show*), and deputy head Jimmy Large.

We talked about our hair that we were forever combing in those rose-tinted days. *The Goon Show* was compulsory listening and Henry Crun and Minnie Bannister were two prime characters. I had a trendy haircut back in the day and we're talking early 1960s here. For a while I had the 'Tony Curtis' that was the rage for a while. This was a style where it was combed at the back of the head so that it resembled a duck's arse. Thus it was also fondly known as a DA. Today it's more mature; in other words it's thinning.

Alas, as this astonishing and totally unexpected and now nerve-wracking season has progressed, I have a suspicion that it has thinned even more. No one could possibly have anticipated this remarkable campaign.

SEAN DYCHE – A MAN WITH BELIEFS

IAN Brookes, from Rossendale, near Burnley, is a lifelong supporter of the club, a business adviser and consultant specialising in those companies that wish to improve performance and strategies. He is particularly interested in those qualities that make for good leadership, frequently looking for correlations between business and sport. His website is www.dnapeople.co.uk.

On 3 March after the Derby game he analysed the leadership qualities of Sean Dyche, and has kindly allowed me to reproduce his findings here:

> With a league record of P33 W18 D12 L3, Burnley have sustained a place in the Championship's top three since September. It's a tight-knit squad and Burnley have used the smallest number of players in the division with only 18 starting league games. While the squad is small, manager Sean Dyche believes their togetherness and group mentality will play a massive part in their ability to compete for promotion.
>
> What Dyche doesn't state is the significant impact he has had on the squad, with just one player added for a fee to the team that finished 14th last season, conceding 1.3 goals per game. This time round, the team has let in just 26 goals in 33 games to date, and just for good measure, last season's top scorer Charlie Austin left for QPR for £4m four days before the season started. The Turf Moor crowd have given Dyche the accolade

'Ginger Mourinho' although he is known not to like this tribute.

Sean Dyche played a total of 460 Football League games. Perhaps his most famous match was an FA Cup semi-final against Middlesbrough, when Middlesbrough won despite Chesterfield scoring a legitimate goal that was over the line, but the referee decreed it wasn't. It robbed Chesterfield of a cup final appearance as they lost the replay 3-0.

Dyche won promotion with four clubs as a player, maybe this time as a manager. He is developing his own clear style. There have been tracksuit-class tyrants such as former boss Brian Clough, urbane intellectuals like Arsene Wenger, and egocentrics such as Mourinho with a polyglot sophistication and a touch for the theatrical.

Sean Dyche is methodical in his trade, articulate and intelligent in his analysis and communication, respectful to the opposition and has an enthusiasm for research with a learner's mentality; all this being a powerful combination for an effective manager. Having studied his interviews, watched him closely at home and away matches, and assessed his impact at Burnley, here are my thoughts on Dyche's management principles we can take into business.

A balanced management team: Ian Woan, Tony Loughlan, Billy Mercer and Mark Howard are all different. Dyche uses his management team proactively on matchdays. They are as animated and engaged as he, he works closely on the touchline with his team, constantly observing, pointing out and engaging with them to highlight areas for improvement. Attention to detail and in the moment creates a focus.

Dyche says, 'Then, of course, it's up to me to make the end decision, but it's nice to have that support system of a staff that is very honest and very open with their opinions, in order to get the best outcome we can.'

Who cares wins: There is no denying the phenomenal passion that Dyche has for football and for Burnley. It's a simple truth but one that is often forgotten; the very best leaders care deeply about what they do. Apple founder Steve Jobs said, 'The only way to be truly satisfied is to do what you believe is great work and the only way to do great work is to love what you do.'

Maximum effort is the minimum requirement: Dyche has transformed the Clarets into a well-respected side as a result of a high-performance cocktail of an ultra-dedicated backroom team, meticulous planning, and a team willing to go that extra yard with one of Dyche's favourite sayings as their backbone, maximum effort is the minimum requirement. From that you can see the organisation, commitment, spirit and determination that makes the whole much greater than the sum of its parts.

Dyche said, 'I had a chat with each of them individually and made it clear what I wanted. The demands were laid out openly. It was about mentality, fitness levels, how we were going to play as a team and how each individual was going to contribute. I want to believe it is possible. I always trust my work.'

Connect with individuals: Dyche consciously takes time to connect with every member of his organisation as individuals, from first-team players to office staff, to get to know them personally and understand their different drives and ambitions. This enables him to judge the true mood of the group and tailor his communication to each person individually.

Dyche has personally mentored and supported a number of players this season who have transformed their performances so that they are having the best season of their career – Sam Vokes, Keith Treacy and Scott Arfield are the obvious picks in an overachieving team.

Dyche has a sense of purpose and determination derived from his passion but with a deep vein of humanity, treating people with genuine interest.

I watched a video of him in a training session. He was encouraging Keith Treacy, watching him closely. Treacy stuck at it, 'Decent Keith, decent!' Encouraged, Dyche followed with a celebratory cry of 'Champagne!' as Treacy produced an outstanding piece of skill. As Treacy acclaims, Dyche is capable of connecting with you individually and changing your mentality.

Be the man that makes the difference: another of Dyche's sayings that resonates. His shaven-headed, physically imposing presence belies a sophisticated approach to the game.

More than anything, it seems Dyche's greatest talent is selling his players on the importance of putting the team before the individual as a core responsibility. He's got the remarkable ability to merge individual talent as a team rather than being dazzled by individual brilliance.

Strong at home, strong at work: This communicates a man with strong attachment to his family. I have no doubt he is a great father, husband and brother as much as he is a great manager. There is no point being successful everywhere else and failing to be a hero to your own family. A strong family builds a good strong support structure and ensures a stable and focused mind. Dyche often talks about his brothers and his family ethic.

This underpins Dyche's broader model of man-management that shuns the old-school approach of haranguing people to bad performance and instead treats his team as an extension of his family. The loyalty and devotion he shows to his players is met in kind. He is a master at instilling belief into those he himself believes in. People talk about transformational leadership.

Dyche portrays a confident leader, whether or not he's actually feeling pressurised, able to make a difference to a situation.

Open-mindedness: Dyche attributes Burnley's success to open-mindedness and freeing his side from fear. He has made open-mindedness a mantra, encouraging it from his players and employing the term frequently at press conferences. Once they have done the basics, they have the freedom to play. They are encouraged to do that and it enhances what they can offer as individuals.

I think these players can achieve whatever they want to. It's about being open-minded. They know they're organised. They know they're fit enough and it allows them that mental clarity to go for the performances.

If you don't believe in yourself, you should not expect others to believe in you. You have to trust your own decisions and have faith in your abilities. Often, self-confidence is misconstrued for arrogance, an overbearing, excessive opinion of one's self. Dyche's approach is about valuing and respecting your own perspective and being the best you can be.

Pride: When Dyche took the job, he said, 'They asked me what the thing was I remembered most about Burnley after playing here. I noticed there were always Burnley shirts around the town. You would drive through the town and there would be shirts everywhere. There is an obvious connection between people and the club. It's a good old-fashioned trait that the people genuinely support the club.'

Dyche has used the bond 'our town, our team, our turf' to build a strong connection between the team and the fans, a sense of responsibility that the team has for wearing the shirt and representing the town and the fans. It's become tribal.

Perhaps one of the worst impacts of the economic downturn has been the growing tendency to pass the buck, managers attempting to safeguard or promote their own ambitions, ahead of the wider goals of their team or the company they work for. For Dyche, it's all about the team and there is no question that he inspires fierce devotion in his players. In many ways his large but understated persona ensures that he is a dominant figure. He takes the pressure off his team as he becomes a bigger focus than the players.

At a time when many managers are loath to go beyond the corporate soundbite, the power of a genuine, passionate and honest figurehead should not be underestimated.

Winning is a mentality: 'It's a great feeling when you look into their faces in the tunnel before kick-off and know how hard they are going to go to win. I was promoted four times with four different clubs and that same level of respect and honesty was there each time. I can feel that with these Burnley players. It's not about the money. It's about the glory of winning. You should not be OK with average. As Michelangelo says, "Our biggest tragedy is that we set low goals and achieve them".'

Learner's mentality: 'I tell the players I've had my time as a player but now I have a chance of making you better. My job is to guide them. For my Pro Licence I went and studied the Oxford University Boat crew and I used snippets from there to inspire my players.

'These rowers want to be part of history. They don't get money. In the Oxford boathouse there's this meeting room with massive boards all the way round containing the names of all the people who have been in the boat. They are desperate to get on there. I've said to the players, Burnley is a founder member of the Football League, a heritage to respect. You can make your own Burnley history this year. Be relentless; be limitless in your performance.'

Ask me the secret of Dyche's success so far this season and I will say it's his honesty, simplicity in his communication and the empathy he has for his players. Last season 79 points won Hull promotion. Today Burnley already have 66 points from 33 games with 13 remaining. April sees the centenary of Burnley's 1914 FA Cup Final win, our only cup win. What a double celebration we could have!

1. Our town, our turf, our team, our time – with Dyche's management getting us there.
2. Maximum effort is the minimum requirement.
3. Be the man that makes the difference.
4. Be relentless, be limitless.

DYCHE, MONEYBALL
AND ROVERS:
Blackburn Rovers 1 Burnley 2

THE compulsory buses were out in force again. Mrs T and me elected not to bother with the rigmarole. Not only do you have to put up with a rickety, old, ramshackle, worn-out bus that has seen better days, you actually have to pay for the privilege. I sat down in the comfort of my own home and doffed my cap to those who were prepared to put up with all the hassle, especially those Burnley fans who had travelled from Germany, India, Ireland, Alicante, Norway, Bulgaria and Heckmondwike. In Crawshawbooth, Riley's butchers had created claret and blue sausages using red wine and blue Stilton.

One guy who did return for more hassle was Brendan Flood, returning to the board as a director again. There may well be days when being a director is rewarding. I can well imagine there are days when it is not. When last we heard, there had been a state of disagreement between Flood, Mike Garlick and Clive Holt. Flood had been specific in his comments, that he felt he would not wish to work with Holt and Garlick again. I remember thinking at the time that he had been quite frank in his comments.

It had been Garlick on the club website who had revealed that Flood was no longer permitted to be a director because of the IVA he held then. Football League regulations specified that this was not permitted. Flood had retaliated, saying that he felt there was a lack of leadership and a lack of belief and that he had been forced out. It was all so very public.

What had prompted all this, for those who have forgotten, was the news that thanks to John Sullivan the Russians were coming with new investments and the club and co-chairmen were involved. It was reported that Flood's resignation had allegedly slowed things down. It was this that provoked the Garlick statement; that the Russians were definitely not coming and that Flood was, in any case, no longer permitted to be a director at that point. Perhaps we should all be relieved that the Russians didn't come. The image of troops surrounding Burnley Town Hall does not sit easy.

Following his resignation Flood said he wanted to get away for a while and recharge his batteries, regain his enthusiasm; that perhaps one day he would return. He still retained the largest individual shareholding and the lure of football did not go away. Now, the enthusiasm was back and so was Flood. It was good to see that bridges had been mended.

The negotiations that would see his return had been on the go for some while. We can all make guesses as to who might have brokered the 'peace deal', in all probability John B, who just seems to do more and more for the club behind the scenes (it was John B who 'found' one of the newest directors, Terry Crabb), but Flood brings something to the table that is crucial – contacts and ambition.

By the end of that momentous promotion season his financial support had dwindled but no one can underestimate his importance in supporting the bid for promotion in 2008/09. He and Modus injected enthusiasm, money, 'get-up-and-go' and vigour into the boardroom when he first joined. If his business ventures suffered, then so did many others. It was a global problem that knocked him back.

Flood certainly took a hit but entrepreneurs have that knack of bouncing back. The University College of Football Business was, and is, his brainchild. At the year ending 31 July 2013 it had made a loss but the new Wembley campus could well change all that. The UCFB could have been the club's to own. In time, when the initial loss-leader years have run their course and all three year-groups are in residence, it might well generate serious income for the owners, but in the boardroom there was early scepticism about it. All it brings in at the club for the moment is rent.

The QPR directors' report made for entertaining reading, unless you were a QPR director of course. Their names made for interesting reading too; Fernandes, Bhatia, Meranun and Maheshwan. The first line of the intro was the chairman expressing his delight at presenting the report. He reported a loss of £65.4m. It was said to reflect the continuing investment in players and management and supported the focus on regaining Premier status.

At this point you could be forgiven for smiling at their predicament. Automatic promotion was by now slowly disappearing on the horizon like a mirage. Meanwhile that little club from the north, Burnley, whose team had cost only a few quid, a book of Green Shield stamps, and some old Embassy coupons someone found in a drawer, were nine points ahead of them in second place. And their directors: six locals from Burnley, good, honest Lancashire lads, and one that had been resident oop t'north for 30+ years.

Things were a bit glum at Nottingham Forest too. They'd lost a mere £17m under their owners, the Al-Hasawi family. I bet they're not from Bacup. Neither Forest nor QPR had managed to beat Burnley all season. While they had struggled through the previous weeks, Burnley's Sam Vokes had been named the Championship's Player of the Month. At Birmingham, owner Carson Yeung had been jailed for six years for money laundering. No one can launder money at Burnley – there isn't any.

And in the meantime things were hotting up in readiness for the fixture to come. On Facebook, Twitter and all the websites fans were counting the days down to the game on Sunday. There was a real feeling that this would be the day. Blackburn and Venky's had been quiet of late. Things seemed calmer and more stable there. It wasn't quite the 'chicken-in-a-basket' joke club that it had been in previous seasons with the Indian owners although in their last game they had been clattered 4-0 at Bolton.

Journalist, Clarets fan and publisher Tony Dawber wrote a superb Sean Dyche derby piece for SportNW (worth a Google for news and sport) as part of the build-up, which has been kindly reproduced here:

> There's a lot more to the Burnley boss than meets the eye. Don't be fooled by the stick your head where it hurts centre-back image, although there is a fearless and relentlessly positive air about the Clarets chief. Dyche is also a deep thinker about the game and a keen student of sports psychology. Indeed it was in pursuit of more knowledge on that particular subject that he read the opening chapters of *Moneyball*.
>
> The gist of the book, if you're not familiar with it, is that Oakland A's were skint, so general manager Billy Beane wanted to find a way his penniless team could compete with the big spenders.
>
> 'There are rich teams and there are poor teams. Then there's 50 feet of crap. And then there's us,' was how Beane bluntly but brilliantly put it.
>
> He went to work and discovered a strategy which held that too many sports teams are carried away by emotion, assumptions and hearsay in terms of buying and selling players and running the team. Beane removed all the collected wisdom, prejudice and emotion of experienced coaches and pundits, and signed players based on pure and in-depth statistical analysis. The tactic disgusted his wizened old coaching team, especially his team manager, played in the film by the recently deceased Philip Seymour Hoffman. But guess what, it worked. Unfancied cast-offs came good and season after season the A's confounded the critics and made the post-season play-offs, defeating bigger spending rivals over and over again. And they're still doing it today.
>
> Sound familiar? It might do to anyone who has been at Turf Moor this season and watched a vibrant Burnley team dismantle the expensively assembled QPR, Nottingham Forest and just a few days ago, Derby County, despite operating on a fraction of that trio's respective budgets.

Now, I'm not saying that Dyche has faithfully adapted the *Moneyball* method. He hasn't and he gave the impression it hardly registers at all in his general strategy as he stressed that reading the early part of that book was merely one of the countless tasks he took on to try and widen and improve his managerial skills. But: there is clearly an echo of Oakland A's story in Burnley's achievements this season.

Let's also strip away the stomach-turning bile from both sides that has seen gross and personal insults bestowed on former chairmen or backers on both sides of the fence. And let's strip away the emotion and adrenalin this most passionate of games inevitably sparks. What you have left, as far as the Burnley standpoint goes, is a fantastic season in which the Clarets soared in the early stages, dug in when they did not hit the heights for a spell, then surged on again.

Consecutive home wins against two of their closest challengers on the last two Saturdays have brought new highs, especially in view of the manner of the triumphs. And now, they face a trip to a mid-table side whose squad has much more quality than their league position suggests, but one which has long since lost the chance of automatic promotion. Indeed, it is a side that needs a fairly striking run of form to even make the final play-off spot, a run that shows little sign of materialising, particularly after an abject showing against a similarly under-achieving Bolton last week.

Imagine, after those wins against Forest and the Rams, Burnley were travelling to Leeds, Brighton or Watford, sides in a similar position to Blackburn and with similarly-decent squads, who might have been expected to do better. You'd be fairly confident. But in the cold light of day, you would have to say a draw would do.

The hard work was done against Derby and now it's just a case of keeping things going. In the light of all that, the question is would I take a draw? And the answer, which might surprise one or two, is yes. I'd be lying if I said I wouldn't dearly love Burnley to end the hoodoo and win an east Lancs derby at last, and what satisfaction that would bring after years of taunts and derision, many from fans who have long since deserted the listing Ewood ship.

With Burnley in good form and with a fully-fit squad, there's no reason why they can't do it, especially as Blackburn have a host of injury problems and the central defensive area looks particularly vulnerable. But, my point is that a draw would be far from disaster and while a defeat would be a huge blow to our local pride, the cold facts of the table say that if that did happen, Burnley would still be second and still have everything to play for.

'You don't support Burnley for 42 years without being a glass half-empty man sometimes,' Tony continued. How many more of us might say the same? Mrs T, me and little Joe settled to watch the game on Sky. Below us QPR had caught up three points, but Millwall, bless 'em, had beaten Derby. The butterflies felt like they were wearing clogs at the prospect of an eight-point gap opening up if only Burnley could win. I'd had the offer of a ticket but would have felt a cad, leaving Mrs T and Joe behind.

Unchanged for the eighth game, no win against Rovers for 35 years, Rhodes hadn't scored in eight, Ings hadn't scored in five; 4,500 Burnley fans there fervently praying for the win that would become the stuff of legends, a win that folk would say 'were you there' and would tell to their grandchildren. People like me would say 'I was there on the sofa…'

The obligatory chicken clucked its way on to the pitch; little Joe beside me was beside himself with laughter. He didn't know that sometimes hens sneak in down someone's trousers to watch a game. In some pub or restaurant in Blackburn that chicken probably ended up in a basket with a pile of chips later in the day.

Vokes in the early minutes had a goal disallowed for offside. TV replays showed him to be in line with the defenders. It was a good goal. Only his big toe could possibly have been offside. You feared the worst, that this, even so early, might already be the defining moment of the game.

We feared that even more when totally against the run of play Rhodes scored, given room and space by three defenders around him. He turned and scored. The air went blue in the lounge at number 12 and probably hundreds of other rooms and pubs all over the UK.

Half-time, 1-0 down, and the conviction before the game that we would not lose began to turn to gloomy thoughts that this was going Blackburn's way. But in the dressing room at half-time Dyche had told them to keep going, that they were on the cusp of history.

And so it proved. Rhodes broke clear courtesy of a loose pass that came to him and hammered the ball against the post as we sat with our eyes closed. Another turning point, because after that Burnley upped the tempo, kept possession and the Dyche substitutions, when they came, were sprinkled with the stuff of romance as the Barnes–Wallace combination took to the field.

Barnes was bundled over; Wallace curled the resultant perfect free kick and Shackell headed home. Irony: he scored last year only to see his goal equalised in the most ridiculous fashion when Blackburn had players a yard offside. Football is like that sometimes when sweet justice is granted by the gods; even more so when Ings pounced on a ball 12 yards out that had swung around the area from player to player until it came to his trusty (at last) right foot and he struck it home.

Delirium, ecstasy, and that was just chez nous but 11 minutes to hold out. The plane that flew overhead with the pro-Burnley banner was another magic moment as it buzzed the stadium.

There were Herculean performances all over the pitch. Ings had a sparkling game, Arfield and Kightly ran and harried. Trippier was, well, just Trippier; superb from start to finish. Heaton held the fort in the final minutes when a lesser goalkeeper might have caved. But it was the 12th man that was outstanding, roaring and supporting and singing and dancing and producing a volume of noise that I swear we heard in Leeds.

We, on our sofas in parlours all over the UK, the away end, the world, went mad. Tears were shed. The banners came out. Tweets flashed round the universe. Blackburn faces were glum as Rovers piled on the pressure in the dying minutes and Heaton was magnificent with one superb save and others that showed his solid quality. This was the stuff of which history is made and legends are born. The names of these guys will be remembered for years to come.

And: the bonus, the wonderful bonus of going eight points clear, had Derby and QPR fans no doubt gnashing their teeth. It was tempting to say we had a foot in the Premier door, but no, a toe maybe, just a toe and not even a big toe, just a little one. This is Burnley, broken dreams have happened before. I still haven't got over how we weren't champions in 1962 and blew it all over the last ten games.

Mrs T and me watched the whole thing again in the evening, the build-up and the post-match, savouring every moment, every kick, every tackle, every interception and roaring with delight all over again when the Shackell and Ings goals went in. Dyche said the win was for us the supporters. The league table looked amazing.

Forgive my language, but it was all just f*****g ace.

WRITTEN IN THE STARS:
Birmingham City 3 Burnley 3

IT was a pleasure to read the papers after the win at Blackburn. I bought three. I knew my pal in Burnley would save me the two he buys. I woke up thinking, 'Jeez did we really win at Ewood?' A bright blue sky and a rising sun said yes we did. The world looked good. The toast tasted better, the coffee perfect. On the walk to the paper shop I felt like saying to everyone I walked by, 'Hey did you know Burnley beat Blackburn yesterday?'

Two goals in the last 17 minutes to come from behind; this was a win that was written in the stars. It just had to happen and it had to be Shackell and Ings that scored. The pictures that flooded the websites were fabulous. Was this the day that the balance of power began to shift from a declining Blackburn to a Burnley that if they reach the Premier League will have five years of huge secured income while Blackburn's dwindles further and further and their crowds slowly vanish?

But nobody was counting chickens just yet except Venky's and the Blackburn allotment holder who found he had one missing on Sunday lunchtime. Apparently he saw it on TV and yelled at his wife, 'Hey that's my f*****g chicken.'

Dan Black wrote in the *Burnley Express* about the balance of power shifting. The article is kindly reproduced below:

Matt Smith (Dr Who), Margaret Thatcher, Lee Mack, Jim Bowen, James Beattie, Jack Straw, Phil Jones, Robbie Savage, Jack Walker, Gary Bowyer and David Dunn – your boys took one hell of a beating.

Remember the date, 9 March, 2014. Treasure it, savour it and store that episodic memory indelibly in the mind. Nobody can touch it. Nobody can take it away.

Remember the unison of 4,500-plus fans housed within the Bryan Douglas Darwen End. Remember reactions and celebrations. Remember the joy and elation shared by supporters, players and staff alike. Remember captain Jason Shackell's primal scream and the despondency on the faces of the opposition. Remember how that triumph made us more than just record-breakers. It embodied our progression, ambition and just how together we are as a club.

It was a moment that ranked among our two Wembley visits, that night at Stamford Bridge, the Carling Cup semi-final tie with Spurs, and an unprecedented triumph over Manchester United. It was reward for our patience, our perseverance, our endeavour. It was a privilege to witness such a comeback, not just in terms of the result, but in the fortunes of the respective clubs.

And now, Rovers' only hold over Burnley that had stretched close to 35 years has gone up in smoke. Which antiquated claims of superiority will be regurgitated by those at Ewood Park now? Premier League champions of 1995; who cares? We've been champions of England twice and we didn't buy it once.

The performance at Turf Moor earlier in the season suggested that the margins were tightening, but now that tangible string of hope which Rovers had been desperately clinging on to has finally thawed. The East Lancashire rivalry has seen a reverse and Rovers have been usurped. For a club that was just a single game from oblivion in 1987, competing against neighbours who would go on to enjoy a lucrative two-decade spree of splashing the cash courtesy of Walker's riches, it's a phenomenal achievement. That dominance has been dented so vehemently by those just 15 miles down the M65 – ever since the club inherited the fortune to make £5m striker Chris Sutton the first £10,000 a week footballer.

But those halcyon days, where Rovers were once cast in Burnley's overbearing shadow, could be set at last to return. A huge gulf separated the clubs when the Clarets returned to England's top tier as Second Division champions in 1973, with Rovers glued to the hierarchy's Third Division following relegation in 1971. That's where folklore suggests, the phrase 'No Nay Never' was coined and popularised. And that historic expression could soon have renewed meaning in the current clime.

Talk of a return to the Premier League could still be premature. But promotion could postpone one of the country's fiercest and most passionate derbies for some period. Or at least negate that competitive edge. This group has shown no fear and, Michael Duff aside, they don't know how it feels to lose a derby. That has enhanced the trepidation down the road.

While Burnley's books are balanced, although promotion would rocket the numbers well into the black, the accounts at Ewood are seemingly less assured, hence Rovers's managing director Derek Shaw has slammed the Football League's Financial Fair Play rulings. The club had gambled on making the Premier League and that is not going to happen.

The accounts revealed a £36.5m loss for last season and it is highly unlikely that the club will cut its losses to the necessary £8m limit for this term that the FFP guidelines specify. A failure to do so could result in a transfer embargo that would come into force in January 2015.

That could spell the sales of £8m leading scorer Jordan Rhodes, who cost nearly three times the amount of Burnley's starting XI at the weekend, as well as skipper Grant Hanley. They either sell to survive or face the consequent penalties.

For the Clarets however, it's now four years since they last endured defeat to their arch nemesis, while the 23-point gap manifests the significant shift between the two. Memories of the 5-0 loss in April 2001, the FA Cup defeat, Martin Olsson's dive in the Premier game, David Dunn's controversial leveller last term, and Rhodes's fortuitous equaliser at Turf Moor earlier this season have been eradicated.

It's all about the here. It's all about the now, No Nay Never.

A few people on the estate know I'm a Burnley fan. 'Doin' all right, good win,' said Stuart from next door. He's a Leeds fan. The lad behind the counter in the bank grinned. 'You won,' he said. I needed more money; bus and tickets for Charlton to pay for, and Barnsley and Watford. We won't know until the season's end if history has been made. But in the meantime you have to help in the attempt to make it.

There was a nice six-minute highlights package on the Sky website that I saved. I must have watched it a hundred times. How brave was Shackell? How lethal was Ings? How totally shattered were those long-faced Rovers fans?

The papers were generous with double-page spreads, 'Danny Ings was not even born, Sean Dyche had hair and Alastair Campbell was about to be a trainee journalist when it last happened. So forgive the good people of Burnley for their wild celebrations at Ewood park as 34 years and 11 months of hurt turned into joy and expectation,' wrote Alan Nixon in *The Mirror*.

'Every journey is made up of single steps but some may seem more significant than others and Burnley's first victory over their East Lancashire rivals for 35 years could be pivotal in their pursuit of a Barclay's Premier League place,' wrote Pete Oliver in *The Times*.

'Hunger takes you so far, class the rest of the way. In a typically intense East Lancashire derby, Blackburn Rovers' desire gave them the lead, but Burnley's talent took them to the win,' wrote Ian Ridley in *The Daily Telegraph*. 'I told the players to enjoy these magic moments because they are part of history,' said Sean Dyche.

And back in 1979 *The Mirror* was quick to point out that a gallon of petrol was 98p a GALLON (repeat, a gallon), VAT was 15 per cent, Sony introduced the Walkman, McDonalds put the Happy Meal on the menu, Sid Vicious died of an overdose, Pink Floyd released *The Wall*, Maggie Thatcher swept to power, and the average house price was £13,650. Harry Potts was manager at Burnley.

Dyche praised the board for Burnley's success, 'There was a nice honesty from the board when they came out in pre-season and called it how it was. It was when Charlie was sold and they said, look, it has to happen to safeguard the future of the club. OK, that maybe re-aligned everyone and they thought OK there are realities to our club. We still want to be successful, we still want to move forward and we still believe in the group of players we have.

'That galvanised everyone. We thought let's get back to what we are which is a really good club with a rich history, not with massive resources but we want to be competitive and we want to punch above our weight as Burnley have done many, many times before. There was a nice reality about it and slowly but surely because of what's been achieved on the pitch so far, it's galvanised that feeling and the feeling is as tight as it's been in many years at Burnley. We're enjoying that and we'll safeguard that. We want to continue the journey and we do this one game at a time.'

Before the Birmingham game he talked about being limitless and relentless. Blues boss Lee Clark was full of praise for the Burnley side, citing them as an example of what can be done with a never-say-die spirit and their unbelievable attitude when every single player has a fantastic work ethic.

I was actually in Burnley on Wednesday. Alison Leigh at the Crooked Billet in Worsthorne became a sponsor of the Buchan book. I'd never set foot in this pub before but even when empty first thing in the morning it felt homely and welcoming. Spanish classes, cyclists groups, quiz nights, Thai nights and a list of ales as long as your arm. But the thing that appealed to me was the pie and peas with a taxi to the game on a Saturday for a fiver. Now that's a bargain, I thought. How good is that?

Next, it was across Burnley and up to the printers, Hudson and Pearson at Dunnockshaw, to give the green light for the Buchan book, and then next, back across Burnley again to collect Jimmy Mac for pork and apple pie at the Queen in Cliviger. The point of this little travelogue is simply to say that everyone I met had a smile on their face and was still buzzing after the win at Ewood. All that plus another gorgeous blue-sky spring day. Conversations centred on something else as well, that IF, IF Burnley should beat Birmingham then an astonishing ten-point gap would open up between Burnley and third place.

Nobody hardly dared say it or think it, but the tantalising prospect was there. QPR had lost at Brighton as we hoped they would. Derby had only drawn at home to Bolton.

The lead stretched not to ten points but a very healthy eight after a controversial injury-time leveller resulted in a 3-3 draw in front of over 1,500 Burnley fans. As soon as it was scored virtually the whole Burnley team chased after the referee, remonstrating and claiming that there had been a handball.

Shackell continued remonstrating long after the final whistle had gone. This is a guy who is the epitome of cool. When he is upset you know something is wrong. Three times Burnley had taken the lead, Vokes's goal coming as late as the 86th minute. Before the game most of us might have settled for a draw, before the game I'd guessed at 2-2, but to lose the lead deep into injury time and in such a manner was hugely exasperating. Added to that was an injury to Ings who left the stadium on crutches to protect his damaged ankle.

Marney, Duff and Vokes scored the goals. 'If Ings doesn't score, Vokes does,' said the Sky anchorman. Trippier got yet another assist to add to his remarkable tally.

Birmingham manager Clark kicked the boards and leapt up and down like a dervish in delight at the final whistle. But he fumed at the referee for allegedly mocking his captain, Paul Robinson, following Burnley's second goal and Robinson's booking. In truth, I suppose, this was a poor Birmingham side and nobody should mock the weak.

M6 travel problems, a controversial Birmingham goal, pictures showing that the ball went in off Macheda's arm, and an injury to the talismanic Ings left a sense of deflation even though it was yet another unbeaten game at a place where Burnley have rarely done well in recent years. But the thought occurred: in the long run could that late, late contentious equaliser be very costly?

There were dozens of stories of how long it had taken people to get back home, be it north or south. Not only were there motorway closures and detours through Wolverhampton, but thick fog as well. Many said it was the worst football journey they had ever experienced.

The pundits and neutrals all agreed that this had been a thriller, end-to-end stuff, a game that Burnley could maybe have had dead and buried by half-time. In total 22 shots and just four on target was one reason why it was just the one point gained. But credit gutsy Birmingham as well, they all reported.

And so Leeds: in two home games Leeds had shipped nine goals with their prospective Italian owner, Massimo Cellino, accusing them of being chickens after the massacre by Bolton. He missed the 4-2 defeat by Reading having returned to Miami to await news of two things. It was perhaps as well; if he'd seen that debacle, you wonder what he would have said next. A Football League board meeting on Thursday would tell him whether or not he was fit and proper. In Sardinia he was waiting to hear the outcome of a tax evasion case.

'The question of what happens next hangs in the air like an unpleasant smell,' wrote Phil Hay in the *Leeds Evening Post*. As a Leeds resident and a keen follower of Leeds United's misfortunes, it has been a smell that has hung over the club for far longer than just the last few weeks.

MASSIMO MASSIMO WHEREFORE ART THOU:
Burnley 2 Leeds United 1

THE group, the collective, the one-club mentality; Sean Dyche's reference points for so much of what he does at Burnley. It was 'togetherness' that was on display at both ends of the ground when Leeds United arrived in town.

But while the togetherness at Burnley encompassed supporters, management, town and team, at Leeds that togetherness was relevant only to supporters as they heroically rallied round their ailing club despite all the chaos that surrounded them. What a mess that club was in. It showed no signs of getting better as Massimo Cellino was kept waiting yet again regarding his purchase of the club. And yet the crowds still roll up on a Saturday at Elland Road desperate for some sort of salvation. Credit where it's due, the Leeds crowd were superb at Burnley.

How different Leeds's history might have been if only their directors of the time had sanctioned Jimmy Adamson's plan to bring Kevin Keegan to Elland Road from Hamburg. But they would not back him and Keegan went to Southampton instead and totally galvanised the city and the club. Imagine Keegan at Leeds and the impact he would have had at a club with their stature. Not even the kindest person could say that Southampton then were a big club. But Leeds were, even though they were in the doldrums.

The Leeds club shop would not stock the Adamson book *The Man Who Said No to England*. Someone there decided that the two Adamson chapters focused on a time at Leeds when things weren't too good and didn't reflect too well on the club. So they preferred not to stock it. That's a shame. It might have opened their supporters' eyes a bit regarding what went on there at the time.

Adamson was abused and derided at Leeds, but the Keegan bid was real. Contact was made according to Dave Merrington, his right-hand man. But when it was scuppered by directors who would not fund it, Adamson as good as decided, what's the point of bothering? What am I doing here? These were directors he said he could never trust. He left by mutual consent with a nice pay-off and then successfully sued the club for things said about him by the incoming manager. His successor, Allan Clarke, then took the club to relegation and yet remains a hero and legend.

If things went pear-shaped with the Cellino bid it was quite possible Leeds would enter eventual administration yet again. They were borrowing money simply to pay off existing loans and new loans had been paying the players' wages. Leeds supporters who were genuinely 'in the know' didn't know in fact where March's wages would come from. Owners GFH hadn't paid the wage bill for months, according to the influential Leeds website The Scratching Shed. Cellino had already loaned the club money and if his bid was unsuccessful wanted it back. GFH were desperate to unload.

Chris Boden at the *Burnley Express* must look across to his counterpart at the *Leeds Evening Post* with a degree of envy. Phil Hay has had juicy material, crises and problems to report on at Leeds for years. He already has one book under his belt about the financial woes that existed under previous owners. Hay yet again filled page after page in the build-up to the game at Turf Moor with questions and articles about the ongoing shambles.

Leeds is a goldmine for a journalist, with endless scoops, revelations, drama and mysteries. At Burnley the only drama is finding the culprit who left the lights on in the empty boardroom, or would Ings's ankle recover for Saturday. It didn't.

On 13 March, Hay asked ten key questions about what the hell was going on at Leeds, not the least of which were; how big were the club's debts? Who was in charge? What happens if the takeover falls through? What was McDermott's future? How was the club being funded?

Supporters' tweets made fascinating reading, 'if this takeover falls through, no plan B, administration, relegation and the possible return of Dennis Wise, I can see it now'; 'Burnley away has to be the day we make a stand. There's no better occasion to put this horrible year behind us'.

Peter Lorimer, in his column, came out with, 'Being boss at Leeds United is like no other club in the Football League.' Perhaps that was what Jimmy Adamson discovered all those years ago. There was no love lost between him and Lorimer, according to Lorimer himself in his book.

On 14 March, the day before the game, McDermott was 'defiant', reported Hay, with Leeds 11 points from the play-offs. Meanwhile the Football League said it could be ten days before they made a decision on Cellino. The majority of outstanding issues had been resolved, they said, but they still awaited news from Sardinia about Cellino's tax evasion case.

The Football League by the way were seemingly backtracking on the Financial Fair Play rules they had introduced knowing that they were about to be legally challenged by the big clubs that faced debt and sanctions; no surprise there then.

On the fans' page in the *YEP* the mood was gloomy:

'Fans face up to more misery on matchday'; 'we go into this game against a form team like Burnley thinking we will be lucky not to concede four'; 'Only a fool would predict anything other than a home win 3-1'; 'Manager Sean Dyche has proved that you can succeed in this division on a small budget and yes I am going for a Burnley win'; 'There will be another huge following making the trip to Burnley more in hope than expectation, displaying a loyalty that frankly this club does not deserve'; 'The work Sean Dyche has done at Burnley over the last 12 months has been nothing short of a miracle'; 'Our squad built on a significantly bigger budget than Burnley's continue to embarrass'; 'Burnley 3 Leeds 0'; 'I fear another hammering this coming weekend as this Burnley side is the best I have seen in the Championship, fast, well-organised and my tip for automatic promotion'; 'They have players who know their jobs and do them well'; 'Burnley 3 Leeds United 0'; 'My head just can't see us winning'.

But then there was one glimpse of optimism, 'But it would be just like this Leeds side to win the most difficult game of the last three, Burnley 0 Leeds 1.' Chilling words to bring any Burnley fan down to earth with a bump. Such things and unexpected results happen in football. Some of us have never forgotten a scoreline of Burnley 0 [non-league] Wimbledon 1.

For me and Mrs T this was a Leeds game with a difference. Hush, but we were bringing a Leeds fan with us. We'd met on holiday last September and turned out he was from Leeds. We'd listened to Leeds 1 Burnley 2 on the internet. He'd squirmed and we'd whooped and hollered. We collected him from Birkenshaw and commiserated (as one does) at the last results he'd had to sit through at Elland Road. He was totally convinced there would be nothing in this game for Leeds United.

The Scratching Shed came up with some pearlers in its 'Lambs head for Slaughter' piece:

> 'It would take an incredible degree of delusion to believe this Leeds United side can win tomorrow's encounter'; 'The fat lady has finished her swansong and the Whites have nothing left to play for'; 'If you're inclined to throw good money away betting on a three-legged rocking horse race the odds on Leeds winning will be astronomical'; 'As team news goes, Leeds United's is terrible. Jimmy Kebe is too ill to travel which I think is code for cowering in a corner'; 'Anyone predicting a Whites clean sheet should head to the nearest psychiatric hospital'; 'There's more fight in a frozen chicken than our current ensemble'.

The stats were ominous for Leeds. Burnley had averaged two points a game through the season, automatic promotion form with a win ratio of 54 per cent. Leeds had averaged 1.29 points a game with a win ratio of just 35 per cent. Burnley's defeat percentage was an astonishingly low eight per cent. Leeds's was 41 per cent.

To any outsider this was surely a game that Burnley would win with only a minimal chance of losing. But football has a habit of kicking you in the teeth, we worried. And all this talk in Leeds of the sacrificial lambs rolling over and being given a mauling by Burnley seemed just too good to be true. It was 4,000 Lemmings hurtling towards a cliff, wrote Leeds fan Andrew Butterwick on his website, as they drove to 'the dark, satanic mills of Burnley and one of the most ancient and worst equipped stands in the Championship. Only alcohol and blind loyalty was firing up Leeds supporter enthusiasm to an absolute buzz,' he mused.

All winter the *Daily Express* had headlined with horrendous but continually wrong forecasts of ice and snow lasting for weeks. Two days before the game it was headlining with 'Ten Days of Sun'. It was wrong again as we woke on Saturday to cold, grey skies and a vicious wind that had blown up a couple of days before. The news that Ings would be missing was not unexpected but increased the feelings of apprehension.

If the stats were ominous for Leeds they played as if nobody had told them. They were certainly not lambs for the slaughter. For most of the first half they were up for it while Burnley were nervous, edgy and slow out of the blocks. The ball spent more time in the air than any ten previous games put together. Leeds pressed, harried, and it was hard to tell which team was second in the table. A goal seemed inevitable, and not for Burnley.

Were Burnley out of sorts because not just Ings was missing but also Kightly and all the irrepressible, up and at 'em energy and tracking he brings? Was it because this was the third game in just six days?

Mental tiredness could well have been the cause of the careless, suicidal Jones back-pass when it looked odds on that Ross McCormack would score as he pounced on it and raced for goal. But like Rhodes a week earlier the ball smacked the post with Heaton quickly lessening the space to aim at. Shackell cleared it away. Yet again luck came to Burnley's aid. But why shouldn't it? At Birmingham three points became just one thanks to a last-minute goal that should never have stood.

Slowly Burnley began to wake up as they started to impose themselves and at last got the ball down on the floor. But a Leeds goal came when Connor Wickham took a good throw-in, the giant Matt Smith got the flick-on and McCormack scored with a bullet header from nine or ten yards out. We feared the worst.

The makings of an upset were clearly visible but then any possibility of a Leeds 1-0 win vanished when Trippier broke clear, whipped over a superb cross, and a hapless Leeds own goal got Burnley right back into the game. This time it was the Burnley fans that went ballistic, the eruption almost as colossal as the one that followed Blakey's goal against Manchester United; everyone now fully conscious that Burnley were standing on the brink of a quite astonishing if not miraculous achievement.

Barnes, Ings's replacement, grew more and more into the game. He ran, worked, chased, hustled, and took more than one clattering. Vokes became increasingly influential. And Arfield was immense.

Fittingly it was Arfield who scored the winner, rifling home a shot from 12 yards as Burnley became dominant. By now the vocal backing for Leeds was diminishing while Burnley's grew. Stanislas had by now replaced Wallace, bringing some badly needed threat, guile and craft. The minutes ticked by and a series of Leeds corners in the final minutes in front of their 4,000 howling fans had Burnley supporters nervously screaming for the whistle. Shackell, Duff, Mee et al held firm, the ball cleared each time.

A Burnley win then, gutsy Leeds players crestfallen, fans filing out morose and downcast, many not quite believing they had lost, Burnley players leaping with joy. But the game was never pretty. This was a win that was the result of grit, determination and the never-say-die spirit and 'relentless mentality, physicality, quality and organisation' that Dyche had instilled into them.

This was a victory for 'passion and desire', when the team ethic and support for each other compensates for any player having an off-day. Dyche has said several times (with a degree of false modesty I suspect) that he was never much as a player but what he had was a relentless desire to win.

This was the first double over Leeds United since 1926. The crowd of something over 18,000 was the best of the season. Our Leeds chum was magnanimous. But like so many other Leeds fans he has grown used to the continuous disappointments that come these days to the Mighty Whites, and they are all on pins now desperate for news of the Cellino takeover. If it fails they know that things will get even worse and defeats at 'little' clubs like Burnley may well become a regular event.

Andrew Butterwick's thoughts on the way home were plaintive, 'Burnley looked a well-drilled and very hard-working side who have taken advantage of some astute signings to mould a team who seem to have one of the automatic promotion spots tied up. If Burnley can do it on a shoe-string, why can't we?'

For 'little' Burnley the giant prize edged a little closer. Derby could only draw so Burnley were now ten points clear of third place, but that good news was soured by worries that Ings's ankle may not be so quick to heal. A visit to a specialist was planned. Next up Charlton, our tickets booked. Little Joe was envious. 'When can I come to an away game?' he asked.

Ten games to go; tweets and texts asked the same thing – can they do it?

TASTELESS SANDWICHES AND REGGAE MUSIC:
Charlton Athletic 0 Burnley 3

WE'D tried to get coach seats to the Birmingham game but left it too late. Instead we booked for the London trip to Charlton, a long and gruelling all-day journey, but what the hell we thought. In such an enthralling season you just gotta be there.

Charlton were another club that had been in the news. The new owners were Belgian. Manager Chris Powell had been sacked. The new man was Jose Riga, a former coach at Standard Liege and conveniently available. Supporters were worried that this once-proud club would simply become a feeder for someone elsewhere. Some of the players had been brought in on the new owner's recommendation. This was the club that had won the FA Cup Final in 1947 against Burnley. It had been a club of repute and stature. Not too long ago it was in the Prem. Now, it was another club where fans asked what the hell was going on.

It was alleged that owner Roland Duchatelet was telling his sacked manager who to play in the team. On principle Powell refused to play the goalkeeper who Duchatelet had imported so Powell paid the price. Duchatelet is said to own six clubs dotted around Europe and nobody really knows why he would buy Charlton as well unless he had eyes on its youth set-up and saw a gold mine of young players he could sell on or shift the best to his key club, Standard Liege.

Monday morning in Leeds and their supporters weren't too despondent having seen a spirited fight at Burnley. Ross

McCormack tweeted to his pal Scott Arfield that he hoped Burnley would now go and finish the job. He was generous towards Danny Ings when Ings won the Football League Championship Player of the Year award and McCormack himself had been one of the other two nominees.

Eddie Gray in the *Evening Post* was generous in his praise of Burnley and suggested they should be the model for Leeds to aim at. That was ironic; Jimmy Adamson years ago had brought his Burnley team away from Elland Road after a tubbing and said that Leeds was the team to emulate.

But with or without promotion at the end of the season, clubs and the media everywhere were looking at Burnley and seeing how a good, organised side could be produced on a shoestring and be up there in an automatic promotion place. But at Burnley, it was still feet on the ground, one game at a time, especially with the injury to Ings.

The 'p' word was avoided. 'You won't get talk of promotion here,' said Scott Arfield. 'Not from me, not from anybody.' But, it was hard not to imagine those boys as they nodded off to sleep last thing at night dreaming of playing in the Prem.

Phil Hay in the *Yorkshire Evening Post* described Burnley as the essence of relegation fodder at Elland Road in April 2013. Those of us who were there will remember it well as Burnley lost 1-0 and were utterly dire in a depressingly awful game. The only consolation was it took just half an hour to get back home. At that point we looked at the bottom three with growing alarm.

'But their win on Saturday stretched the gap between the two clubs to 29 points which says as much about United's standing as it does about the huge steps taken by Burnley. Sean Dyche has taken the club to the brink of automatic promotion inside one full season and 70 league games. His expenditure on transfers has been low enough to suggest that money is less of a factor than managerial aptitude and the ability of his players to exceed their presumed talent,' Hay continued.

'Leeds need to follow the Clarets' example,' wrote Eddie Gray. 'When you look at them they are not a team of superstars. They are now not that far from getting over the line and are the only team who look like holding on to Leicester. They haven't lost a game at home for over a year. Everyone is surprised how they have maintained it this season and you have to give them a lot of credit.'

Unusually for me I bought yet another edition of the *Yorkshire Evening Post*. It was filled with the news that Massimo Cellino's bid to take over at Leeds had hit the rocks again. He had been found guilty of tax evasion by a Sardinian court. The Football League therefore would surely be unable to accept him as a fit and proper person to own a UK football club. Fans were in meltdown and despair. It was front-page news on Wednesday.

And so to the Belgian Republic of Charlton: depart Leeds 6.30am for the 8am bus from Turf Moor, a bag full of bacon sandwiches and more feelings of nerves as the next game became yet another of huge significance.

Charlton were out of the bottom three thanks to a win over Bournemouth but with games in hand they still had everything to play for. The midweek results had been kind to Burnley with a falling-apart QPR losing 3-0 and a rampant Wigan held to a draw by lowly Yeovil. While those games were going on and Russia was upsetting the world and Malcolm Rifkind was issuing a stern warning to Putin, and the EU was threatening embargoes, and Cameron was threatening sanctions, the ITV Champions League coverage was sponsored by GAZPROM. You couldn't make it up. But comfortingly my garden chiminea was still in one piece, the woodpile was fully stocked, and the ten-point gap remained.

People had spent the week working out the permutations. Seven Burnley wins would definitely do it. Five would probably do it. Four might do it if other results went Burnley's way. Local psychiatrists were doing a roaring trade. The number of people seeking counselling rocketed.

Ten games to go and just six weeks remained. The word was that if Ings's meeting with a Leeds specialist was the bringer of bad news, then the club would look at a loan signing as cover. Meanwhile as we all fretted the night before his appointment, the lad himself was relaxing and dining at The Three Fishes in the Ribble Valley, established in 1814.

Fish pie is £12.50; a pure breed Angus rump steak £36. You can have a Sauvignon Blanc at £16.50 a bottle, or a New Zealand Mudhouse red at £9.95 a GLASS. On top of the Ings worries was the news that Trippier was also struggling and could be out for two weeks. The consolation was the signing of Chris Baird.

A footballer's life is a precarious one and unpredictable. Roger Eli wrote about all that in his book. At 32 and a highly-respected Irish international, Baird was out of contract and training with Reading who couldn't afford to re-sign him. Suddenly he found himself plucked from obscurity to travel to Burnley for a two-month contract as backup during the final run-in. He and Dyche had played together at Watford some years earlier.

Faced with such a long trip, I took Mike Smith's new book on the coach to read; *The Road to Glory*, the story of Burnley's 1914 FA Cup win. If you want detail and research this is the book. The time that went into it must have been phenomenal. April will see the 100th anniversary of the cup win.

In just the first few pages I found out how the Bee Hole End got its name, why horseshoes were so lucky in one game, and that the club was so hard up at one point the ground was used as the site for a travelling menagerie of wild animals. But the elephants couldn't pull the wagons on to the pitch so the club only got a tenner out of it. At Blackburn Rovers the tradition continues, but only with chickens.

When it came, the news about the Ings ankle was glum. While George Osborne was delivering a budget that makes life much better for beer and bingo fans (remember how George Orwell wrote about governments controlling the masses via gambling and drinking), Ings was poked and prodded and advised it was settling quickly, but he'd be out for a few weeks, although no one was really saying exactly how many. For anyone who liked beer, bingo AND Danny, this was a mixed day.

'Top geezer,' said the guy who met Ings in Barrowford, walking up the 'fair hill', past the White Bear and up to Pasture Lane, and chatted to him. Danny himself confirmed it would be OK but he'd be out for a few weeks.

On the coach to Charlton the resident stato was quick to point out that of Burnley's last nine goals, only two had come from Ings or Vokes, and of the last 17 points from seven games, Ings had scored only once; hardly the stats of a one-man team.

Pre-match, Mrs T was confident, she always is. But cautious moi would have settled for a scrappy point. Charlton had been on a roll, three unbeaten games and a goal – impressive. Derby had won 5-0 at lunchtime. The day had the makings of an upset. The pitch we were warned was a muddy gluepot. Eddie Howe, after his defeat, said it wasn't made for today's players, or something like that. And Charlton when they came out looked like giants.

The coach journey down was superb; Burnley to The Valley in under six hours including a stop. At 2pm the crowds were already milling around; in a patch of sunlight we ate tasteless sandwiches in a children's playground nearby, bought at the motorway stop. There'd have been more taste in an old sock. Reggae music blasted from someone's open window.

The pitch even at its best looked dreadful, the goalmouth just feet away from us down at the front like one of our veg patches – rolled and ready for planting. Heaton was covered in mud by the time the warm-up finished. Behind us the away end was packed; this is the end where to get in or out everyone funnels in to make one almighty slow-moving crush negotiating your way past the queues at the bar. How it passes a health and safety inspection is beyond me. It makes the James Hargreaves concourse look like the Ritz.

Penpal John Gibault from Seattle was over, Seattle! I rarely use exclamation marks, but Seattle deserves one! He was over for long enough to see three games and had picked this week especially.

Originally from Jersey, as a lad he'd picked Burnley quite arbitrarily as his team to support. He told his mum one day at home, assuming she'd think he was mad. 'Oh,' she said, 'did you know you had a cousin in Burnley?' And so began a long love affair with all things claret and blue. The stories of how so many long-distance supporters became Clarets would no doubt fill pages. I've got one Clarets penpal who lives at the Double D ranch in Driftwood, Texas. He rides round the ranch in his claret shirt on his horse, calling out, 'Howdy pardners, up the Clarets.'

We weren't disappointed by the game that Burnley played; their organisation, their approach, their adjustment to the god-awful pitch, the slow and steady stranglehold they exerted on the opposition so that when they scored it was just reward for their patience and the way they'd weathered the Charlton storm.

Actually storm is a bit of an exaggeration, brief shower might be better. Whatever it was, it was over the minute Barnes headed home Stanislas's sublime cross in front of the away supporters, a lovely thumping header that as good as eliminated Charlton the minute it was scored. It was the tonic Barnes needed. He grew into the game more and more despite receiving pushes, shoves and being leaned on all afternoon, conveniently ignored by a referee we can only assume could only see out of one eye. But of course if a Burnley player as much as sneezed, the whistle was in the official's mouth in a blur.

A penalty by Vokes calmed our nerves, but in case the blessed Sean wonders why Burnley fans are so cautious, a generally disbelieving lot, someone might just gently have a word in his shell-like and explain that it is in the Burnley fans' psyche from years of experience that only when we are leading a game 3-0 do we relax a little – and even then it is not both buttocks but only one.

Kightly's goal was then the icing on the mud. Having run Charlton ragged, Stanislas was taken off and the energy of Kightly was unleashed to torment Charlton further still. He duly obliged by cutting in from the left, nutmegging one hapless defender, skipping effortlessly past another, smiting a mighty shot from an impossible angle, and the ball careered in off the third Charlton goon before looping over the bearded Moses lookalike goalkeeper.

Now, we at the away end, felt totally euphoric. With just a minute to go, Charlton were buried. Now we could all return from whence we had come, by coach, Tube, train, taxi or whatever, with smiles on our faces, unless…

My pal Tim emailed to say what a helluva shift they'd all put in. But afterwards it was chaos on the rail in south-west London. The wrong sort of lightning had wiped out most of the network and Waterloo station was like the evacuation of Saigon. No such problems on our smooth coach journey home to the frozen north, passing the team coach on the way and waving. Pendle, all bathed in white, had looked magnificent early in the morning as we drove over.

Yes, the shift they all put in certainly shifted Charlton out of the way. Arfield stood out in a team performance for which all of them deserved their pay packet. Baird shone, looking like he'd been a fixture at Burnley for months. They were all the man of the match. After Derby's brief and impudent catching up, the ten-point gap was restored.

Relentlessly, you might say.

SEAN DYCHE AND OLD-FASHIONED VALUES:
Burnley 2 Doncaster Rovers 0

'IT'S very difficult to be successful without key core values. They are called old-fashioned but they have never been more modern: respect, good manners, good time-keeping, pride, passion, hard work, belief, integrity. They are the glue that holds everything together.'

There was another fine media piece about Sean Dyche. He was already being nominated as his choice for manager of the year by Stuart Pearce.

Dyche was squashed into his small, windowless room at Gawthorpe for the interview, with his red-stubble haircut and a goatee beard that allegedly glows in the dark. A decent journeyman he described himself as a player. He is only 42 but has his feet on the ground and common sense pours from him. He does find it strange that foreign managers come into the English game rather too easily. Nor is he deceived by flattery such as comes his way at the moment. People haven't always called him the 'Ginger Mourinho' he laughs. 'Man-management is the key now,' he says. 'Having 25 players is like having 25 mini companies.' He is pragmatic, 'Passing like Barcelona is all well and good; but only if you have the best players in the world.'

'Look at what you've got, not what you haven't got,' is another of his key mantras. 'Look at what you have got and that's the unit to make effective.' He is as down to earth as Brian Clough who he looks back at with fondness, doing his garden, sweeping the leaves, brushing the drive, and then Clough would give them a tenner and cook for them. Today, camaraderie, team spirit and respect in the group are what he looks for.

But if some players are strong others are fragile like china cups, he maintains. Empathy with that is important. Most players are like this.

Perhaps never playing in the Premier League has made him more human and given him his core values and a little more humility than many in the game. How grounded and honest to say 'people like me come and go', meaning that no manager stays forever unlike some who may say things that prove to be empty and hollow.

I was looking through an old scrapbook and found this that was said by one previous Burnley manager. 'I'm here for as long as the club want me. We have a responsibility to do the right thing. We have a moral duty.' That previous employee left the club in mid-season.

In another old scrapbook is the account of the night that Celtic came to town and caused mayhem and bloodshed, when hundreds of their fans were filled with drink and had Burnley fans reeling on to the pitch to escape the violence.

Back on the coach home from Charlton and filling the hours on the journey I continued with Mike Smith's new book *The Road to Glory*, and came across this about the time Turf Moor hosted the English League versus the Scottish League, 'Some five thousand football excursionists came into Burnley early on the Saturday and for the rest of the day the town was turned into what is usually styled a pandemonium, a general assembly of evil spirits, whisky in this case appearing as Beelzebub, the chief of spirits.

'Disorder, drunkenness and extravagance prevailed, respectable people avoided the town and shopkeepers suffered and a sigh of relief was raised when the railway companies again swallowed up the pleasure seekers whom they had disgorged early in the morning.'

That was in March 1914. The Reverend Whitfield, who was incensed by the Scottish fans, didn't spare Burnley fans either, 'Take the English Cup competition at Sunderland. Thousands of our Burnley working men spent the whole time from 6am on the Saturday to 6am on the Sunday to see this match at Sunderland.

'We are told that the whole week's wages were selfishly and meanly taken up in many cases for the excursion; that families were cruelly left un-provided for, that tradesmen were unpaid for the week's goods supplied to the homes which had to depend on further credit, that the pawnbrokers did a roaring trade the day before. The railway journey was largely taken up with gambling so that many found themselves pounds in debt on their return and many unfit for work the day after.'

Mike Smith's book is rich with snippets of social history in between the match reports. In 1913 Burnley's groundsman was called Onias Pickles. Burnley Suffragettes disrupted Ramsey MacDonald in Nelson. And in 1914 the eight-month strike at the Albion Bobbin Works ended. These are the things that bring the book to life.

What brought the game at Charlton to life, as well as the goals, was the marvellous away support. Sean Dyche is right to say that people like him come and go. But a club's supporters are there for all time. That's what makes the situations at Charlton, Leeds and Blackburn so sad. They are just three of the clubs where fans scratch their heads and wonder where their clubs are heading as ownership moves around like pass the parcel.

At Burnley we know what's what. Charlton fans on their blogs and websites were filled with praise for Burnley and how well run they are. How many other clubs, they asked, have a chairman and directors who meet up with the away fans before a game in a local pub and buy them a pint, for that is what John B and Barry Kilby were doing.

The singing was splendid. The sound of 'In our Lancashire homes' reverberated around the ground. 'We speak with an accent exceedingly rare; the Longside of Burnley will always be there.' Imagine three sides of the ground at Turf Moor singing that at full volume – awesome. 'Who needs Mourinho, we've got Sean Dychio,' was another one. And the best of the lot, 'Who put the ball in the bastards' net, who put the ball in the bastards' net, who put the ball in the bastards' net… super Jason Shackell.'

On the coach home we had to give our nominations for goal of the season and player of the season. Just where do you start? More often than not it's an easy choice for player of the season, but this time it was not. Heaton, Trippier, Marney, Jones, Shackell, Ings, Vokes, Arfield can all say they've had their best ever seasons. All of them got a mention on the coach.

And goals – so many of them have been outstanding. For player of the season mine was Jason Shackell, the unflappable rock at the centre of the meanest defence in the Championship. Goal of the season – Ings away at Yeovil, a rocket of a shot that came quite out of the blue, a masterpiece of opportunism, accuracy, surprise and power. Then there was his solo effort at Derby. There was the Stanislas goal at Turf Moor against Blackburn, a beautifully placed shot that followed some intricate passing. But you can only pick one.

Tuesday 25 March and Doncaster at Turf Moor: Billy Davies had been sacked at Nottingham Forest. It was confirmed that Massimo Cellino was unfit to finalise his takeover at Leeds United, leaving them in total financial chaos. It made you appreciate the achievements and stability at little ol' Burnley even more.

Nobody was assuming there would be a Burnley win. Nobody was taking things for granted. We continued to pinch ourselves after each win and three more points. We looked at the ten-point lead and yet again blinked. Alas there was still time for things to go pear-shaped, we fretted.

It was a feeling that manifested itself during most of the first half. The crowd was mute, still, on edge and apprehensive. The continuous songs and chants that 2,000 fans produced at Charlton had vanished.

Doncaster were neat, tidy, industrious, breaking down the flanks several times. A free header flashed just wide. Burnley, meanwhile, were uncertain, in attacking mode yes, but there was always a gear, you felt, they could shift up into. It was almost as if the prize on offer was too big to contemplate so that nerves and extra care were playing a big part. Passes went to Doncaster players all too often.

Even so the Burnley shots mounted up, but alas were either wide or high or saved by the goalkeeper. There was plenty of play that was slick and inventive but relentlessness was replaced by tentativeness. The longer the half went on without a Burnley goal the more you wondered if this was the night for the kind of horrible upset we all feared.

Then the moment came that we felt sure would give us the deserved lead. It looked like it was Barnes who was held in the penalty area when a defender clung to him as he tried to rise to his feet. That alone was surely enough for the whistle. But no: then the defender hauled Barnes to the ground again but still the referee waved play on. It was as clear a penalty as you could ever wish to see.

Dyche calculated there have been seven clear penalties denied during the season. For a brief moment the crowd woke up, incensed by the lack of action by the referee. But quietness descended again, the mood resigned to just one of those nights.

Around us, during half-time, Brian from Settle, Joe from Ormskirk, Paul from Stansted, John from Seattle (and we're from Leeds) wondered if Burnley would manage to break through.

There were one or two thoughts that it had been a poor game so far, that Burnley were listless and off-colour. But not so, I thought, the shots had continued to mount up, the goalkeeper had made two stunning saves, Stanislas was causing havoc; Vokes was winning everything, Mee was having a superb game, and save for the one Doncaster header they had been totally ineffective once they got in the area. But with the crowd so quiet, the atmosphere was dead. The game was badly in need of a goal.

And it arrived in the most bizarre circumstances within a minute of the restart. A corner drifted over, Stanislas rose at the back post and the referee blew and pointed to the spot. Paul Dickov was mystified at the end of the game and when the ref blew, we, right in line with the incident, had no idea why.

Mrs T texted her friend, watching things on TV at home, to ask why was it given. Apparently it was a shove on either Vokes or Barnes. Vokes strode up, put the ball down and then took a deep breath. We all did. Would he miss? Was it going to be one of those nights? Vokes looked at the goal, approached the ball on the spot and smacked his shot into the top-right corner. The cheers and chants were as much relief as jubilation. And that was as good as game over.

Now the crowd came to life. Now Burnley came to life. Now we should have been singing 'In our Lancashire homes' (but we didn't). Burnley turned on the style, Stanislas having a stonking game. And fittingly he scored after a lovely move that carved Doncaster apart. It was no more than he deserved. On his day he is a match-winner and a player to excite when he takes defenders on and gets the cross over.

It took Eagles a long time to impose himself at Burnley. Maybe it's the same with Stanislas. Blokes like this are thorough-breds not carthorses, artists not labourers; they dance the tango not the hokey cokey. In the snow they leave no footprints. Blokes like this have to be cossetted, stroked, and forgiven for when they do lose the ball or a dribble doesn't come off.

And Vokes: this was a textbook centre-forward display. Winning the ball in the air, leading the line, laying it off, holding the ball, using all the spaces, beating his man on the ground, working his socks off all over the place, closing down defenders, winning the ball, retaining possession, showing a delicacy of touch and control that belies his size; and all capped by his masterful penalty. Ings player of the season… hmmm… don't forget Vokes.

More shots rained in, 26 by the end of the game but alas only eight on target. Yet more superb saves from the goalkeeper; yet more brave last-ditch blocks by defenders. Burnley began showboating, passing the ball around with contemptuous ease to the cries of 'ole, 'ole'.

Yet again there had been another display of relentlessivity (a new word). Ease into the game, test the water, keep 'em out, wear 'em down, deny 'em space, hustle 'em, harry 'em, make 'em play the ball back to the goalkeeper over and again and then unleash the reborn Stanislas. Dare I say that Ings and Trippier were barely missed? Barnes might not be the prettiest, most subtle player in the division but by God he makes defenders work with his presence and running.

Derby lost, Wigan lost, but QPR won so the points gap on third was not increased. And one really sour note: Marney was booked and would therefore miss the next two games. He knew immediately and raised his arms to the heavens in dismay.

The ten-point gap was still there but still eight games remained. One of the statos worked out that assuming QPR won all their remaining eight matches, Burnley needed to win five. Only five weeks to go but we felt afterwards that this was feeling like the slowest run-in ever to a season's end. And while the finishing line inched agonisingly closer, there was still no certainty that little Burnley would make it in second place, thereby creating one of the biggest and most unexpected football fairytales of all time.

BACK TO EARTH WITH A BUMP:
Burnley 0 Leicester City 2

THE Foxes were in town: top versus second in the Championship match of the day. An articulate Leicester fan had been on the Claretsmad message board to say that his team had been listless and out of sorts for the last couple of games.

They had stumbled to a draw at Blackburn but wound up the Blackburn support by singing 'We're going up with the Burnley.' They had stumbled to a home draw against lowly Yeovil and only equalised in stoppage time when goalkeeper Kasper Schmeichel came up and scored with a bullet header. The Leicester fan was expecting to lose.

Out of interest I looked back at this time just about ten years ago in *It's Burnley Not Barcelona*. Leicester had been to Turf Moor and won 2-1. And then there followed a 1-1 draw at home to Grimsby. It was that weird and wacky season filled with ridiculous scorelines, mostly with Burnley on the wrong end of them. But the write-up of the Grimsby game made for interesting reading:

> Of this for the moment we will say little… save to say, the sun shone beautifully and we got half a suntan. During the first half I read the programme from cover to cover. The chap behind me actually fell asleep (honest I do not make that up). Pigeons settled happily on various parts of the pitch, there was so little

to disturb them. In fact sometimes they settled on a player's head.

Grimsby were so bad it is a mystery they aren't marooned at the bottom already, 90 points behind the rest, and this had all the ingredients, passion and interest of listening to Iain Duncan Smith. This was the classic end-of-season game that neither players nor crowd were interested in.

And yet at that point ten years ago there were still nine or ten matches remaining. Contrast that to now and the end-of-season run-in. The game then was described as passionless garbage, 'huge expanses of time taken up with nothingness', and the money alarm bells were ringing loudly as crowds dwindled. The next game was Bradford City at Turf Moor, 'two struggling teams battling for mid-table inferiority'.

Fast forward ten years and supporters couldn't wait for the next game. Yet the attendance for the high flying 'new' Burnley against Doncaster was only 1,000 more than ten years earlier even though Ings and Vokes had between them done something never done since the heady days of Lochhead and Irvine over 40 years ago when both strikers had bagged 20 goals or more. While Leeds supporters were in agony at the fast-approaching meltdown of their club, where the players and staff were now wondering if they would be paid for March, happy Burnley fans were packed into the James Hargreaves Suite attending a Radio Lancashire fans' forum with Sean Dyche, Lee Hoos, Mike Garlick and John B.

At Leeds, owners GFH were denying responsibility for paying the wages, claiming that this was still Cellino's job; the same man who had been deemed an unfit and proper person. GFH claimed that notwithstanding the league ruling there was still an agreement that he would fund the club for six months.

He was said to have paid the wages and running costs for January and February already, paid off a loan of £1.7m to a sponsor, and bought £7m in shares, believing his appointment would be a formality.

Here is a club, one report said, that never mind they didn't own the stadium or the training ground; they didn't even own the tables and chairs.

GFH, according to Cellino, didn't even have the money to pay for the washing powder and he had allegedly told GFH to f**k off in response to their claim that it was down to him to continue stumping up the lira. Manager McDermott was reported to have said that all the talk at player level was whether they were going to get paid. It was reported they got 50 per cent.

It was therefore with a degree of pleasure that I tuned into the forum on Radio Lancashire. Those who were there agreed it was a superbly successful evening. The panel took questions for nigh on two hours.

'You have vol au vents in Burnley?' smiled Dyche wryly at the mention of the words.

With things going so well, someone mentioned why not a Sean Dyche Way, as well as the Harry Potts Way? 'Last year it would have been Sean Dyche No Way,' he responded, laughing.

Transcribe the complete broadcast and you'd fill a chapter but along the way there were a few things that stuck in the mind:

> 'You're a custodian, not just a manager'; 'the club has a rich history and it has got to be protected'; 'being ginger is a unique selling point'; 'I'm flummoxed half the time with referees' decisions'; 'there are no plans to rebuild the Cricket Field Stand but we are looking for painters and decorators to spruce it up'; 'the signings we have made have been fantastic, the players have been fantastic so far'; 'group mentality has been the key'; 'the best thing is seeing a group become a real team believing in each other'; 'taking away egos has been key, each accepting the others for what they are'; 'behind my façade of being the ginger beast I can in fact be quite light-hearted'; 'if Lego are listening I think they owe me a few quid'; 'the voice of the fans is the most powerful thing in football'.

The Lego reference was in connection with a new model figure that displayed an uncanny resemblance to Dyche. Hoos revealed that season ticket sales had passed the 9,000-mark that very day. And then a most telling comment after listing all the foreign owners of Leeds, Leicester, Derby, Nottingham Forest, Reading et al – 'Burnley owned by Burnley folk.' There in a nutshell was the uniqueness of Burnley and its provincial distinctiveness.

Friday night before the Leicester game: we knew Ings and Marney would be missing. The word on Trippier was that it was touch and go but he was unlikely to play. With the deadline day approaching for advance-price season tickets both the upper Jimmy Mac and the Bob Lord were approaching a near sell-out.

Leeds United players received a 'proportion' of their wages. Folks arrived in Burnley from all over. One lad posted on Claretsmad that he was coming up from Southampton, 'But my mum thinks I'm coming to see her.'

A 2-0 win would see Burnley go top. The mere prospect was astonishing. Facebook, Twitter and fans' sites were filled with messages from people who couldn't sleep, were on pins, couldn't stop thinking about it; couldn't wait for the game. This was the match of the day.

But it was a game too far.

Ings missing, Trippier missing, and Marney missing: nevertheless Stanislas was there and he'd been magnificent during the week, and big Sam Vokes was there. But then it was four missing as he twisted a knee as early as the fifth minute and lay prostrate on the turf by the dugouts. We looked at each other and groaned. It was game over from that moment. Alas it was then five missing as Stanislas never looked like running the show as he'd done against Doncaster.

Burnley fought and battled as any Dyche side would do but with Edgar on from the bench, in preference to Wallace, or Treacy or Stock, and Barnes on his own up front it was an impossible task that faced them.

It looked like they might make it to half-time with a 0-0 scoreline but then Burnley's nemesis Nugent cut in and from 20 yards curled and guided the ball into the bottom corner with

Heaton powerless to do anything other than make the dive. Until then neither side had come anywhere near scoring, neither goalkeeper had anything of note to do. But it was clear that Leicester were by far the better team as they imposed themselves and controlled most of the play. There was never any doubt where the points would go.

In the away end the massed ranks of Leicester fans all decked in blue t-shirts given to them by the club – along with a bacon roll and coffee breakfast – sang and chanted as we did at Charlton. Going up, going up, and they knew it and it was hard to see this powerful and talented side losing another game all season.

You always hope for a breakaway goal, or a stroke of luck, or a free kick and a referee's decision going your way. In a Burnley attack, and there were several, there were loud claims for a handball and penalty but the claims were waved away.

When Leicester scored their second, the ball carelessly given away cheaply then swept upfield for the forward to run on to and nudge Duff out of the way, the referee waved play on. Others might have blown for the foul. The finish though was sublime with a shot from 20 yards that dipped and went in like a rocket.

Leicester had striker options on the bench that Burnley didn't. If there was one huge difference, that was it. This was a game between a club with resources and finance, and one without. This was a game between a side with players on the bench who could make a real impact, and one that did not. This was a game between a side running on a full tank, and one that was running into the fuel-low warning zone. It emphasised how brilliantly Burnley had done to get this far in the season and still be in second spot.

And yet, ironically, for all Leicester's power-play, it was hard to recall a single save that Heaton had been called on to make. But there he was, on the wrong end of two goals.

Burnley battled on. Kightly had a terrific strike that Schmeichel punched away. Treacy put in a 20-yarder that tested him. But it was Arfield who had a plumb chance to equalise when the score was still at 1-0. The defender slipped on the edge of the box and suddenly Arfield was clean through with only Schmeichel to beat. But the shot was from an angle and though on target it hit Schmeichel and away it bounced. You knew then even more that this was not to be Burnley's day. We applauded our boys loudly at the end. They'd given their all. The defeat had to come one day. And now we had to wait and see what Derby and QPR would do.

They both had 'easy' home games, QPR to Blackpool and Derby to Charlton. No one could see anything other than three easy points for the picking and them moving three closer to Burnley. It was a very quiet drive home and we drove home thinking that to run out of gas after all the superhuman efforts so far, would be heartbreaking. On went *Soccer Saturday* and we watched the results coming in just as nervously as if Burnley were playing.

Football is filled with surprises. Derby won comfortably but QPR could only draw. So Burnley STILL remained nine points clear and still had the better goal difference. Suddenly things didn't seem quite so bad after all. The disappointment lifted considerably. And the injured brigade had a week's rest to come.

Dyche took the defeat on the chin and his reaction was pragmatic. Look where we are in the table, he told the players, see what we have done; that it had been a year since anyone had last come to Turf Moor and won. This was no time for recriminations. The players he had remaining had done the best they could.

This was also a day when two more major pieces featured him in *The Guardian* and the *Daily Mail*. If the *Mail* is correct he would return home after the defeat and let the time with his family expunge the memory and freshen him up ready for the next round of preparation.

'If you go into my house there's not a thing about football. You wouldn't know whether I was a bricklayer, a builder or an IT consultant. Why would I want to keep thrusting it in my family's face? I don't want my wife constantly reminded of what her husband does, or the children. I want them to lead their own lives.

'I keep all my memories locked in my head. I've got a couple of scrapbooks and my mum and dad have my Chesterfield shirt from the semi-final; no signatures or anything, I wasn't interested in anyone else's. Collecting souvenirs has never been my bag.'

Dyche was sticking to his one game at a time mantra, no talk of promotion, but said he was human.

'I'm human. It's smashed in your face every turn of the page, every news channel. League tables are for fans to look at and the media to speculate about. I'm more interested in performances and getting the preparations right for the next game. I won promotion four times as a player and I'm not going to deny I would enjoy another as a manager but you can ask any of the clubs I went up with and they will tell you the same.

'My focus was always dead calm, always on the next game. I know what I believe and what I think the group can deliver but outside expectations are a different thing.

'I'm aware of what the media suggests; I'd be naïve not to be. Every single week there's someone linking us with promotion but I never even mention it and I won't until the job gets done. But what I can say is that the stats show that we are getting stronger, working harder, covering more ground. We are not tailing off and that gives everyone encouragement.'

At the end of the day, seven games remained and the table still looked damned impressive. The sensible thing was to shrug it off and accept that all good things must come to an end. Next up Watford v Burnley, Bournemouth v QPR and Middlesbrough v Derby. Not quite the home stretch, but almost.

April

BATTERED AND DEPLETED:
Watford 1 Burnley 1

IN our homes, pubs and clubs, on Facebook, Twitter and assorted websites we endlessly debated the number of points and wins needed. But then came the news that none of us wanted to hear. With the prize so tantalisingly close, the injury to Sam Vokes was serious.

Cruciate knee ligament damage was the announcement. There couldn't have been a Burnley supporter anywhere, a Burnley player, the Burnley management, or anyone connected with the club, and many neutrals too, who wasn't devastated.

And then there was Sam himself. Lord only knows what he must have been thinking with months out of action in prospect. Twenty league goals, a wonderful partnership with Ings; his season was finished with months of recovery ahead of him. What made it all the more numbing was that we had taken this guy to our hearts.

For most of his career Vokes has been a wandering footballer on loan here and there, and never settled. Then he has his best ever season at Burnley, develops superbly, man of the match on several occasions, signs a three-year deal, well in contention for player of the season, and then suddenly, with everything going so well, hit by a lengthy spell out of the game. Football is cruel and unpredictable. One minute a player is at the top of his game, man of the moment, and then in an instant his season is over.

Some said that on 79 points the season was now on a knife-edge, even with a nine-point cushion. Would those points be enough? Could we scrape together the remaining points needed? Others were still confident, that Trippier was near to a return, maybe even at Watford. Marney would be back for the Barnsley game. Ings might see the final two or three games.

There was enough ability and resilience to gather the required points. Just two wins would do it, some said. By contrast at this time in 2013 Burnley were just four points above the bottom three.

In the meantime, could this battered and depleted team find the energy, the spirit, the bottle, to get a result at Watford? Recent games there had been not quite meaningless but almost. The last one of any real significance had been way back in 2003 when Stan Ternent's side played an FA Cup quarter-final there. The semi-finals beckoned but what followed was one of the poorest games and performances of that or any other season as we lost 2-0.

If I had a pound for every time I've sped by the Watford turn-off on the motorway I'd be a wealthy man. I've seen it signposted so often I used to feel the car veering towards it before swerving on to the M25. We head for Kent or Sussex regularly. Southern folk think that the world ends just north of Watford. Hertfordshire's own Xanadu, wrote Igor Wouk ten years ago.

'Cultural oasis of the south with their fantastic one-way system, the outstanding curves of the inner ring road, the place that gave the immense cultural talents of Elton John and Geri Halliwell, big shops like B&Q and the redundant power station next to Vicarage Road. It's hard for a down-to-earth place like Burnley to match the architectural majesty of the jewel of the M25 and the Parisian-style sophistication of downtown Watford.'

But Watford fans didn't think much of Burnley either, 'Can I give you a piece of advice? Always try to avoid a trip to Burnley if humanly possible because, quite frankly, when God created a waiting room for all the evils bound for hell, he twinned the place with Burnley. Furthermore if you ever feel hungry in Burnley, try to resist all temptation of food. Burnley is a God-awful, pus-filled hole of a place. It has no redeeming features whatsoever.

'It is as much home to all the grossly generalised stereotypes of the north held by southerners as Essex to the north's equally blinkered picture of the south. Narrow-minded, coarse and hostile are three descriptions that come to mind. A trip to Burnley is among the least pleasant of the football calendar.'

Clearly the guy who wrote this needs to visit the Crooked Billet at Worsthorne on a Thai night, or a Saturday pre-game and sample the pie and peas. Or visit the Queen at Cliviger and sample any one of half a dozen pies on offer there. And by the way it's two-quid Tuesday every week there.

Anyway, Watford shouldn't grumble. On our last visit there ten years ago we noted the splendour of the nearby Watford General Hospital, the cemetery over the road from the ground, and nearby assorted allotments of all shapes and sizes. It's where if the football was dire and there was no fun watching the paint dry, you could turn your gaze to the chrysanthemums, cabbages and cauliflowers. Today it has a John Lewis so Mrs T was well impressed.

Come 1 April the FA had a great April Fool gag. The newest England kit was out and they were asking £90 for the shirt. I saw through it straight away and fell off the chair in the office laughing when I saw it. It was up there with the best ever 1 April gags. Like the story that Holland had beaten England at cricket.

The shirt, designed by Nike of course, modelled by Rooney, Gerrard, and Hart et al, was made up of space-age technology materials and was described as keeping the body at the optimum temperature required for an early exit from the World Cup whereupon the shirts would be down to £10 which punters wouldn't have to actually pay, but would be given by the FA to persuade them to take the piles of shirts off their hands.

And then I gulped. This was not an April Fool joke. This really was £90 for the shirt. Even cash-rich Premier League superstars were Twittering that this was too much, even for them. And Holland really had beaten England.

Sometimes you feel you just HAVE to be at a game to show solidarity and support in times of adversity. Watford was one of them. The last one when we felt such an emotional pull was when the promotion team of 2008/09 had been knocked out of the League Cup by Spurs in extra time after scoring three goals to level the semi-final at 4-4. It was the emotional equivalent of being kicked in the head by a donkey. We were just distraught at coming so close to a fabulous win that would have taken us to the Wembley final.

Following that we headed for the Midlands to see them in the FA Cup against West Brom, simply to be there. It felt the same when we heard the news of Vokes's injury and that he would be out for months.

It just seemed such a massive blow to the promotion push. And thus we headed for Watford with the thought ringing in our heads; your team needs you.

It was referee Stuart Attwell's first game at Watford for five years but their fans had not forgotten him. Five years ago against Reading he had given 'the goal that never was', when a linesman had imagined that Reading had scored and flagged the referee to insist that there had been a goal. Experts are still baffled as to the sequence of events that led the linesman to suffer this hallucination. Football being football, hardly anyone remembers the hapless linesman, but football does remember Attwell and he goes down in the history books as the guilty man copping the blame.

Thursday night and even Sean Dyche was saying things were a bit stretched, intimating that there were people outside the camp almost thirsting for this to happen. Ings was still out but 'back on the grass'. Trippier was 'on the cusp' of coming back. Junior Stanislas had a tight hamstring. Marney was still suspended and of course Vokes was missing, his operation delayed for a week to allow the swelling to subside more.

Thermopylae this was not. Rorke's Drift this was not. It was only Watford. But nevertheless this was still backs-to-the-wall stuff in a desperate attempt to hang on to some kind of points cushion until injuries had healed and reinforcements could be brought up to the front.

Bullish thoughts of a win were far from our minds; a point would be welcome. Watford, still with their Italian connections, were a good side at home, free-scoring and well organised. It was a return to a place where Dyche has such strong connections. He had been player, captain, youth coach, reserve coach, assistant manager and then manager.

Ever the rational pragmatist, his departure he described as 'a business move'.

'Well how did you spend your Saturday?'

'Er well, we went to Watford for the day.'

So did nearly 2,000 other Clarets. With a full team all would have been confident. But this was a Burnley side playing with one arm behind its back. The odds were with Watford and Leicester had won the night before. They were as good as up. Not even the thick Saharan dust and cloying European pollution that had blanketed the country for days had any effect on Leicester's progress, as the health experts advised folk to stay indoors with people coughing and sneezing their way around with irritated weepy eyes.

Not bad is it when you can be back in Leeds from Watford by 9pm without breaking a speed limit. In fact much of it was at 50mph thanks to long stretches of roadworks. And what a mood we came home in, a mix of yet more astonishment, incredulity, more admiration and more respect for this gutsy team that never knows when it is beaten.

Marney, Trippier, Ings, Vokes and Stanislas all out: you could have been forgiven for thinking the worst. Even more so when Watford took an early lead as Deeney scored with a shot that might, on another day, have hit the top of the hospital behind the stand, but on this day became a stunning strike that flew in over Heaton's head. You feared the worst from that moment on and then could only hope that both Derby and QPR might lose.

From those games the news was good, both of them falling behind while Burnley did their utmost to get back in the game with their makeshift, patched-up side shorn of its key players.

And how they tried: Kightly was everywhere; Jones was in the thick of everything. Mee got down the left over and again. Barnes battled away in the lone role and was magnificent. But enter Mr Attwell and his linesman.

If Attwell is infamous because of the goal that never was, the one he allowed at Vicarage Road five years ago, this was the game where he disallowed the goal that was, again thanks to a flag-happy linesman desperately in need of a trip to Specsavers. No way was Barnes offside when he swept in from behind the defenders to force Treacy's superb cross home and equalise.

The Sky crew were nearby with their monitor and summariser Matt Murray assured us at half-time that the goal was good. It left you thinking that this was going to be just one of those days and this soufflé of a season was about to collapse.

But this Burnley side is rugged, robust, resilient and remorseless, the image of its creator. It wasn't one of their better days up front in the box; how could it be minus Ings and Vokes? But nevertheless they soldiered on with Barnes leading the charge, Kightly buzzing like a hornet, inroads being made, Heaton, the back four, and superb defending at the other end keeping Watford out, and all of us willing them on to salvage something knowing that Derby and QPR were losing.

With the score still at 1-0 our hearts were in our mouths when it seemed Watford must surely score a second and put the game to bed. A slide-rule pass cut Burnley in two: a masterful through ball that the great Jimmy McIlroy couldn't have bettered and a Watford player ran on to it. Heaton dived but the player went round him and struck the ball homeward.

Suddenly the ball, with not a player near it, was rolling in slow motion towards the Burnley goal line just feet away from us. We stared at its progress, mesmerised, hypnotised, horrified until it was just inches away from a goal. And then, just as you thought it must trickle over, in swooped Baird from nowhere, a blur of claret, to hack it away to the utter elation of the away support. Maybe then, we thought, there was still something in this game for Burnley.

And there was. Wallace replaced Treacy. Burnley turned on the pressure. Attacks became more frequent until Baird played a ball for Arfield near the edge of the box. Arfield moved on to it, turned beautifully and struck a shot into the bottom-left corner of the net. It was so far away from us at the away end that at first it didn't register. Had it been fingertipped by Almunia, had it hit the post, but then we knew it had gone in and Arfield had scored to rescue a precious point just four minutes from time.

I always think of the goal at Blackpool in the storm scored by Christian Kalvenes as one of the defining goals of the 2008/09 season. Maybe the goal at Watford scored by Arfield will be one we look back on in the same way.

All of us knew that Derby and QPR were still losing. The whistle went. 'Going up, going up, going up,' the away end sang, knowing there was now a ten-point gap over QPR and just six games to go. Any one of half a dozen could have been Burnley's man of the match; Kightly, Jones, Barnes, Baird, Mee or Shackell. If they were the props, then the others weren't far behind.

This was a supreme team effort, a triumph for the never-say-die spirit instilled into them, the day spoiled only by the terrible news that Jay Rod had been stretchered off at Manchester City earlier in the day.

'Nobody is going to catch Burnley now, are they,' said a dejected Harry Redknapp at the end of the day. And all of us hoped that Harry would be proved correct.

In *The Daily Telegraph* on Monday after the game, Ian Ridley wrote a telling opening paragraph to his report, 'Fans of cheesy 1980s TV will remember fondly the darts quiz show where the host, Jim Bowen, would rub salt into the wounds of any pair who had failed with their final test by showing them the glitzy star prize and taunting, "Have a look at what you could have won."'

Old Jim, had he been at Watford, might well have said just the same to the Watford fans as they exited the stadium, reminding them how different things might have been if the Pozzo family hadn't ditched Dyche in favour of Gianfranco Zola. Their loss, our gain, as the old saying goes.

BARNES MAKES THE DIFFERENCE:
Barnsley 0 Burnley 1

THE euphoria of the result at Watford would not go away; but from the press and media you'd still never really have known that Burnley, barring disasters, were heading towards the Premier League and the pot of gold.

My pal from Watford, Matt Rowson, has written regular reports for years. His latest made for a nice view (albeit abridged) from the other side. He has kindly allowed me to reproduce it here:

I was reckless with my routine today, trains instead of cars, Mexican food with Dad instead of the pub. And as the match kicked off, with the spring weather unsure what to make of itself, things began to shake themselves out rather well. With Lewis McGugan prominent, this was as effective and dynamic a 45 minutes as I've seen him put in, in yellow, we looked bright and prominent in the early exchanges, kicking towards the Rookery with Sean Dyche presumably having advised flipping the ends.

Ten minutes in and we were ahead, the irrepressible Deeney latching on to Pudil's pass and belting us into the lead. We got a break, a deflection off Jason Shackell's thigh looked critical in lifting the shot over Tom Heaton; everything Troy strikes is going in at the moment. Minutes later, another break; what looked like a tight offside call denied Burnley a decent equaliser…

Burnley's disallowed goal was greeted with a rousing rendition of 'One Stuart Attwell' from the Rookery. Coming hot on the heels of the inevitable mock-celebration in response to the first shot drifting wide of the Clarets' goal this briefly suggested that the much-discussed first return of Attwell since the ghost goal of 2008 would be commemorated with sarcasm and wit rather than ire and red-faced barracking.

That it didn't prove that way was in no small part down to an erratic display from the official, albeit that the only decision that had the potential to directly affect the outcome was, if failure it was, down to Attwell's assistant… which sounds familiar. That call got the visitors on his back and he was never going to get much leeway from the home end, so both sets of supporters were on his back as he left the pitch at the interval…

Faced with the absence of his two prolific strikers Sean Dyche had selected his only available forward, target man Ashley Barnes, who remains as respectful of the rules of engagement as Beppe our manager is to the boundaries of his technical area, in front of a five-man midfield. This begged the question; do Burnley score a lot of goals because of Ings and Vokes, or do the forwards score a lot of goals because of the players they are in front of?

The truth appears to be somewhere in between, for while Burnley on the day could be summed up as 'a striker or two short of a very good side' and struggled to turn their possession into clear-cut chances, they did not look blunt and, as one would expect of a Sean Dyche side, were utterly single-minded and focused on their task…

My youngest daughter is four. At story time she delights in re-hearing one of a limited number of favourites, even if we have read it the previous evening, and the evening before. In some cases such as that of 'Hairy McClary from Donaldson's Dairy' the scope for silly character voices makes this tolerable; in others, 'Elvis and her bloody Magic Ponies', less so. Elder daughter, seven, rolls her eyes, demanding greater variety. I can cope with the whimsical demands of a four-year-old, but am less able to respond calmly to this same old story being played out in front of us at Vicarage Road.

It should be acknowledged that the visitors DID play a role. They had turned up the pressure a little, inevitably, and threatened for the first time. Brian Stock's free kick from wide on the right was whipping inside the post until Abdi's forehead intervened. From a corner, Ben Mee's header was clawed out of the top corner by an astonishing Almunia.

Worth noting, too, that it's tempting to attribute every late goal to our inability to concentrate for the full 90-plus-whatever. Sometimes opponents do just score late goals. In context, however, this was a complete pain in the arse. Scott Arfield, a fringe player at Huddersfield and an odd-looking recruit by Dyche in the summer, hit his eighth of the season, turning sharply in the box and driving low past Almunia, who got a hand to it but not enough…

Meanwhile in the real world outside of football, it was indeed spring and an old man's thoughts turned to the garden. There are different ways of looking at spring; firstly that it is a wonderful time of Easter eggs, rebirth, fresh greenery and things warming up; or secondly, it is a time of great irritation to a gardener when the list of things to do seems longer than the number of MPs fiddling expenses and mortgages.

As ever the decking and shed needed painting, the furniture needed checking to see which legs had fallen off, the grass needed the first cut, the hose needed disentangling; plus I must be nice to the neighbour next door because sure as hell I'll need to borrow his power wash.

And then there are the potatoes to go in. I swear I once knew someone who thought that early potatoes had to go in before 8am.

Then there is the neighbour opposite who is so organised and his drive is so clean and immaculate that he even power-washes the fencing.

It is the time of year when our wonderful Prunus sheds its almond blossom all over the street and out he comes with his leaf sucker-upper glaring daggers at us. In truth though, there is so much of it, that if it were snow you'd be out building snowmen and sledging down the slope.

And thirdly, I suppose, it is the time of year when promotion and relegation issues are sorted, especially in the old days when clubs played three games in four days.

It was with that in mind that Barnsley beckoned, the 'Tuscany of the North' as it once liked to describe itself to get one over on Rotherham because Rotherham once christened itself the 'new Milan'. In fairness there is some gorgeous countryside around the area and the scars of pits and mining on the landscape have long disappeared.

Some years ago Barnsley had one season in the Premier League and Peter Ridsdale was once chairman. Michael Parkinson wrote stories about them and their legendary players. One of them, the tale goes, used to headbutt his way out of the main door of the club as a party trick. This worked well and caused him no problems other than an occasional migraine until one day the hinges were changed and doors replaced so that they swung the other way.

Of course no one told the unsuspecting clod so when he did his usual *piece de resistance* he knocked himself out cold and lay there for an hour while folk stepped over him and went about their business without batting an eyelid, as Yorkshire folk will inevitably do, especially in Barnsley.

The news on Monday was good. At Leeds Massimo Cellino had completed his takeover so all of us who enjoy the wacky world of football would have more fun and games to follow. There was no truth in the story that Massimo would be contacting Maria Miller for mortgage and financial advice.

At Burnley, Marney would be back. There was nowt wrong with Jones following his early exit from the field at Watford due to feeling unwell. Trippier and Ings were back in contention, said Dyche. Burnley folk were expected to be there in their thousands having snapped up 3,000 tickets with more then paying at the gate.

Unfortunately Barnsley has never been a happy hunting ground for Burnley and every year I've sworn I'll never go to this place again having seen so many dire games there. The 1-0 defeat in an FA Cup game not long ago was typical. It was the last match for Brian Jensen and his sad goof cost Burnley the result when a long Barnsley hoof made its way three miles up into the sky and the Beast made a total hash as it came down from space. It was an ignominious end to a great career for Burnley although he was still, at the age of 38, keeping clean sheets at Bury.

Barnsley then: Tommy Boyle's first club, a classic encounter in prospect, third from bottom against the second-placed favourites to go up; both teams desperate for the points. QPR were at Blackburn and Derby at Blackpool, providing a rare occasion when we wanted local rivals to win.

A motorway accident held up hundreds of fans with the supporters' coaches trapped in the delays. The game had started by the time the coaches arrived. The car crash victims were two sisters, both Clarets, on their way to the game. The car had been clipped by a lorry and then flipped over and over and landed facing the wrong way on the verge.

Burnley fans are a tough breed. The sisters got out, brushed themselves down and managed to get there for the second half of the game. They, plus the fans there for the kick-off, almost filled the away end. The songs, the chants and tributes were non-stop on a par with the vocal support at Charlton. The roar that greeted Barnes's goal in the early minutes had the foundations of the stand shaking.

What a goal and what a start: Kightly, once again on fire, whipped over a superb cross and there was Barnes stooping low at the near post to bullet the ball home. It was no more than he deserved, especially after the one disallowed at Watford.

For the rest of the night he was superb; brave, bullish, here there and everywhere. It was one of those nights when the ball stuck to his feet, he won the headers, he played the ball off, he held it up; he played the right passes and was a handful for the Barnsley defenders all night, including the giant centre-back Lewin Nyatanga, so big he can head lampposts.

Ings was back as well, to the delight of the supporters. Vokes limped in on his crutches and received a warm welcome. Trippier was fit but remained on the bench. Marney was back from suspension. Ings got most of the game under his belt and showed several moments of sheer class. A goal for him would have been the icing on the cake but it was not to be.

Any thoughts after the early goal that this would be a walkover were soon dispelled as Barnsley fought all night. They harried, stopped Burnley playing and were quick and sharp. But all of it then came up against the wall that was the Clarets' back four so that other than a half dozen routine catches Heaton had little to do other than read the programme. Certainly he had no saves to make since Barnsley, for all their possession, industry and neat, tidy play made few inroads into the box. On the occasions that they did, Duff and Shackell vigorously ushered them straight back out again. For all their good play they never looked like scoring. Did they even have a shot at goal on target?

On the radio afterwards, after the hour or so of the obligatory drooling over the Chelsea win, at last the programme spared a moment to look at Burnley's result and listen to callers. The rich earthy tones and broad accent of a Burnley chap joined the programme. He spoke passionately about the season and the miracle of it all. He spoke about how little had been spent on this marvellous Burnley team. And then he mentioned the values and costs of Premier League players that cost £50m or more.

'And ey, you could buy all of bloody Burnley for that,' he said, to the delight of all of us listening.

QPR lost at Blackburn so temporarily we all loved Rovers for a fleeting moment, about a nanosecond. But a plummeting Blackpool could not beat Derby so they took third place, 11 points behind Burnley. It was an astounding thought that should Burnley beat Middlesbrough in the next home game and Derby fail to win, then Burnley would go up. Not only that, Leicester City lost at home. Could Burnley go on and even win the Championship if Leicester had a bit of a wobble?

So a night for samba football this was not. If footballs had feelings, this one would have had a headache from the battering it got. This was a night of industry, resilience, digging in, dogged defending of the precious lead, and restricting Barnsley to the edge of the box more or less all night.

This was a night when the result was more important than the performance. Not that the performance was poor, far from it, but it was functional rather than flowing, determined rather than dazzling. They went out and did a job but this was not winning ugly, this was winning with calm professionalism.

The following morning the *Yorkshire Post* waxed lyrical about the carnival atmosphere and the whole team on the cusp of promotion, 'Well-drilled, physically strong, swift and purposeful.' But all season Sean Dyche has urged all his players to be the man that makes the difference. It was Barnes who was that man at Oakwell.

EVERYTHING BACK ON HOLD:
Burnley 0 Middlesbrough 1

HOME to Middlesbrough: 12 April and on the cusp of an achievement of staggering magnitude. The mantra held firm, one game at a time. Don't mention the 'p' word. But how could we not? It was so close you could feel it, sense it; almost taste it.

Before the game things were by no means certain. The worst could happen – Derby could win all five remaining games and Burnley could somehow contrive to lose all five. The cruellest things can happen in this game. There were plenty of folk on the message boards playing around with the possible points totals and comparing Derby and Burnley's final games.

Yet how could we not fall victim to conjecture and imagination? The point that was salvaged with just four minutes remaining at Watford and the three points gleaned at Barnsley; these were things that made us almost sure that the finishing line was within one outstretched hand. And not only that, but Leicester's defeat opened up the absurd possibility that even first place was not impossible. You wondered too what the players were thinking the night before. The day that lay ahead of them might make them heroes at Burnley Football Club, with their names in the history books forever.

Scott Arfield might well have been relaxing with his guitar. Michael Kightly talked about how he felt he was playing better. He still wasn't satisfied; still felt he wasn't at his best. Playing was all about confidence, he said. It's simple, he added, the more confident you are, the better you play. Junior Stanislas was aware that he would be looking for a new contract at the end of the season but for now he was concentrating on the matter in hand, winning and helping the team. He would like to stay. He was settled. He was happy in the area with his young family.

But it begged the age-old question. What happens to the fringe players at the end of a season like this? They have helped bring about something special but they face the axe if promotion is won and the manager decides he must release players in order to attract new ones. This is a player good enough to find a contract elsewhere but he could be forgiven for worrying that he is dispensable. Where's the security in that when you have toddler twins to clothe and feed?

David Edgar, at the end of the Watford game, stood and looked at the cheering Burnley fans for an age. I'm sure I saw the question in his face; will I be here next season? Triumph and reward for some might be bittersweet for others.

The inevitable comparisons appeared with triumphant teams of previous seasons. Comments such as, 'This is the best Burnley team I have seen,' were common. But perhaps the most intriguing was the mention of the team of 1947, the team that lost the FA Cup Final at Wembley on a sweltering day, but won promotion to the First Division.

It was the team of Alan Brown and Harry Potts with the nigh-on impregnable iron-curtain defence. It was a team that could win a game handsomely but if during such a game a goal was conceded, long inquests were held and even arguments, not at the manner of the win, but how and why just one single goal had been given away.

The thought occurred that Brown and Sean Dyche would have got on well; both men with firm moral codes, both firmly believing in the team, the group with a one for all and all for one mentality. If Potts was D'Artagnan back then, then maybe this season it has been Sam Vokes. Didn't Dyche say something quite profound that wasn't really picked up on at the time in an interview; that his players must buy into the group mentality, if not they must be moved on. Quite simply they must be willing to fit in.

So many people were agreed. This was a season no one wanted to end. 'This is the best season ever, even better than 1972/73,' said one guy coming down the stairs after the last-gasp equaliser at Watford. But yet, the little warnings would not go away. Nothing was settled. Nothing was certain. Be it horse racing or athletics there have been plenty of instances when the leaders of the field, with the winning line so close, have fallen or pulled up.

So at Turf Moor, in Burnley, in places the length and breadth of the country, or far away overseas, no one was taking anything for granted. The word 'if' was the word of the moment, and usually in capital letters. There was still trepidation mixed with anxiety. 'Can we really do it?' the question most often heard.

Two days before the game I'd wandered around the 1914 FA Cup exhibition at Towneley Hall. Communing with history you might say, wondering what thoughts went through those players' heads on the morning of the game. They wouldn't have been about money, that's for sure.

A century separates that team from today's. But wouldn't both teams have been thinking about the possible achievement in front of them, the sheer wonder of it along with the pride and triumph? One hundred years ago the season had begun with nothing special in prospect, so what they had done was immense. Today's team began in much the same way, with the smallest this, the smallest that, so the final victory in prospect was just the equal of the team of 100 years ago. And both teams had a manager who uncompromisingly drove them on, John Haworth back in 1914, Sean Dyche today.

The underdogs; both teams unfashionable, underestimated, the little team from the little northern town that some southern folk still think is the back of beyond, that some still think is all mill chimneys and cobbled streets, cloth caps and whippets. The common bond: both were teams that no one expected much of at the beginning of the season.

The comparisons could go on with the lists of similarities and the lists of differences, the boots, the footballs, the shirts, the haircuts, and the money. But Dyche said something fascinating about handling today's players, that each one is a sort of mini-company, each with its own individual needs, with their agents and lawyers and complicated contracts.

Handling players today is so hugely different but once on that green grass it all boils down to the same thing – winning. Tommy Boyle might recognise that bit but the rest he might just shake his head at with both wonder and bewilderment.

Towneley was vibrant, the grassy areas newly cut, the smell of the mown grass filling the air. Families strolled around, children played; the Stables restaurant was full. The day was fine and warm. In the exhibition hall there were all manner of things; the medals, the replica FA Cup, newspapers, programmes, photographs, postcards, framed pictures, actual shirts, menus and tickets; an absolute treasure trove of exhibits, the prize perhaps being the congratulatory letter from His Majesty the King, and everything all beautifully lit and put together.

Down the bottom end was the hugely-enlarged, almost life-sized photograph of the team. Slowly you walked towards it, but before it you came to the life-sized figure of goalscorer Bert Freeman. Nor was he a stripling, it could have been Sam Vokes such was the resemblance.

One hundred years ago, then and now, history, tradition; this is a club where there is so much of it, so much to be proud of, identify with and feel part of. This has been a season where there really has been what Dyche has advocated all season, a one-club mentality. In 1914 the town of Burnley was well and truly placed on the map; the whole town was united in its pride. It was repeated in 1921, 1947, 1960, and in all the subsequent occasions of triumph that followed, the last one being 2009.

Wandering round the Long Gallery I wondered if 2014 would be the next, exactly 100 years since the first. The ghosts of Bert Freeman, Billy Nesbitt, Tommy Boyle and all the rest would surely look down and be as proud as the rest of us.

I looked with especial wistfulness at the images of 'Little' Billy Nesbitt, who weighed just 7.5st and was deaf. He was from Todmorden so there was the link between us. On a train to London to see the FA Cup Final in 1962 I think it was him I met, though I didn't realise who he was at the time. He would have been 70. Did he know we were talking about the game? He spoke to us and said he'd once played in a cup final and pulling back his jacket he showed us a medal he wore on a chain that hung from his waistcoat.

But Ed and I were only 15 and in what must have seemed to him to have been rude indifference, took barely any notice. A few moments of polite acknowledgement and that was it. We never chatted to him or asked him questions about his day at Wembley playing for Burnley. He must have been so proud travelling down and yet we as good as ignored him. To us he was just an old man. And now I'm nearly 70 and it embarrasses me still, to think about it.

At the Turf it was ladies' day. I went to Beverley races one ladies' day and vowed never to go again. Never have so many drunk so much, fallen over so much, been carried out so much and behaved so outrageously. Some of the horses refused to go to the finishing line.

At the Turf it's the day that all the lasses and mums get dolled up and set out for one thing only – to have a good time. Last year we caught fleeting glimpses of them through the large windows. Some of them ventured out into the seating areas in their frillies and fineries. You wonder if some of the young 'uns think they might snag a footballer if any of them are 'on duty' guesting in there.

Alastair Campbell was once a celebrity guest and said he'd never had his bottom felt so much. It was difficult to tell whether he was shocked or delighted.

The Middlesbrough manager, Aitor Karanka, was complimentary about Burnley, 'Every team can learn from Burnley. The coach has made a very good team. I don't want to say Burnley don't have good players but I think they are the best in the league as a team.' Dyche lauded his players again, 'They have been relentless in their nature.'

We were reminded too of the bell that hangs in one of the main corridors of the club in a glass cabinet. It was locked in there never to be rung until Burnley were in the Premier League again. It was Jimmy McIlroy and then manager Eddie Howe who locked it in. Later in the week supporter Tony Scholes bumped into Jimmy in Tesco and mentioned the bell.

'I think I'll have to live another 80 years before I hear that bell ring,' said Jimmy, laughing. We probably all thought the same.

Andy Lochhead has lived in Burnley for decades. He has seen so many managers come and go. He played for several at Burnley, Leicester, Aston Villa and Oldham Athletic. He is still a Burnley matchday host and knows his football inside out. He could still give masterclasses on how to attack and head a football.

Andy was pinching himself, still unsure as to the reality of what he was seeing. One of Burnley's greatest ever centre-forwards during the 1960s, a superb header of the ball with no little skill in his feet, his partnership with Willie Irvine was one of the best seen at the club. He saw a whole town that was buoyant, united with the club, with a manager that in less than two seasons had cracked the problem of aligning everybody.

Everybody was living the dream, Lochhead said. What was happening was no fluke and the manager was the man who had done it. People had bought into everything Dyche had said, he was immaculate on the touchline, but with the right passion that everyone wanted to see in a manager.

'He was a manager I could have played for, no-nonsense, straight talking, telling his players what he wants them to do and always expecting hard work. He has done a good job with existing players. You only have to look at the transformation of Sam Vokes to appreciate that.

'There are plenty of others who have improved under his watch. He keeps his messages to his players simple. You can get bogged down with information if you are bombarded with it. All you want to do is your job and do it well.'

Kick-off was at 3.07pm for this game in memory of the 96 spectators who lost their lives at Hillsborough. It was the 25th anniversary, and a quarter of a century down the line, the families of those who died or were injured were still fighting for truth and justice.

And at 3.07pm Burnley Football Club, if all went well, was just one game and 90 minutes away from football glory and an achievement that would rate as one of the greatest ever; that could elevate them in the opinion of so many people to no matter what the sport, team of the year and Sean Dyche to manager of the year.

'Clarets are almost there!' headlined the *Burnley Express*.

And then Middlesbrough came. And won. And everything was back on hold. And all of us filed out, shaking our heads, wondering how on earth we had lost that game, and praying that there would be no final heartbreaking twist to this astonishing story.

BLACKPOOL ROCKS:
Blackpool 0 Burnley 1

IMAGES of the Middlesbrough defeat would not go away. The build-up to the game began early on Sky with live cameras at the ground, the possibility being that this would be the day of triumph. Lee Hoos was interviewed. Ground staff gave the pitch a final cut.

Sky was relentless with their message that if Burnley won and Derby did not, then Burnley were up. Supporters were interviewed in the club shop snapping up matchday shirts on offer at £10.

The cameras went into the ladies' day lounge. It was only 11.45am and Burnley's beautiful were already on the champagne and cocktails. The cameras homed in on four of them. These four girls were indeed stunning. Burnleh? This could have been the red carpet area at the Hollywood Oscars.

'So this is ladies' day?' asked the man from Sky, clearly impressed by the flesh and flash on parade in front of him.

'Ey we won't be ladies by th'end of it,' said one of them with an accent exceedingly rare.

A crowd of over 16,600 filed in; the biggest line of photographers seen for 50 years behind the Boro goal waited for the defining pictures and player celebrations. All was set bar the carnival weather with a dull, grey, almost wintry sky, with fine rain swirling around in and under the stands.

The minute's silence in memory of the 96 at Hillsborough began well. And then the hordes from Middlesbrough defiled it with singing and chanting. It was shameful, embarrassing and a stain on their club. What you wished for was chastisement, a comprehensive Burnley win to put them in their place. But it was not to be.

Football is funny sometimes. Burnley had hardly given one of their best football performances at Barnsley but had come away with the 1-0 win. At Turf Moor against Middlesbrough they played marvellous football, dominated the game, hogged possession, piled up the shots on goal, yet lost this game 1-0. It was just one more instance of that basic football lesson that you don't always get what you deserve.

It was one of the most one-sided games seen at Turf Moor for years and Burnley gave as good a passing performance as there has been all season and once or twice had me thinking, hell this IS Barcelona. For all apart from a fleeting 30 seconds you could not fault them but the ball just would not go in the Boro net. Days later we still hadn't forgotten how Kightly hit the bar, Ings volleyed wildly when he had time to think; there were several goalmouth scrambles, shots were blocked, Shackell had a header cleared off the line, Duff headed over, Wallace hit a screamer, Stanislas hit a screamer. In the second 45 minutes the shots and free kicks rained in but no one could beat the inspired Greek goalkeeper who pulled off at least five fingertip saves. Crosses and passes shaved the post, balls were played across the six-yard box with no one to meet them; the pressure was continuous. But still Boro's single-goal lead remained intact.

The ball had been at one end for a Burnley corner and 30 seconds later it was in their net when Boro picked up possession from a hoof-it-anywhere clearance and raced upfield and scored. In that second half you could count on one hand the number of Middlesbrough forays into the Burnley half. The goal was the result of one of them. From that point on it was all Burnley with the shots, the corners, pressure and possession.

And it was all Burnley with the penalty claims, all of them ignored by a blinkered referee. Commentator Phil Bird, with the benefit of monitor replays, counted three clear calls. Manager Dyche identified two. The clearest of all was the one we were right in line with when Ings was blatantly hauled to the ground. He was incandescent. Dyche marched to the referee at the final whistle demanding to know how he had not seen any of them.

Derby won later on and clawed back three of the 11-point lead. The results had been the wrong way round. Dyche assured us and his players that there had been nothing wrong with the performance, save for the mistakes that led to the goal. It was, he said, difficult to speak because the officials had made such a difference to the outcome of the game.

'The ref had spoken to players about not pulling shirts in the box but when it happens to Danny Ings, he doesn't give it. I asked him, what was the point in speaking about it, if you are not going to give them? That's nine penalties not given this season.' But play like that again and some team would be turned over, he added.

Watching *The Football League Show* that night served only to leave us wondering more than ever how Burnley hadn't won. Dyche had worked a miracle, said Neil Warnock, and now they had to limp over the line. And yet these things happen. That evening Barcelona versus Granada: Barcelona with 81 per cent of possession, 29 shots to five, 13 corners to one, and lost 1-0. Perhaps over there they were saying, 'Hey if it can happen to Burnley it can happen to us.'

In his programme notes Tony Livesey described the plight of Burnley folk; that being a supporter was the most stressful job in the world with every waking moment spent running through all the permutations that would take Burnley up. The 'p' word in question was not promotion, but paranoia or pessimism. We could only hope that at Blackpool, there would be a Groundhog Day repeat of the scenario needed for the Burnley promotion party, a Burnley win and Derby to drop points. But Derby were playing mind games suggesting that Burnley were having a wobble, that they were catchable and vulnerable. It had crossed our minds, too.

Of course people were nervous. Just like the previous game there was the possibility that Good Friday would seal promotion, something that seemed so unlikely, so improbable when the season began. The *Daily Mail* reported that players were fined £500 if they mentioned the 'p' word. Absolute fabrication the club responded. On Claretsmad one trembling poster said he was immobilised with nerves about the game.

'How do you cope with a real crisis?' asked another, derisively.

'Well I don't know about you mate,' responded another. 'But I can't concentrate on porn, let alone work.'

One permutation for a while had been that it would be at Blackpool that things would be settled. People were desperately searching for tickets. Many of those who had them were making a day of it, or even a weekend, since this was a Sky game with a 5.15pm kick-off. There were even people going without tickets but who planned to watch on TV there and stay overnight.

Years ago the mills closed for a week and Burnley workers decamped to the seaside for Wakes Week. It wasn't quite that this time but it was reckoned there were maybe 5,000 Burnley folk made the journey. The train journey from Burnley Rosegrove to Blackpool was a short one and was a reminder of the old days of football specials.

The memories and reminiscences poured out, of broken windows, attacks by other supporters, of so many people squashed on, that people lay in the luggage racks overhead, and you could pull the safety cord and stop the train every half a mile or so.

Sean Dyche was adamant, 'Our focus has been clear all season, one game at a time. We look fit and well, we're delivering performances. There's a nice clarity to the way the team is playing. We just look to take that into the next game. The "next game" mantra is a real one. We believe in it. We look to deliver a performance on Friday and see what the outcome brings. Our focus has been clear, pushing the levels and pushing the boundaries.'

Oh we do love to be beside the seaside and after getting the result both team and supporters craved, the seaside was a great place to be. Two moments of outstanding skill settled the game. Kightly cut in and bent the ball around Gilks from 20 yards to send it high into the top corner of the Blackpool goal. 'A sublime finish,' said Dyche. And then with just minutes to go Trippier made a breathtaking, balletic headed clearance from a strike that like Kightly's was heading for the top corner; a clearance that defied both description and gravity. In truth it was Blackpool's first shot on target.

Other than these highlights there was much to forget other than the glorious weather and stunning blue sky. Nobody cared about the nervous, tense performance (just a different way of winning, said Dyche). Three points and a pink Kiss-Me-Quick Blackpool hat for some, and a suntan was all that mattered. Walks on the beach, strolls down the prom and pints in the pub completed a grand day.

The Guardian described it as a regulation result in a campaign notable for relentless industry, clean sheets and sprinklings of magical moments. It was a fair summary. If the unbeaten home record had gone, the away record stood firm with no defeats in 11 games.

Nerves might have been settled far earlier if Kightly had scored within minutes of the start of the game when a poor back-pass played him through one on one with the goalkeeper. We were all screaming at Kightly to go around the keeper but Gilks saved the shot with his feet.

'Michael Kightly has Burnley dreaming,' said *The Independent*. Dyche had built a side around 'graft and camaraderie'. But if folk thought this would be a straightforward game it wasn't as Blackpool battled for their Championship lives.

Any other drama came off the pitch. On 53 minutes came the threatened protest by Blackpool fans, fed up with the way they see their club run. Hundreds of tennis balls were thrown on. An expert said they were supposed to represent tangerines, in fact there might even have been a few tangerines mixed in. Blackpool players initially threw them back into the crowd until realising they were being thrown straight back at them again, providing a nice comedy moment, something sadly lacking at Bloomfield Road of late.

And then there was a near punch-up between one of the Blackpool coaching staff and substitute Stephen Dobbie on the touchline, something to do with the substitution they were making being so slow. One report said that Dobbie was slapped on the face.

The Burnley mantra is one game at a time; at Blackpool, one slap at a time. Over the season Blackpool fans have seen their club fall from an early top end of the table position to the bottom three. 'They have some interesting times,' said a wry Dyche with delightful understatement.

Kightly sang the manager's praises, 'What he's done is not far short of remarkable. It's unbelievable. When I came in the boys said we were fourth favourites to go down. It's a testament to the manager. He's been different class but I knew that from my time at Watford.'

The last Championship manager to win the coveted Manager of the Year award was Steve Coppell at Reading in 2006. Kightly was adamant that Dyche was a candidate for 2013/14. After the game *The Daily Telegraph* reported he had headed back to spend the evening with his family, and catch up with the final episode of *True Detective*. The climax to it was stunning, like Burnley's season we hoped.

The perfect evening did not materialise. Derby beat Doncaster to remain eight points behind, hanging on to Burnley's coat tails, stubbornly refusing to be shaken off. We watched that game on TV as well, all of us temporary Doncaster fans, the fish pie on a tray and a glass of grog in front of the TV nearly going all over the floor when Derby scored their first.

And so it agonisingly dragged on with 86 points still not guaranteeing second place. Cardiff in the previous season had been champions with 87. Hull had taken second spot with just 79. Burnley had 86 and we were still sweating.

Such is football; such is being a Burnley supporter. Derby had an easy home game against Barnsley ahead and Burnley were at home to a more difficult Wigan. Queues for tickets stretched down Harry Potts Way.

Eight points clear with just three games to go. Not even Nostradamus or Old Mother Shipton could have predicted this way back at the beginning of the season.

THE BURNLEY LORD MAYOR'S SHOW:
Burnley 2 Wigan Athletic 0

HYPERBOLE abounded: the date with destiny, a day to rival Wembley, this is it. There were those who were confident and those whose nerves were on the brink. A few were recovering from long-weekend Blackpool hangovers. Dozens queued for tickets. Over 19,000 eventually made it inside and saw football history being made.

The signs were not good. Wigan were powerful, the team that most people had tipped to walk the Championship and back into the Premier League at the first attempt. And then they appointed Owen Coyle. It's reasonable to think that had Uwe Rosler been manager from the start they would have arrived at Turf Moor in top spot.

Over the last six games Burnley had won three times and lost twice, both of those defeats at home. The points return was reasonable but the goals had dried up, just five in six. It was the defence that had held things together by conceding just four.

No wonder the goals had slowed to a trickle; for a number of games both Ings and Vokes had been missing. Although his toes still twinkled, Ings's goals on his return had dried up. Vokes was still hugely missed. Kightly was the man in form. Dyche was adamant that the team was still strong, full of running and energy. In fact they were even increasing. The stats said so, he said.

Wigan had just crushed Reading 3-0 and had staged a wonderful performance in the FA Cup semi-final against

Arsenal, although they had lost. Wigan fans were therefore a little concerned that at Burnley they might have an off-day.

'After the Lord Mayor's Show comes the dust cart,' one blogger worried.

The scenario for this game was simple. A Burnley win and they were up. Match Derby's result and they were up. If Derby only drew Burnley were up, even if Wigan won.

We chewed all these things over endlessly in our heads, in our sleep, out shopping, in the pubs and on the message boards. But it was hard to predict anything other than a Derby win at home to Barnsley and at Turf Moor history said Wigan would not have an off-day; the stats said that over the years Burnley had a poor record against them. The sense of foreboding grew a little more.

Yet again Burnley remained unchanged but Rosler had rotated his squad. A friend the previous day had remarked, 'Hey, haven't you got a terrible run-in, don't Derby have it easy?' It's what most of us were thinking and if you were a Derby fan you'd be thinking, 'We can do this.' For Burnley fans, how was it possible to have an eight-point lead and feel nervous? Would the last-minute Macheda goal, bundled in with his arm that equalised for Birmingham and cost Burnley two points, prove to be so very costly after all?

The fans were nervous, 'Traipsing round the house like an expectant father in a maternity ward'; 'nearly there'; 'please let it be today'; 'can't cope with any more of this'; 'our fate in our own hands'; 'we are Burnley, super Burnley, we are Burnley from the north'; 'barely slept'; 'going to enjoy it whatever happens'; 'one game at a time, this is THE game'.

It was indeed THE GAME. 'That was better than Wembley,' said Mrs T.

They did it. They did it handsomely. They did it with style. They did it with two wonderful goals. They did it in front of a packed house. They did it for themselves, for the club, for the town, for the people. And when the final whistle went, they brought the house down and Burnley's name flashed round the world. The significance of promotion is immense; Burnley instantly became a marketable brand around the globe. Within minutes a friend emailed to say it was plastered all over the news in Australia.

This was a Burnley day, not just for the club but for the community. They flocked to Turf Moor in their extra thousands, the young, the families and the elderly, some on their walking sticks. Some of them gasping their way step by step, quite painfully to the top of the James Hargreaves and you feared for their health and wondered if they'd make it. But they did, determined to be there.

At the end, the pitch invasion was not just the teenage numpties, it was families, it was lads and dads, it was grannies and granddads and it was even the disabled on their mobility scooters not quite doing wheelies but almost. It was fabulous, wonderful, awe-inspiring, and every other superlative you could think of. It was just a special, special day, so unexpected, so unforeseen.

My head jumped forward several months to that interminable BBC Sports Personality of the Year show. The team of the year, Manchester City, no doubt will garner the accolade, but why not Burnley; this Brad Pitt *Moneyball* team fashioned and cobbled together from other folk's bits and pieces that has gelled, becoming something truly extraordinary and attaining the unthinkable.

The day warm and dry, pale sunshine bathing the ground, the conditions perfect, the pitch looking fresh like it was being used for the first time, the atmosphere electric, tingling with that magical sense of excitement and frisson of anticipation, along with more than a few hopes and prayers. A bit of fun too when the Wigan fans sang 'Owen Coyle is a wanker, is a wanker,' and the Burnley fans laughed and applauded. Opponents and rivals yes, but brought together by football's gallows humour.

If we were worried about Wigan, we had no need to be. It was indeed the dust cart they arrived in for the Burnley Lord Mayor's Show. This was a game between footballers and true comrades in claret and blue, against brute force and a disparate collection of individuals in black who for the first 45 minutes could do little other than pump and hoof the ball high into the Burnley half, while Burnley danced their way through their defence for the first and then curled the ball in for the second with a free kick from near the touchline that would have graced the Nou Camp. The first was textbook, intricate passing and first-time touches, rapier sharp and unstoppable.

'If this was Arsenal it would be shown 400 times,' said Dyche later. Of course Wigan gave a better show in the second half, but the fabled Burnley defence gave them little joy. George Halley, Tommy Boyle and Billy Watson would have smiled with appreciation. There was never a moment that the two-goal lead looked in danger.

At the other end Ings hit the post and all game he'd twisted and swerved and trick or treated, and led the Wigan defence a merry dance. Barnes had led the line magnificently; Kightly was electric, now it was he that was the man who made the difference. A Barnes second-half volley from a ball that came at him at 100mph was punched away by a goalkeeper who could only have seen a blur; what a goal if it had gone in.

The minutes ticked down. You knew the end was near when dozens of stewards began to line the perimeter. Leading 2-0 and coasting, Duff, Shackell et al in total command; thou shalt not pass.

At half-time the great Jimmy McIlroy appeared with the news he was at last to be inducted into the Football Hall of Fame. How that man was not inducted years ago is one of the great mysteries. We worked on his two books for a year and it amazed me then that he was not included. It just seemed so ridiculous.

Five minutes to go and Arfield and Ings began the age-old routine of playing for and wasting time by the corner flag. How we loved it. Jimmy Mac must have watched with approval. He invented the routine and it became known as doing a Jimmy Mac.

Tick tock, tick tock, the clock wound down and we laughed and smiled at Wigan's futile attempts to win the ball. The crowd by now knew that the club, the town, the supporters were all on the edge of a truly great football achievement.

Four minutes of extra time the board showed. We knew then the game was ours. We knew the prize was ours, the Premier League, the bloody Premier League and all its great stars and teams that would visit Turf Moor. And all the money it would generate. We knew that the glory was ours. Our time, our team, our club, our Turf and all the rest of it was seconds away and within our grasp.

All those games during the long hard slog of a season in all conditions and all weathers; yet another clean sheet, the meanest defence in the division, just five defeats and one of those only because there was a crass referee who couldn't see a penalty if it had hit him in the face. And then goosebumps and emotion and lumps in the throat as the whistle went and try as they could the stewards could not hold back the surging crowd racing on to the pitch.

Goosebumps when Ings fell to his knees with his head buried in his arms just like Phil Malley did all those years ago at the end of the Orient game. And then Ings was gone, vanished beneath the tide of supporters who engulfed him. Goosebumps when at last the team and Dyche and all the staff walked out and local lad Tom Heaton collapsed in tears; when suddenly Ashley Barnes spotted his little boy and arms wide gestured for him to join him. Goosebumps when Danny Ings found Joe Skinner in his wheelchair; when Sam Vokes limped along on his crutches; more goosebumps when Danny gave a fleeting glimpse of his famed body-popping dance routine.

Goosebumps too when you thought of the story of Scott Arfield, a young lad who at the beginning of the season had no club to go to, tagged along on the pre-season Irish trip hoping to scrounge a game and a meal, all of us wondering who he was, and then found himself a key member of a team bound for the Premier League.

Twelve months earlier he was on the football scrapheap, shown the door by Huddersfield Town. Before Huddersfield he had been a bright talent in Scotland linked with top clubs. New managers can mark the end of football careers. It had happened to Arfield and now here he was having had the best season of his career. Fairytales do come true. At Burnley he'd found a club with history, 'a strong club with a great group of players'.

And then the sheer wonder of it all. Just how did it happen? How was it possible that this little group, this happy band, this united squad of buddies and pals and clean-cut, well-spoken lads with respectable haircuts, had achieved the impossible?

Not a single expert at the beginning of the season had given them one tiny chance of an automatic promotion place. Just 22 players had been used all season and of those some had made just a handful of appearances.

At the end of the game Sean Dyche was hoisted by the players on to their shoulders. Of course he paid them tribute and there was that word 'relentless' yet again when he said they were such a committed group 'willing to be relentless'. To achieve automatic promotion as they had done, with the points they had amassed, within such constraints, using so few players, was a 'marker in history' he doubted would be repeated.

I bought a bundle of newspapers the next day. What more pleasure could there be than to sit back and read and relive the day? Little Joe had been there too. The five games he'd seen had all been wins. It was Manchester City he wanted to see the most. We had to explain that Burnley might one day lose and at that he'd looked just a little nonplussed; the thought had never occurred to him. But we'd be able to collect Panini stickers and make a Premier League scrapbook together.

The Sunday Telegraph, 'Playing with organisation, skill and positive thinking, it felt inevitable that Burnley would realise what once seemed an improbable target. Burnley were too powerful and too dogged to disappoint...Burnley is a town where the average annual salary is £7,000 below the national average. This promotion felt like an achievement by a community, against all the odds.'

'"Burnley are back," boomed the thousands who saw the Premier League dream become a reality,' wrote Alan Nixon in the *Sunday Mirror*. 'Burnley lives for its football and does defiance pretty well. Once again they take those qualities into the millionaires' playgrounds.'

'Thrust into orbit,' said *The Guardian*, opening with Dyche being asked if this was his greatest achievement. He rolled his eyes and insisted to laughter, "No, I've had a few mate… a year ago there were people questioning me." Now they are celebrating and serenading him.

'It feels like the destination at the end of a long journey. It is the people's club.'

PART THREE

May

MAKING SENSE OF IT ALL

IT was the day after the win over Wigan but the headline news was not Burnley's gigantic achievement; instead the sacking of David Moyes at Manchester United. One statistic was churned out, that in his short reign of less than a season he had employed 51 different starting line-ups. Contrast that with Sean Dyche at Turf Moor who had used the same line-up in game after game. It had paid off spectacularly dispelling any notion that a large squad was a necessity. Even in the very last game at Reading when the job was done, promotion was assured, it was the regular starting line-up, minus Sam Vokes, but still the tried and trusted group that had astonished us all.

Nor was there any slacking when you might have supposed that it would be a game simply for going through the motions and anticipating the summer break ahead. Reading were desperate for the win in order to cement their play-off place, but Burnley displayed every single attribute that had won them such acclaim and the Premier place; the never-say-die spirit, the running, pressing, and relentless determination to compete. 'We finished in style,' said Dyche, the match ending in a 2-2 draw. As a result Reading were beaten to sixth place by Brighton. It was an outstanding display of commitment.

Journalist and broadcaster Adrian Durham was at the Wigan game and wrote glowingly of Dyche. He made direct comparisons to Jose Mourinho that were less than flattering to the latter, pointing out that Dyche doesn't resort to hammering officials to the point where they are left vulnerable targets for abuse, thus deflecting from any deficiencies in manager or players. Durham wrote that Dyche hasn't criticised referees to the point where his staff think any referee or official is fair game and it is acceptable to behave in an aggressive way towards them on the touchline.

While Mourinho's football is sometimes merely functional, Dyche has had Burnley playing a brand of football that has been a joy to watch. They pass the ball, they get forward, the full-backs attack and they attack relentlessly with Dyche getting far more from his strikers than Mourinho. And then he asked a telling question. Pound for pound this season, who has done the better job, Mourinho or Dyche?

We'd missed the final two games. In our wisdom we'd booked a week away but thought we'd be clever, play safe, and in the hope that we'd be in the play-offs, left that particular week free. It was further evidence of how no one, way back in September, viewed an automatic promotion place with any degree of seriousness.

But there we were, sitting by the pool in Sunningdale village, Golf del Sur, Tenerife, while Burnley, in their one-off centenary shirts with the royal crest and all the razzmatazz the club and fans could muster, played Ipswich Town. In fact we didn't miss seeing it; there it was on TV in the restaurant. What felt good, as well as the sun on our backs, was the sure knowledge that there would be no play-offs to face, shredded nerves and chewed fingernails, or scrambling for tickets. It was yet another win, 1-0, Kightly the scorer.

The distance, however, seemed to serve a purpose in as much as it was a chance to sit back, think, and try and figure out how this dreamlike tale had evolved. The words 'romantic', 'fairytale', and 'magical' would not go away, not words you'd normally associate with Burnley, even though the mills, the chimneys and dense black industrial smoke and billowing steam had long gone from the landscape.

The other word was 'Moneyball' and the parallels were striking. A team unable to match the bigger budgets of the fancied clubs was struggling, but with the right blend of carefully chosen newcomers, many of them players who had wandered from club to club, some of them underachievers, others just needing the right leadership, all of them unfancied and raising eyebrows, a new team was fashioned, welded, and proceeded to perform at new-found levels.

And that was the baseball team in the film. The football team at Burnley could have taken their place with a modified script and the outcome would have been uncannily similar.

Goalkeeper Tom Heaton, at his previous club, had been part of a team that had conceded something like 80 goals in one season. Then Dyche signed him. At Burnley he conceded not even half that and was outstanding in the final Reading game, another on TV, that ended 2-2. His contribution was such that he would not have looked amiss in an England shirt.

Defenders Trippier and Mee had been released by Manchester City. They were not signed by Dyche but he took them to levels of performance not seen before. Michael Duff at the heart of the defence was the 'old man' and had risen through eight divisions of football to the very top once again with the Dyche team. Jason Shackell found himself at Burnley playing for his sixth club.

Midfield pass-master David Jones was at his eighth club, successful at two of them but underachieving at others. Sam Vokes and Danny Ings, the goal kings, had been cast aside by Southampton at a very early stage. Ings became prone to injuries before his renaissance in the Sean Dyche team. Vokes wandered around seven other clubs before finally finding a home at Burnley.

For Michael Kightly Burnley was his eighth club until Dyche brought him in from the cold at Stoke City where he was slowly languishing and becoming one of the game's forgotten players. Dean Marney had been at six clubs before Burnley and was another who had one of his finest ever seasons.

But it was Scott Arfield who, more than any other, symbolised the nature of the achievement. 'Who on earth is Scott Arfield?' we all asked when he was signed. By the end of the season we, and the rest of football, knew full well who he was, especially as he slammed in one of Burnley's final two goals of the season at Reading.

A reject at Huddersfield, without a club to go to, Sean Dyche saw his quality and took him in, and he became an ever-present in this all-conquering collection of other people's bits and pieces.

David Blackburn summarised the parts that made up the whole, in a piece kindly reproduced below:

> Quietly almost sneakily the squad was assembled at Burnley that fully justifies the league position. The defence is statistically the second best in the league and the personnel explain it. In Tom Heaton Burnley have a goalkeeper who is as complete as anybody in the division. He rises above the euphemism of 'good shotstopper' by commanding his box, cutting out threats and organising the team in front of him.
>
> The team has archetypal attacking and defensive full-backs. Right-back Kieran Trippier has the deadliest cross from deep in the league, while Ben Mee is a stalwart on the left. Both are the product of Manchester City's formerly formidable youth academy, cast cheaply into what was the wilderness at Burnley by the multitude of expensive signings before them.
>
> Central defence sees the real strength; the combined experience of Michael Duff (who joined ten years ago for just £35,000) and Jason Shackell is a real killer. Despite a real lack of pace nothing gets past them. Both are capable of moving the ball forward effectively and neither gives the opposition an inch.
>
> Midfield is no weaker. The partnership in central midfield is incredibly good. The guile of David Jones, veteran of promotions at Derby and Wolves, combined with the workmanship of Dean Marney who made it to the Premier League with Hull City, is able to control football matches both with and without the ball.
>
> The widemen couldn't contrast more if they tried. Michael Kightly, a veteran of the same Wolves side as

Jones, has worked hard to recover a career that stalled at Stoke. He combines work rate with trickery. Scott Arfield on the other side is about as far from a winger as a wide player can be. Augmenting the midfield and attacking the far post from crosses though has turned out to be hugely opportune for the Scot. He allows Burnley to dominate central midfield with three men, while holding the fort on the wing, scoring goals along the way.

If this is the picture of a brilliant team, then the best part has yet to be reached. Bournemouth youth graduates Sam Vokes and Danny Ings are a rather substantial icing on a delicious cake. Comprising a modern twist on the classic little and large combination, they have contributed 41 league goals. Both fulfil the role one expects, Vokes the target man and Ings the pacey, creative scorer.

Yet they swap roles freely. You expect Vokes to win the ball for Ings to score, yet just as easily Ings can supply for Vokes to beat the keeper. It's been an incredible combination and a joy to watch.

To call them 'journeymen' would be unkind. To be a 'journeyman' implies, heartlessly, that these might not be the most skilled of players. Far from it, 'wanderers' is maybe more apt and a deal more romantic and appealing; their skill grew and flourished throughout the season and their fitness was phenomenal. Dyche had referred to it as they entered the home straight pointing out that even approaching the last bend of the race they were in fact getting even stronger and were extracting every ounce of potential.

'Statistically we're still outrunning teams. That was always a question mark, could they, should they, would they? Well 30-odd games in we're still full of energy, belief and quality. We just look to continue that. You can add to fitness in different ways; it might be balance, lean body mass, good dietary control, all sorts of things.

'There are a lot of games but there are also better support systems, dietary support, and understanding from coaches about the mental and physical side of the game. The lads can keep going, make no mistake, they can play as many games as they need to; I'm convinced of that.'

It was a conviction that came from the work of fitness expert Mark Howard. If fitness is high on any manager's wishlist then Howard was the man who delivered at Burnley. It meant that Burnley began with the same starting line-up more than any other club in the top five divisions. Dyche employed an unchanged starting line-up on an astonishing 21 occasions.

Howard moved to Turf Moor only a year ago after working with Sam Allardyce, a genuine pioneer in the field of sports science. While the Dyche mantra might well be one game at a time, Howard's is 'any injuries are too many injuries'. On his arrival it was his pledge to Dyche that he would 'make the players available as often as possible and as fit as possible'. Daily coaching briefings reveal if there are any injuries, 'If there are any injuries, it disappoints us. We feel it's our job to make sure that doesn't happen. That's why, when we've had such a special year it's good to be able to say we've managed to get the squad available for the manager.

'One thing we don't have to do here is worry about players not having done enough. When they do train they train properly. The sessions delivered by the manager, assistant manager and the coach are set up to give them the appropriate amount of work and because we know if they apply themselves properly in the work that we set them there are no problems with fitness.

'We train so hard that sometimes the games feel easy, it's been mentioned. It's about hard work and getting things in the right order. Nutrition is a big part of what we've done this year. We like the lads to be lean and if you get the nutrition right they'll be healthy and will recover and be ready to play another game. There's no way of cheating the system; taking a tablet to make you recover and perform.'

Burnley writer and diarist Phil Whalley spotted one of the iconic pictures of the season of Dyche himself. Taken by Christopher Thomond for a *Guardian* feature, it showed a square-jawed Dyche staring at a window like a convict contemplating his future freedom, wrote Whalley, surrounded by ascetic signifiers: the white-washed breezeblock, the plain mug of tea and the broken clothes hook, all of which said the same thing that this is the school of hard knocks where everything has to be earned and accounted for.

Whalley saw that photo as the encapsulation of the sheer unlikeliness of the promotion achievement. Not just from the customary no money/small squad angle, but also the spectacle of this former lower-league defender inspiring all those around him with a mixture of no-nonsense grit and dare-to-dream glitter.

This no-nonsense ability to deal with the reality of situations is one of the foundations of his management style. His handling of the situation that saw star striker Charlie Austin sold before the season started was a lesson in coping with what might have been adversity and gloom to someone else.

'We were in Cork on a pre-season tour,' he said, 'when I made an agreement with the players. Charlie had already had a move fall through but the reality was that he was going to go. The club needed the money and we were going to lose him. The players knew that and I knew that. Then he does go.

'So I suggested to the players that every one of them, whatever his position, has the right to be the next version of Charlie Austin. We can only do it one step at a time but if we train right we can give it everything every time the whistle blows. That's all we agreed. There were no promises, no targets.'

Co-chairman John B paid tribute to Dyche's attention to detail, 'He actually brought a PowerPoint presentation for us to the interview. How many managers would give a PowerPoint presentation to the board of Burnley?'

Dyche remembers, 'It was something to give them, a feel of what I was about, the depth of how I work and how the staff should work, and what I felt would be important for the club.'

Banaszkiewicz made it clear what the situation was, 'If you haven't got a lot of money you have to be careful with what you've got.' Both co-chairmen were agreed. 'At Burnley we have to make the best of what we've got, polish the diamonds and make them shine. A lot of managers just want the money and instant success. Sean's got patience and can develop players.'

Impatient fans were given a gentle rebuke in the previous season during a mediocre spell when Dyche suggested to them they needed to be more realistic. The manager said, 'I knew the demands were high. It takes time. Everybody wants something instantly and it's just the way it is now in life and in football but I was suggesting then that there was good work behind the scenes in progress. We were making changes that I thought would benefit the team and the club for the future.'

On his appointment Dyche took the unusual step of actually giving the players a questionnaire to encourage open lines of communication and to help make the place a good place to be.

'Players are human and if you can make it an enjoyable but informative environment, that's the right way to work. The first thing really is to align a new group with what you can offer them. That's certainly what I did. I thought there were things we could put in place to enhance their individual potential and collective potential. I gave them a brief presentation on what they'd get from me and laid down some – not firm – but straight and simple ground rules to move the group forward.

'In the same presentation I gave them a question and answer sheet to get some feedback on where they thought they were at and where they thought training was at, and what their thoughts were on what was needed to progress.'

They were offered anonymity. 'I wasn't looking at handwriting to try and catch them out. I was trying to get them to understand that I was interested in their thoughts. You're trying to build a professional rapport. It doesn't have to be best mates but there has to be a respect, certainly between the manager, the staff and the players and to build on that as quickly as possible is important.

'Winning galvanises that because if you lay down certain criteria for what you want and you can reinforce that with wins, then everyone buys in quicker.'

What he also made clear to everyone was the one-mentality factor. 'When I came here I made it clear that managers can only guide players to what they think is appropriate. Despite what people think, I don't scream and shout at them all the time. I talk to them about what is important for them as individuals and the team. If they realign, then fantastic; if they don't, we talk some more and if they still don't, then they disappear out the building.'

Those who remain are accorded his trust. 'I've made them aware that I absolutely trust them and it's for them to decide if they let that trust down, not me. I think they trust what I do and what the staff give them. If you're asking them to give everything, which we are, you need to be psychologically and mentally rested. The reason I give them days off, and not many by the way, is just to shut down. Then they come in fresh and that freshness is the key when you're asking everything of someone.'

This 'trust' has been at the heart of the campaign. After the 1-0 win over Ipswich and with the promotion place assured, the only game remaining at Reading, medals collected, Dyche trusted them with two days off.

'I think the lads earned the right to enjoy it so we gave them a couple of days off, but they're so respectful this group, they knew to come back in on Thursday knowing how I work and how the staff work. They knew that we were not going to take their foot off the gas. I'd like to think we affected that and they've taken responsibility. They've been doing it all season. My personal belief is if you do it right all the time you don't need to flick that switch and turn it on.'

Is there a right way to play? What comes first, winning or style?

'The modern thought is that there is a "right" way of playing. I don't know who said that and I'm intrigued by it to be honest. If the so-called right way of playing is 500–700 passes a game and rolling out from the keeper and having 50–70 passes up to the other end and scoring, then you'd better have some good players.

'I have a pragmatic philosophy. I look at the group I've got, then I decide what strengths and weaknesses they have and then I formulate what I think is an appropriate way that those players can work in order to be individually and collectively successful to win games.'

If the key word is successful, then the type of play that has brought results and goals was summed up by the manager himself when he outlined his faith in fast, accurate passing 'through the units'. In a season that saw many wonderful passages of play and a score of stunning and memorable goals, there was one that will live long in the memory and was a goal that Dyche lauded to the skies as being everything that football was about and had it been scored by a 'name' team would have been shown on Sky Sports over and again.

Significantly it was in the Wigan game and was a move that began with Tom Heaton rolling the ball out, and what came next was a sequence of swift and incisive passes that took but seconds and finally ended with a sublimely deft pass from Ings to Marney who then raced forward, crossed low and hard into the six-yard box, and there was Barnes hurtling in to sweep the ball home.

It was football at its very best, at which you could only stand back and marvel that this had been created at Turf Moor against a top side that was simply swept aside. It won the Goal of the Season award. If there is such a thing as a textbook goal, then this was it.

And yet Dyche well remembers the pre-season friendly at Morecambe. 'We played our first pre-season game at Morecambe and had two different teams in each half. We lost 1-0 and someone shouted "rubbish Dyche" with a few swear words thrown in. In truth it was a continuation of criticism from the previous season. That was incredible and just shows the demands.'

Contrast that with the acclaim and applause with which he was received at the two Player of the Year functions at the club nine months later; his standing in not just the town but the football world in general sky high. At every speech he has given, be it in a low-key interview or at a public function, he has continually preached the same message; that in everything he does he is mindful of the need to be responsible and to do things in a sensible manner.

From the moment he joined Burnley he understood the constraints and what he was working with. And within those constraints, by the season's end he had amassed three Manager of the Month awards, the only Burnley manager ever to do this.

At the two awards evenings the records and accomplishments witnessed during the season were announced, the highest this, the best that, the record number of points, the clean sheets, the individual recognitions heaped on the players and defeats that you could count on the fingers of one hand.

And yet from Dyche there was no boastfulness, no ego, no extravagant claims, but definitely a wry sense of humour that suggested that this was a manager you'd enjoy working for on a daily basis. Midway through the season, despite the defeat in the FA Cup at Southampton, a game in which Burnley had played incredibly well and could have caused a major upset with their slick play, Dyche burst into the media centre, sat in a plush leather chair and announced, 'Look at this eh. This is a Premier League chair; we've got to get ourselves some of these.'

During a post-match media session after a game at Turf Moor, a journalist's phone went off. The entertaining consequences of that can be viewed on YouTube. Jovial banter and self-parody, you suspect, is never far from the surface. You also suspect that this is a manager unburdened by pressure even when there is £120m-worth of it at stake. Add to that the ability to shield the players from pressure with the one game at a time mantra and there is another huge reason for the success that came.

'Wouldn't it make going to work fun,' wrote Chris Dunlavy. 'Listening to Dyche wisecrack his way through interviews you'd assume he was talking about a five-a-side with his mates, not a promotion push with so much at stake. In a sport where victory can be decided by tiny percentages, simple psychology can make a huge difference. And it cannot be denied that Burnley's players have looked utterly unburdened by pressure.'

'My management education has cost about £35,000,' says Dyche. 'You could probably do a Masters for that. People suppose you are great if you win and rubbish if you lose. Well, whatever the result I know what I'm doing. I've put all the hours in and there's a depth to my education.

'There are a couple of brain cells in there, more than you might expect in a six-foot-one ginger skinhead. I started asking questions when I was in my mid-20s at Chesterfield and why.

The manager, John Duncan, was a bit suspicious at first, but once he realised I just wanted to be more involved, we got on fine. That was a breakthrough. I wasn't thinking in terms of a managerial career but once you start taking an interest in the planning and organisation that goes into a team, you are on the way.

'I encourage my own players to ask questions now. I'll often ask their opinion because it's important to get feedback. Players are not always open to it, at least not everyone wants to verbalise it, but if you give them a phone they would probably let you know in a text.'

Being happy with what he's got is something that Dyche continually expresses. 'You can't have everything and we certainly don't have everything here. You have to acknowledge reality [there's that word again]. I hear a lot of managers saying I haven't got this and I haven't got that but I always prefer to look at what I have got. I'm pretty happy with what I've got actually. I say to the lads all the time they are like magnets. If you work really hard and get it right, then things start coming to you.'

All Dyche ever wanted to be was a footballer, especially after he left school, 'I had the drive to think I could make it work.' At school he was in the top sets, had good friends, and still maintains those friendships. Traditional values are close to his heart. His friends are the same ones he had at school. His strong moral values came from his parents; his home was loving and caring. The family lives in Lincolnshire but he stays in Burnley three nights a week.

A strong private and family life keeps Dyche grounded and provides the getaway. Jane has been his wife for 15 years and their relationship goes right back to primary school. He tries to keep football and home life separate. Son Max is a talented footballer and tennis player. Daughter Alicia is also a talented tennis player, maybe not surprising when Jane is a tennis coach.

Relaxation comes from TV programmes like *24* or *True Detectives*, the cinema with his children and holidays in Portugal. He admits to being extravagant with watches and handmade leather shoes. But, when promotion was certain his relaxation was not with bottles of champagne.

'I sat on the M6 for three and a half hours. I cut some logs. Then I cut my nails and had a shower. Made a few phonecalls, got a bed delivered for my lad Max; I made that. My hands are still sore. Then on the Wednesday night me and my wife had a bit of dinner. That's more my style.'

But try as he can to find relaxation the job is never far away. Already he was thinking about the needs for the new season and the types of players that had to fit in with the Dyche alignment process. There was a strong story that one earlier player deal was sorted until he decided that this was a player that simply would not fit in with the group. Character is as important as quality in the Dyche world.

Already he has warned fans (and if he hadn't the co-chairmen certainly would have) not to expect marquee signings. 'We won't be signing anyone from Manchester City, put it that way,' he laughed. 'We'll be shopping in the lower end finance-wise. We've just got to shop wisely and it's more difficult now because of quality costs. We have to be sensible, not to break the bank and kill the club for the future.

'What I've got to do is build a team with the same mentality but increase the level of talent, organisation and power. I care deeply about the players but I understand it is a professional business and I'm paid to make decisions.'

Within a day of the final celebratory dinner and awards evening it was announced that four players would not have their contracts renewed. Three of them, Keith Treacy, David Edgar and Brian Stock, had all played a notable part in the season. Treacy, a talented player, had battled hard with Dyche's support to conquer his personal demons. In a masterstroke he was offered the incentive of a trial before the new season. In other words, 'Show me you're still worth my investment and faith.'

Dyche was candid about the type of players to be brought into the club and his approach, 'I'll be looking for players who can affect the group. They know I'll be pushing whoever comes into the building for even better results and to perform at a higher level because that's what it's going to take. We've moved up a division, it's as simple as that. If you are investing money, no matter how much money, you want it to work. You want it to be right.

'I believe in working with people, not just players, so it's fair to say I'd like them to be the right types but you can't guarantee that. You would take a maverick. You want someone who's loose and free and can play and can change the look of the team, but you don't want someone who would undermine and will undermine the fabric of what you do. They are the most awkward signings to make.

'You need a mixture of them, you need a mixture of real solid players; you need a mixture of great mentality, energy, physicality, all of those things. That's what makes a team and makes a squad.'

THE BEAUTIFUL GAME, THE BEAUTIFUL SEASON

THE 2013/14 season was one that so many people didn't want to end. This was a season of wonderful flowing football and sublime passages of play. It was a season of one-touch passing and quick movement. It was a season of players who could dance with a football at their feet. It was a season when Danny Ings thrilled us with his dancing on YouTube. It was a season of wonderful goals, some spectacularly individual but many of them the result of marvellous team-play. It was a season when all were agreed that this was one of the finest teams to have graced Turf Moor.

If football is the beautiful game, then this was the beautiful season. This was a team that was up there with all the teams that had won titles and promotions. For younger fans it was the best they had ever seen. For those a bit longer in the tooth there would be endless debates about how it would have fared against the Harry Potts 1959/60 title team, or Adamson's 'Team of the Seventies'. Such topics are part of the ceaseless fun of football.

One thing, however, that all were agreed on, was how difficult it was to choose any one player of the year. Sean Dyche was of the same opinion, saying that he had never known a season when it had been so hard to single out any one player, believing that it was a reflection of how much of a team effort the season had been.

'You could go through virtually every player at some stage of the season and think what a season they've had. I could name the whole team. There are some who don't catch the eye as much as Ingsy or Vokesy. But they are all invaluable to the team, the people at the back and in midfield who don't always get the accolades.'

One thing he was emphatic about was that, 'There have been magic moments, consistency, great performances, team performances, people have been under the radar, people have done the unnoticed work well. Eventually, all those things make a real team and that's what this group has been. There are things I talk about a lot; the tactical framework, the understanding the players are finding, the energy, the effervescence, but most of all the quality. It's been a real team.'

The words 'unexpected', 'unanticipated', 'unforeseen' and 'unpredicted' appeared over and again. Writer and columnist Stephen Cummings wrote, 'Outstanding, scarcely believable, astonishing, brilliant; trying to describe what has been witnessed at Turf Moor over the course of the last nine months will only lead to adjective fatigue.'

Reactions were of delight and incredulity, joy and astonishment. An estimated 20,000 fans crowded round the Town Hall and lined the streets for the parade to the ground on Sunday 4 May. Stuart Pearce and Neil Warnock both advocated that Dyche should be named Manager of the Year.

Of course the usual 'celebrities' voiced their pleasure, Alastair Campbell, Tony Livesey, John Kettley among them, but the most intriguing was from several thousand miles away. Not many in the football world are aware that one of Burnley's most avid followers is Cardinal Wilfred Fox-Napier of Durban, South Africa.

He contacted the *Burnley Express* and said, 'The manager had a definite plan and he made sure that the squad knew the plan and fitted into it like a glove. Of course the inspired performances of Danny Ings and Sam Vokes had to be seen to be believed. To gain promotion with two games to play and to do so on a squad of players that was developed rather than bought, is so reminiscent of Harry Potts in 1959/60. In that side too there were some magicians, Jimmy McIlroy, Ray Pointer, Jimmy Adamson and Adam Blacklaw to name some of my personal heroes.

'I'd love to recruit Pope Francis as a Clarets supporter, but being Argentinian he will probably shout for Lionel Messi and the like. Nonetheless I will ask him to keep Burnley in his prayers.'

He had already tweeted, 'En route for Rome and Ad Limina visit which will include meetings with Pope Francis; will have to tell him about BURNLEY'S great achievement.'

And, 'Who knows, with Pope Francis's influence, Burnley might surprise even the big boys. Can't wait for the next season!'

Cardinal Napier would no doubt include Andy Lochhead in his list of favourites. Andy had already sung the praises of Sam Vokes earlier in the season. Now he was even more fulsome.

'Sean Dyche has gained automatic promotion on a shoestring budget. I think it shows that with organisation and the right manager anything can be achieved. Burnley should be an inspiration to other small clubs that a Premier League place can be gained without spending huge amounts. I think Sam Vokes has been brilliant. I was undecided when he first came to the club. He had been on a lot of loans but Sean has turned him into a great centre-forward.

'His playing style reminds me a little of myself and he has been a great foil for Danny Ings. We were there celebrating in the chairman's lounge until about 10pm. It was a great night and a relief to finally get there. I'm looking forward to next season with optimism. We should have nothing to fear.'

That most distinguished servant of the club, Michael Duff, described his second promotion to the Premier League as the greater of the two.

'I think this season has got to be seen as better really, because of being around the top since August and everyone expected us to go away. Players talk to players and speaking to players in the past week or two they said themselves that they expected us to fall away. Everyone did. But we've almost got stronger. Someone said we stumbled over the line, second or third in the form table. That's not a bad stumble.

'It's been a fantastic achievement and that's because of the consistency. Last time we got promoted we were almost like a cup team. We did unbelievably well in the FA Cup and the

Carling Cup and sort of just sneaked our way into the play-offs, sort of a cup competition in itself. I'm not taking anything away from that but I think to show the consistency we have this season has been just brilliant. It just shows what you can do with a bit of hard work and togetherness which almost sums up the town mentality.

'I think that's why the supporters have come on board because they've seen that we work our socks off in every game and every day in training. It does mean a lot when they stick with us. I don't care how being promoted at Turf Moor compares to doing it at Wembley. I've done them both.

'The challenge is to stay there. I don't think there's unfinished business after the last time; it's just a hard league to stay in. We wouldn't be the first that went up and came back down and we've already been written off. It's hard to say about next season because you don't know who's going to be in the league yet and because you don't know who's going to be here and who's not.'

Tom Heaton said that manager Dyche should take the bulk of the credit for what had gone on.

'I think most of it can probably be poured his way. He sets the standard, the expectation, the format, what he wants. He simplifies it for players. We knew from pre-season there was something special and we managed to keep it going. He's been fantastic to play for and he should be very proud. The manager sets the stall out where he simplifies it for the players and I think once you get that physical conditioning that we've got, that we certainly had in pre-season, we've kept that going and once you apply that physical conditioning to the game, it simplifies things.

'We know we've got quality, so if you can put the work ethic and the application in there which we've done in every game this season, you're already going to give yourself a chance, especially in the Championship where fine margins make a big difference. It's been superb. It's been a brilliant achievement, just incredible really.

'There are some great sides in the Championship this year and we're one of them. We're there on merit and there's certainly a lot of pride in that. I set out when I started playing football as a kid to play in the Premier League. When I left Manchester United a few years ago it was the aim to get back there.

'It was the pre-season period in Cork that was critical,' said Heaton when I spoke to him. 'And the day we knew it had all come together was when we had one particular day of incredibly strenuous work, hard labour in fact, and then ended it split into three teams. Each team had to complete a lap of the pitch in less than 60 seconds. If one team member failed, then his whole team did it again. Not one person from any team failed.

'It was then that it seemed that it had all come together and we had something special going. It said such a lot about the efforts we were making and it left us all feeling really fit and ready to go, fresh and energised.

'Our fitness is science-based and in this area no stone is left unturned, be it diet and nutrition, weight, heart-rate, hydration tests, supplements or pre-habilitation programmes. These are a form of training designed to prevent injuries.

'The chef at Gawthorpe makes sure that food selections are of the right kind. Breakfast is optional. Lunch isn't. And let's just say that you won't get bacon, sausages and a full English. Salads, soups, fruit are the norm at lunchtime along with varied hot food, different options of meat, vegetables and potatoes.

'Lunch is an example of where the manager's little ground rules come in. If anyone sits there texting, that's a no and a fine. Calling the manager "Sean" is a fine. There are no written rules, it's just common sense and the manager has his way of making his expectations clear. Fines aren't always money and Friday is the day when they are imposed in a fun kind of way.

'Anyone can nominate anyone for a fine whether it's being late or using a phone when we shouldn't. But a fine can sometimes be a forfeit, having to sing or dance.

'The daily training depends on whether there is a Tuesday game but is always at high tempo and the application from everyone has been incredible. At some clubs you get slackers but not here. No one has tailed off. That can happen; especially at the midway stage of the season but here everyone has put even more into it as the season has gone on, without any passengers.

'At some clubs the players who know they are on the edge of things don't always give it their all. But here, that's something that has not happened and we've just got stronger as the season has gone on. All of us have pulled in the same direction and that's rare. It's been a pleasure to come in every day.

'It helps that the manager is so approachable. There's a great camaraderie with him but there's also an authoritative line that you don't cross. The ground rules are simply his expectations that he gets across; smartness is one and that comes from being in club tracksuits and club-issued trainers when we're in public. Forget this and it's a fineable offence. He likes smart haircuts and people don't slouch around with headphones in public. We don't wander around texting.

'Team talks are on Friday nights if it's an away game and another on the Saturday morning. For a home game the Saturday team talk is in the dressing room and we are in there at 1.15pm. The Friday night session is spent talking about the other team with a few video clips. It's quite brief. The Saturday pre-match session is about specific requirements from team members, reminders of the basic core values, and strengths and weaknesses.

'I'm often asked when I, or we, thought that promotion was a real possibility but it's really hard to answer. If it did happen it was gradual; there was never any specific game or week that we thought this is it. We had this confidence and belief from day one. We knew from the pre-season in Cork that we were a good, fit, balanced side. I remember that we thought that the 1-0 win away at Bolton was a big result. But in all honesty the best answer is that from day one, we never felt we couldn't do it.'

Ings too praised Dyche in an interview for the Football League website at the Football League Awards ceremony, 'He is a great manager. He is firm but very fair and as long as you buy into what he buys into you are definitely going to get along with him. That comes down to hard work and all of our players are hard-working. Mix that with talent and it's a powerful force.

'He has played the game so he knows the environment very well and it shows because he gets on with all of the lads, and the lads who aren't playing. We have a bond at Burnley Football

Club. We go out to warm up and have a bit of banter, but when the training starts we're serious.'

Ings smiled when he added that Dyche would not have been a player he would have liked to play against.

Dyche, meanwhile, wasn't getting too carried away when the points were in the bag after the Wigan game. 'It's an internal celebration for me. But internally I can assure you I'm more delighted than you'd ever know. I'm extremely proud. The players have achieved so much and there's that pent-up kind of anxiety of getting over the line when you're so close. But I don't get too high with the highs or too low with the lows.

'There are words we've used a lot, relentless, limitless. It's just a mindset. The hardest thing is all the noise on the outside. But it's only noise if you stay focused on what you do. Real achievers I believe stay focused on the job in hand, whatever that job might be. If they don't get caught up in all the noise around them they stay focused on that role and responsibility. And they've done that. The players have been absolutely exceptional this season. Next season all we can do is what we can do. I'm always reality-bound.'

Kieran Trippier was certainly looking forward to the new season, especially the chance to return to the Etihad. There's a song that's sung on the terraces at Burnley about favourite players and it ends with the line 'he's one of our own'. Long after other players had left the building after the awards night Trippier was still there and loving every minute of the occasion. 'Kieran Trippier, he's one of our own,' sang 30 or so people round the bar and they meant every word. Some players have that indefinable quality and character, be it humility or commitment; people see them as part of the Burnley family, one of their own sons. Trippier is one of them.

'I'm looking forward to playing in the Premier League now and I want to play against the best players and the best teams. I'm looking forward to going to the Etihad. City let me go and I don't think I got the opportunity there but I came here and I've enjoyed myself. I've been here three seasons now and been player of the year and got a promotion so it's not been bad.

'I've always said to myself, my dad and my mum; I'll never make a better decision in my career than to sign for Burnley. I'm happy at Burnley; I'm ten minutes away, close to my family and friends. The season has been unbelievable. What a set of lads, you have to cherish these moments. Look at Heats, Tom Heaton, last year he got relegated with Bristol City and now he's part of the defence with the best record in the Championship.'

Skipper Jason Shackell was one of three players winning places in the Championship Team of the Year. The others were Trippier and Ings. Shackell was an ever-present in every game of the season, a remarkable achievement in itself. With promotions at Norwich and Wolves already under his belt he declared this was the best one.

'It's been my biggest involvement. I've played every game this season so for me personally this is the best promotion by far. You see some of the clubs and the money they've spent, so to do it with such a small squad is an incredible achievement. I can't give the gaffer and staff enough credit. They've been brilliant and the lads have been absolutely magnificent. We stay together.

'People have doubted us from the outside so maybe that's galvanised us a little bit more. The lads will always have each other's backs and I think that's shone on a few occasions. From day one we knew we were a good team and a good squad and then the results started coming and that just breeds confidence. We grew and grew and now we can reap the rewards.

'The gaffer gets us working day in day out and the lads have really bought into what he wanted and what he believes and we've been a real tight-knit group from the start.

'Anyone who knows the gaffer knows he wouldn't let us lose focus. His mantra has always been that we do it day in and day out, no matter what happens. From being fourth favourites to go down and then getting automatic promotion with the likes of QPR, Reading and Wigan below us, just makes it an incredible achievement.'

One of Burnley's most well-known supporters is Dave Burnley. He hasn't missed a single game for decades, lives in the Stoke area and doesn't even own a car. He wasn't always called Burnley but changed his original name to honour his club.

For Dave it was one of the most remarkable seasons in the whole history of the club. It was a reflection of the underdog tag that has been affixed to the club since as long as he can remember and was the reason why he first began to follow Burnley.

He remembered when, way back in the pre-season period and the first game against Bolton, it was all doom and gloom. Everyone including himself had predicted a lower-half finish. Nevertheless out of blind loyalty he put a small wager on at the bookies that Burnley would end with a top-three place at 50/1, never thinking he would have anything to collect. He thanked everyone at the club from the co-chairmen to the cleaning ladies but his 'biggest accolade goes to our imperious leader who has transformed our club from apparently going nowhere to where they are today, Saint Sean, the Patron Saint of Underdogs'.

Tony Scholes was deeply affected. In April he wrote a 2,000-word piece, calling it *My Unshakeable Belief*. This is the essence of it:

Easter Monday, 21 April 2014: that date is up there now as one of the best I have experienced as a Burnley supporter. Watching the Clarets so long there have been far too many ups and downs to mention. Given that I started watching us in the top flight and given that's where we are going next season, I've witnessed the same number of promotions and relegations. Seven of each is the total with the first of them ending what was simply an horrendous 1970/71 season.

I'm not sure when I got the unshakeable belief about this season and I'm not sure what brought it about for someone who, despite not being negative, is always worried that things will go wrong. I suppose I'm similar to Barry Kilby, the self-professed club pessimist, who said to me earlier this year, 'My mum used to say if it's that good, it won't last.'

Pre-season started with a defeat at Morecambe. Dyche spoke only in the last week of some of the barracking he received as we lost 1-0 just days into pre-season training. But, we then got off to a decent start and I think we all sat up and took notice at how well we played in game number five at Derby where we won 3-0. Then there was a resounding 2-0 win against QPR, everyone's favourites for promotion. It had been our first massive challenge and we'd passed it with flying colours and more. By now supporters were beginning to believe in the team although it was still no more than a good start.

We'd notched 44 points by the halfway stage of the season and I certainly thought we would be in with a chance if we could repeat that in the second half. What was to come was at times simply difficult to take in.

That unshakeable belief of mine; when did this worrier of a supporter finally realise something very, very special might be on the menu? Blackburn: What a day! So many Burnley fans there had never witnessed anything like it. Many hadn't even been born the last time we beat them. I came home and watched it again, and again, and again. I can tell you on every matchday since, except before the Middlesbrough game, I've relived the moments when the goals went in followed by the final whistle. I love Sky+.

We came home with an eight-point lead over Derby and from that day my unshakeable belief never wavered. When the Watford draw came that's when I referred to the lights at the end of the tunnel.

It was all done and dusted for me at the seaside. No way was Dyche going to allow us not to get the necessary points. 'Are you nervous?' asked a friend before the Wigan game.

I'd watched Shackell scoring at Ewood, then Ings scoring at Ewood and then the hysteria at the final whistle at Ewood. Then I'd gone to the Turf all relaxed. I still find it hard to believe I was so relaxed, so confident. It's just not me; has this bloke with the ginger goatee somehow got inside my head? As it turned out our players were also full of confidence. We brushed Wigan away just as we'd done QPR in October and Forest at the end of February. The after-match celebrations were wonderful. The tears came on Tuesday as I suddenly realised the enormity of what we'd achieved.

It's been one of the most incredible seasons I've had watching Burnley but where does it rank alongside the other good ones? Firstly, I know where I place our manager. When I first started watching the Clarets we were managed by Harry Potts. I adored him and will never forget the first time I met him. No one will touch Harry Potts for me but Sean Dyche, I can tell you, now runs him a close second.

I think most people will agree that this team has outdone that of five years ago. Captain of that team was Steve Caldwell. He sent his congratulations this week, calling it outstanding; an achievement he agreed surpassed that of his own team.

What we have achieved this season is, I really do believe, the finest achievement at our football club since I was first taken to Turf Moor by my dad in October 1960. I'd just missed the championship title season of 1959/60; my impeccable timing again. I cannot think of anything at Burnley Football Club since that title win that can match the achievements of Sean Dyche and his team. The manager's one-club mentality has got everyone pulling in the same direction. I'll stand alongside thousands of Burnley fans watching OUR team playing Premier League football. I really can't wait. I have that unshakeable belief.

Chris Flanagan referred back to 1973 in his celebratory report. It was April 1973 when Burnley last clinched a promotion season actually at Turf Moor in front of a home crowd. Those were the days of Bob Lord, a time of mullet hairstyles, few if any players ever thought about covering their arms with tattoos, cigarette and pipe smoke wafted across the terraces, and dads could carry stools into the ground for little lads to stand on.

Gilbert O'Sullivan was top of the charts and the Carpenters' voices from the tannoy drifted across the ground. They were the days of Jimmy Adamson, Martin Dobson, Leighton James, Colin Waldron, Paul Fletcher and Frank Casper.

There were some uncanny parallels. They beat Sunderland 2-0 that day. Now it was 2-0 again, against Wigan. At the beginning of 1972/73 they sold star man Dave Thomas to QPR. This time they had sold Charlie Austin to QPR. Back then Sunderland were the FA Cup winners that season. This time Wigan were the cup holders.

The co-chairmen and directors were beaming for days after the Wigan game and then the final match at Reading. They knew only too well the financial problems that were facing the club and that now they had miraculously gone away – for five years at least. The club that finishes bottom of the Premier League will earn a minimum £63m for that one season.

The only problems they faced now was what to do with the money; how much to award Dyche for his new budget, how much to invest in club infrastructure, what to spend to develop Gawthorpe and the youth system, and how much of their own considerable loans to the club to reclaim if they chose to do so.

'To finish second in a very competitive league is unbelievable,' said John B. 'We've had a great season. We were written off at the start; we were supposed to be going down. We came 11th last season and if we had improved on that and got in the play-offs, that to us would have been a dream scenario. We've actually done a good job here, me and Mike Garlick, breaking even, compared to a lot of clubs losing money hand over fist.

'A lot of it is down to the manager and to the players. It's a tight-knit squad. The manager has got the best out of the team so he's managed to perform a miracle. We interviewed 16 people for the job and he actually came with a PowerPoint presentation. But he certainly knew how to sort out our little fortress at the back because we were letting a lot of goals in.

'He certainly had all the attributes. He's not only good on the pitch, but he's good off the pitch too. He wants to get involved in everything; sales, commercial and marketing. He's a businessman. I actually offered him a job at my company FIS if ever he wanted to try a new career.'

The man who does have unshakeable beliefs, of course, is Sean Dyche.

'I think it is historic. The challenges of the Championship are getting harder and harder because clubs who are getting relegated are getting richer and richer and others are getting richer by their backers. To do it automatically is something that is getting harder and harder. To amass the points we have with a small budget in the grand scheme of this division, and using just 23 players, I think is incredible.

'I'm not sure those sorts of markers will be done again. I'm unbelievably delighted; it's a marker in history. This achievement might be a marker, not only for the football club, but for the bigger picture of Championship football. We've built something here that's marvellous. It's the destination at the end of an impressive journey with a group of people who are totally motivated and committed to stand the test of a season. I was promoted four times myself as a player so I know what it feels like and what it takes.

'To say that we got here with two games to spare and by then amass 89 points, that's a surprise. But to say we've been competitive in every game we've played in, there's no surprise. That was our marker.

'We couldn't guarantee anything except – it was one game at a time.'

ECHOES OF, AND
RE-WRITING THE PAST

MANY years ago, in the late 1960s when Harry Potts introduced a bunch of kids – including the likes of Dave Thomas, Mick Docherty and Steve Kindon – into an ailing side, their run of success brought reporters flocking to Turf Moor to discover what was the secret and to see how 'the Turf Moor boffins were once again having success in their laboratories'.

The words 'boffins' and 'laboratories' over 40 years later still resonate but in truth there are no magic secrets. In the world of Burnley's sports scientist Mark Howard, what goes on is no great mystery; there are no test tubes or alchemy but just the latest methods of giving the Burnley players 'that extra inch' in a game where the finest of margins can make a difference.

What did Pacino say in that memorable American football speech he gave to his players? 'Inch by inch…the margin for error is so small, one half-second too slow or too fast, one inch at a time, and when we add up those inches they are the difference between winning and losing,' was the gist of it. Those inches come from fitness and training, mentality and attitude. They are rooted on the training fields. And at Burnley that is Gawthorpe.

It was once the legendary Billy Dougal tending to players' physical needs and injuries through the 1940s and 50s and much of the 60s. Now, there are new men and Dan Black in his 'Talking Sport' feature in the *Burnley Express* wrote about them and said, 'Turf Moor physio Alasdair Beattie and head of sports science Mark Howard have certainly contributed to Burnley's winning formula this season, working in unison with first-team coach Tony Loughlan. While the Clarets have excelled on the pitch, the duo has undoubtedly mastered their trade off it.

'It's an intricate fusion of rest and recuperation and strength and conditioning, delving beyond medical assessment and into mentality and nutrition in a bid to maximise physical fitness and guard against niggling soft-tissue injuries.'

The need for a well-planned training area was the brainchild of manager Alan Brown. When it was created in the 50s it was considered state of the art for its time. It was then director Bob Lord who arranged the purchase of the land needed. It was the sweat and labours of Alan Brown himself and several of the players, including the great Jimmy McIlroy, now the club president, that dug it out, levelled the fields, and built it.

Where you now see Sean Dyche and his staff bringing out the best in the players that won promotion to the Premier League, dozens of wonderful players through the decades learned their craft and honed their skills.

Tim Quelch, author of *Never Had It So Good*, the story of the 1959/60 team that won the title, was especially conscious of the parallels between Alan Brown and Sean Dyche. He has kindly allowed reproduction of the following:

> Burnley's unexpected promotion to the English Premier League in April 2014 resounds with echoes of the club's glorious past. For 60 years ago, a fiercely focused, shrewd, innovative and principled Burnley team boss, with a management style not dissimilar to that of the current incumbent, Sean Dyche, also developed a blueprint for football with one of the lowest divisional transfer budgets and average gates.
>
> Alan Brown's Burnley side would eventually snatch England's then Premier League title, the Football League championship, from better resourced rivals, such as Spurs, although it was Brown's successor, the irrepressibly enthusiastic Harry Potts, who presided over the team's crowning glory in May 1960, having

had the good sense to capitalise upon Brown's sound foundations. Dyche's remarkable success at Turf Moor was also achieved with much more modest resources than most of his divisional rivals – a smaller first-team squad, a comparatively smaller transfer budget and a lower average gate.

What Brown lacked in cash reserves, he more than compensated for with eagle-eyed scouting, top-notch coaching, state of the art training drills including 'shadow football', and leading-edge tactics, obtaining the best intelligence available from near and far. Moreover, Brown led from the front in actually helping build Burnley's showpiece training ground at Gawthorpe with its revolutionary all-weather surface, where the team's sophisticated methods could be practised whatever the conditions.

Under Brown's management, Burnley became a thoroughly modern milltown side, capable of defeating vaunted opponents at home and abroad by playing fluent and fluid continental-styled football from back to front, unconfined by the reactionary 2-3-5 system of play.

Under Dyche's management, Burnley became one of the fittest sides in the Championship, defending robustly and relentlessly from the front, continuously hurrying and harrying opposing defenders and midfielders in advanced positions, squeezing them for space, denying them potentially dangerous acceleration room, and forcing countless distributional errors, while pushing forward swiftly once in possession, frequently switching the point of attack in probing forensically for defensive vulnerabilities.

In Dyche's sides, both attack and defence are collective responsibilities with wide midfielders tracking back to assist the full-backs in holding up and dispossessing the opposing flank players on the ball, and the central midfielders and the striking pair helping to ensure that their centre-backs are not isolated and forced into last-ditch tackles in or just around their own box.

Befitting Dyche's Watford legacy, Graham Taylor's pressing style of play is discernible in his current tactics. Perhaps more significantly, Dyche's coaching team raised the level of so many players' performances in terms of their movement, technique and vision. As was said of Sir Alf Ramsey's Ipswich First Division-winning side of 1961/62, what were once ordinary players became extraordinary ones under his management. The same could have been said of Mr Brown's boys, too.

Although Brown was renowned as a tough disciplinarian, insistent, as Dyche is, that his players maintain a smart public appearance and respectful, courteous standards of conduct, he was also understanding and warmly supportive when they experienced personal or family difficulties, a quality that Dyche appears to share.

Brown never resorted to bawling at his players when the going became tough. As Lawrie McMenemy recalled from his days as a coach under Brown, at Sheffield Wednesday, his boss could be deft in his motivational techniques. There was one occasion during the mid-60s when a vibrant, visiting Chelsea side, managed by Tommy Docherty, had torn the Owls apart during a traumatic first half. McMenemy said Brown was coolness personified during the interval as he gently encouraged his players to offer their ideas as to how they might wrestle control from their gifted opponents, knowing full well that he would only disempower them further by tearing strips off them.

As some of the current Burnley players have already testified, Dyche belies his somewhat gruff demeanour in adopting a similar approach.

As suggested by Lawrie McMenemy, Brown was never so intoxicated with his own importance or authority that he failed to listen to his players' views, notably those expressed by his senior players, Jimmy McIlroy and Jimmy Adamson, who helped devise and rehearse a succession of novel dead-ball scams, including the staging of mock arguments designed to distract the opposition at corners or free kicks.

These ruses were so successful that they were still being employed by Jimmy Adamson's 'Team of the Seventies' 20 years later. Sean Dyche's statements suggest that he is an equally inclusive manager, recognising that wisdom does not reside solely in the manager, and that successful teams usually comprise more than one leader, with a multiplicity of leaders representing a strength rather than a weakness, an opportunity rather than a threat.

While Harry Potts was enjoying the fruits of Brown's efforts, his predecessor was immersed in a radical transformation of a failing Sunderland side, ripped apart by unauthorised 'under-the-counter' payments. Once Sunderland finally emerged from the doldrums in the early 60s, Brian Clough became one of Alan Brown's stellar signings. Although free-scoring 'Cloughie' succumbed tragically to a career-ending injury at Roker Park in late 1962, he proceeded to model himself upon his demanding, uncompromising but kindly Sunderland boss as he made his first tentative steps into football management at Hartlepool. In fact, Clough was so in awe of Alan Brown that he treated him like royalty whenever he visited Clough at the City Ground, Nottingham, during Forest's glory years of the late 70s and early 80s.

In introducing himself at Turf Moor in 2012, Sean Dyche acknowledged Brian Clough's influence and example in developing his own management style. In so doing, it seems as if the wheel that Alan Brown had kicked into motion at Burnley, during the mid-50s had completed a full revolution, helped by what had transpired in those intervening years at Sunderland and Nottingham.

Not that Sean Dyche subscribes to any sort of 'personality cult'. Indeed, as he seems keen to emphasise, he regards his team's recent triumph as a collective effort in which the joint determination, dedication and skill of the Burnley players, support and coaching staff were harnessed to optimal effect. Nevertheless, there is little doubt that the management team that Dyche fronts has provided a key lead in setting the necessary standards, establishing the requisite frameworks, supplying the crucial tactical acumen and instilling the essential drive and discipline, all of which have been at the heart of his club's shared success.

Sean Dyche and Alan Brown have another feature in common. Both were combative, no-nonsense, promotion-winning centre-backs. And while Alan Brown led his second-tier Burnley side to an FA Cup Final defeat by Charlton at Wembley in 1947, half a century later, Sean Dyche led his third-tier Chesterfield team to an equally gallant FA Cup semi-final defeat against Middlesbrough.

The teams that Dyche and Brown have managed at Burnley have good reason to name themselves as the 'History Boys' given the enormity of their achievements with such slender resources, a timely reminder, perhaps, that success is not yet entirely governed by money. Amen to that.

Twenty years after Alan Brown, James Mossop had just seen Burnley beat Chelsea and all their stars 1-0 and wrote, 'When the rain comes slanting in at the dark hills and mills of Burnley, in the heart of Lancashire, a special comfort can be found in the deeds of the local football club. It was that sort of morning when I sat with the team behind the football team; the backroom puppeteers who have quietly created the most heart-warming story the game has known for years.

'Burnley are the little team from the sticks who are showing the scrambling, frenetic millionaire clubs how a soccer side should be run. On gate money insufficient to pay the wages they have risen back into the First Division and have produced and sold talent worth millions.'

That was written over 40 years ago just after Jimmy Adamson and his team had returned to the top division. It could have been written today and is as strikingly relevant now as it was then.

Fifty years ago chairman Bob Lord forecast that television would come to rule and dominate football and his prediction is now absolutely true. Burnley are about to enter the world of Premier League television football; their games will be broadcast round the world, the income will be phenomenal.

Actor Richard Moore was also intrigued by the links with the past, in his case by the more immediate comparison with the promotion of 2009 and Owen Coyle:

> It's an old adage that when you're waiting for a bus on a cold and rainy day, two of them will eventually arrive at the same time; a state of affairs recently observed by Liverpool manager Brendan Rodgers, when he claimed that Jose Mourinho, in a cunning Portuguese plan, had not only unfairly parked two Chelsea buses across their goalmouth, but also had the audacity to send both drivers up the field to score two goals against the Reds.
>
> When buses do arrive in twos, like Burnley's two Premier League promotions in five years, the answer may lie in a field of mathematical study known as Chaos Theory, a phenomenon well known to observers of the beautiful game. More popularly known as the Butterfly Effect, the theory states that one small change in one place can result in larger differences somewhere else and would have us believe that a butterfly flapping its wings can result in a tropical storm in the Pacific.
>
> Now, butterflies, like football managers, come in all shapes and sizes.
>
> In 2007, one of the Scottish tartan varieties by the name of Coyle arrived, fortified by Irn-Bru, wove its way across Hadrian's Wall, landed at Turf Moor and with hardly a pause for breath, enthusiastically flapped

its wings on the touchline and propelled the Clarets unexpectedly into the 2009 play-offs and a promotion-winning Wembley final that will live forever in the memory. A memory, in my case, significantly damaged in the champagne-fuelled post-match celebrations that continued for several days and resulted in me being temporarily banned from my Cornish local by my Newcastle-loving publican for crossing her threshold in a Burnley scarf.

Sadly, that same tartan butterfly ran out of Irn-Bru, flew too close to the sun and got his wings burned, falling to the ground in Bolton, where it survived for a while until the climate proved inhospitable. Be that as it may, that same sun shone on Turf Moor for a whole season and how, for the most part, we basked in it.

When the clouds finally descended on Turf Moor, many felt that the good times were probably over. Then, in October 2012, another butterfly, this time of the genus 'Ginger', aka Sean Dyche, fluttered into Burnley after an unexpected flight from Watford and unfurled his muscular wings over the next 18 months to inspire a young Burnley side to automatic promotion, 'One game at a time.'

Promotion, like butterflies and buses can arrive in twos and Chaos Theory would have us believe, and Burnley fans would surely agree, that this is impossible to predict.

Nevertheless it happened. Burnley for the second time in five years are now back in the Premier League, an event that bookmakers and fans alike were not predicting in August last year. If that is chaos then bring it on.

The sun, unexpectedly, is shining over Turf Moor again, but remember as Sean Dyche often says, 'It's best not to over-think it.'

The deeds of Sean Dyche, the football team and the backroom team in 2013/14 have been echoes and continuations of a glorious past. But a past that has also been re-written in so many ways:

1 Burnley's 2-0 win at Doncaster in October 2013 took them to the top of the table for the first time since 2006.

4 Burnley won 3-0 at Derby County to record the fourth successive win at Pride Park.

10 Ten wins out of the first 13 games in the season was Burnley's best start to a season since 1897.

43 The 1-0 at Ipswich Town was the first win at Portman Road since 1970.

3 Sean Dyche is the first Burnley manager to be named Manager of the Month three times.

25 After going top at Doncaster in October, Burnley then spent just 25 days outside the top two for the remainder of the season.

20 Danny Ings and Sam Vokes are the first strike pair to each hit 20 league goals in a season since Willie Irvine and Andy Lochhead in 1964/65.

11 Away wins in a season equalled a club record.

26 Goals for Danny Ings in all competitions.

21 Goals for Sam Vokes in all competitions.

35 When Burnley won at Blackburn's Ewood Park in March it was the first victory since April 1979. The 35-year wait was over.

87 Burnley did the double over Leeds United for the first time in 87 years.

41 The number of years since Burnley had won an automatic promotion from the Championship or the old Second Division to a higher level.

29 The 1-0 win at Bolton Wanderers was the first there since 1985, a wait of 29 years.

21 The Clarets kept 21 clean sheets in all competitions.

51 The number of games played by captain Jason Shackell, who hadn't missed one minute.

15 Burnley gained 15 league points from a losing position this season; three wins and six draws.

27 Burnley scored first in 27 league games and went on to win 22 of them.

37 Burnley conceded just 37 goals in the Championship, the tightest defence in the division.

14 The number of assists from full-back Kieran Trippier.

23 The unbeaten home run stretched to 23 games from March 2013 (Hull City) to March 2014 (Leicester City), lasting one year.

93 The number of points gained in the season, the most since three points a game was introduced. The previous was 88 in the 1999/2000 Stan Ternent promotion season.

26 The number of league wins in the season.

5 Just five defeats in a whole league season.

1 A first ever double over Ipswich Town.

23 The number of players used in the league, of which three made just a single appearance; meaning that in effect just 20 players achieved this remarkable promotion.

1 Danny Ings the Championship Player of the Year, the first time for a Burnley player.

3 Burnley players selected in the Championship Team of the Year for the first time; Ings, Trippier and Shackell.

Most of the above is courtesy of the Burnley FC programme.

THE CO-CHAIRMEN, SEAN DYCHE, AND THE FINAL WORDS

BOTH Mike Garlick and John B offered their thoughts a week or so after the season had ended. I met Mike at the club, and discussed things with John B by email and telephone. The sense of pleasure and achievement was palpable. The sense of relief at the financial windfalls to come was fully evident.

Towards the end of the 2008/09 promotion season, insolvency was a real prospect and it was last-minute director loans that kept the show on the road until the club hit the Wembley jackpot. This time, said Mike, things were not quite so bad, but financial difficulties would indeed have affected the club although not as badly and would have been manageable.

John B revealed, 'We interviewed 15 or 16 potential candidates for the manager's post because we felt this was the most important role for the club. The manager engineers and motivates the team and we didn't want to get it wrong so we took our time. It was also a chance for Mike and myself to put our stamp on the club as the new co-chairmen. The manager's job has come a long way from cigarettes and cold tea. These days it's about sophisticated analysis, diet control, mentoring and support for the players as well as giving them a pat on the back.

'Sean had just left Watford and was working with the England under-21s so we knew he was available. We brought him to a secret hideout where we were doing the interviews; we didn't want the fans to find out who we were speaking to at the time. He gave us a PowerPoint presentation that reminded me of my day job and I was impressed. He showed us amongst other things that although we were scoring a lot of goals we were conceding too many and that this was a recipe for disaster in the long term.

'Sean ticked all the boxes for us, a good communicator, already known for his player relationships and the work he'd done with the youth team at Watford so he really stood out as the best candidate. Some of the candidates were at the time managers elsewhere but I hope it was as useful an exercise for them as it was for us. I think we learned a lot.

'I have an excellent relationship with Sean; we speak just about every other day and he's very definitely on the ball, as involved off the pitch as he is on it. He's great at getting the best out of people, contrary to his rather gruff exterior; he takes time with people and remembers the details. He's a serious, clever guy with lots of commercial ideas too; in fact I've told him that if ever he wants to give up football, he should consider a job with my company Freight Investor Services, where he has got to know one or two of the staff.

'We were very lucky last season to have had a small, tightly-knit squad that suffered very few injuries, but we kept an eye out for loan players. We were always going to be short of a striker if Vokes or Ings got seriously injured but we covered the market really well. Michael Kightly came from Stoke and has been excellent for us. Leicester were looking to pick him up but some good work was done by Lee Hoos and Sean to get him here.

'The funny thing was that as our results got better, the less other clubs wanted to loan us players. I guess they were jealous of our success. The Premier League clubs wanted guaranteed playing time for their players and we couldn't always give them that. It was up to Sean to decide how they fitted into his plans.

'I work in the commodity business and our job is managing risk for clients; you try and steer away from boom and bust and you don't celebrate until the deal is done. At Burnley we knew we had something special with Sean and the team early in the season, but we wanted to bide our time and not get too big-headed about it. It was a one game at a time approach and then perhaps we would surprise everybody.

'Next season we want to imitate what we did in the Championship; get the team fully fit pre-season, find players that fit our model and prepare for the battleground of the Premier League. We have to be realistic about our chances there but we are a very competitive club and I think we can build a future and a legacy by staying true to ourselves and maintaining the belief that brought us here. I will be over the moon if we can get about 17th place and stay there.

'As I write, I have not been contacted by one single Premier League chairman or director since we were promoted. I've read a lot of comments about how surprised they all are that we made it but no one has congratulated us.

'It doesn't take much for the best-laid and funded plans to go astray. The club's wage bill is a matter of public record and accounts for the season are just being finalised but we are in the bottom 25 per cent of the Championship at around £11.4m and that includes bonuses.

'The TV money that we will get this coming season means we have to make improvements to the media facilities and TV gantries. In the old days you might have had longer to do this but when you are signing the cheques these days you can dictate the terms so we will be ready for the start of the season.

'We will make mostly cosmetic upgrades to Turf Moor; we are looking at redeveloping the shop, possibly adding a museum, as well as improving the offices that date back to Victorian times. At Gawthorpe we will be adding more pitches for all the teams, from first to youth.

'Our turnover will go from £14m to £63m; that looks good on paper but much of that money has already been allocated. It looks like a windfall but we are not going to be going out and making any rash buys. It will be wisely and sensibly invested.

'Our strategy is to create a stable, community club with the right players, to be an established higher echelon club, with good interaction between chairmen, board and manager and right down to the fans. Yes we are ambitious but we have realistic targets relevant to the size of the club in this wider money-laden football world.

'Our strategy also means getting a lot closer to the supporters and increasing our fan base by getting involved in outreach with the town and the region. We get a lot of correspondence and I try to reply to as many as I can and really get involved. I think you get the pulse of the town and fans that way.

'We want to encourage more interaction with supporters both local and far-flung; we have informal meetings now with an advisory group which is a source of new ideas from people who care about the club but aren't involved day to day. I enjoy sitting in the directors' box but you can't beat getting into the stands and being with the fans especially when you're winning.

'I don't get recognised and I really enjoyed being at the away end against Blackburn, getting covered with beer when we scored the second goal. I also gain confidence from the good relationship I have with Mike and other board members. We have a great rapport and an honest exchange of ideas. I hope that continues – even if we do lose the first five games of the season!'

Mike Garlick was equally open and communicative when we met in the panelled chairman's room at the club, a room that dates back to the days of Bob Lord and is now lined with framed shirts, pictures, photographs and portraits that give a wonderful taste of Burnley's long history.

Mike was at pains to emphasise that the success gained by the end of the season was rooted in the pre-season work many months earlier.

He said, 'The squad was refreshed, some players moved out, new ones came in; players that had been carefully vetted by Sean Dyche who does his thorough homework on every player he signs. It takes the gamble out of signing a player; a new player is a huge investment.

'At Burnley incomers need to have been "schooled in the right way", conduct themselves with respect and manners. They need to understand another of the basic mantras – "minimum requirement, maximum effort". You don't see silly haircuts or headphones in public places. Sean Dyche looks for solid attitudes, players who put team before self and ego.

'So it was in the pre-season that the foundations were laid, the fitness training, the running, pulling tractor tyres. It was when bonding took place, the new bedding in and acclimatisation, and above all the buying into the Sean Dyche way and development of the one-team mentality. There were strong friendship and groups within the squad but no cliques. Several players had a strong Wolves connection. Jones and Heaton had a strong friendship that dated back to their Manchester United days.

'The sale of Charlie Austin was no surprise and behind the scenes it was known to be essential to solve the cashflow problems. Perhaps the manner of it was a surprise; Hull backing out and then QPR stepping in. But it turned out to be a blessing; up stepped Danny Ings and Sam Vokes and thrived on the opportunity when they came to the fore.'

Mike was adamant that he always thought there were good players to be brought in on frees, and because the Austin sale brought in less than was anticipated, those frees were what they relied on. There was simply no money for a like-for-like replacement. But what they already had was the Vokes–Ings combination that cost less than £1.5m and that investment would come to realise a minimum of £63m.

'The sale of Charlie to QPR rather than Hull meant we faced a £2m shortfall which then meant we had very little budget for transfer fees, which then lead to the "Vings" partnership being born out of necessity. Regarding big Sam I said to Eddie Howe we should buy him as he could only improve; to which Eddie said, "Well he won't score many goals but he will help the team score more." Well, he got half of it right.'

The pursuit of loan targets continued (Tudgay, Phillips, and Wickham) but there were all kinds of reasons why nothing materialised, not the least of which was the fact that some of them wanted assurances of a starting place in the team, or on closer examination it was felt that a player might not actually fit in, or a manager preferred them to go to another club.

If the Austin sale eased the cashflow problems, Mike still felt the early need to announce the £7m losses so that everybody, not just the directors and manager, would realise the constraints the club was under. It worked. The knowledge brought everyone together, brought feet back down to earth, made everyone realise that there was no magic money-pot. Garlick confirmed that no player was on £10,000 a week and the wage bill put them in the bottom third of the Championship wages league.

The impact Dyche made at the interviews he clearly remembers. He already remembered him from the time when he had made an impression when he brought Watford to Turf Moor and there he was in the rain on the touchline in his trademark black raincoat barking out orders and instructions, exhorting his players, clearly passionate and demonstrative. 'It left a real marker and I didn't forget that,' said Mike.

'At the interview Sean walked in with a natural exuberance, energetic and he stood to give his presentation. It contrasted with the way some of the others simply slouched in their chair. He brought his own machine for his PowerPoint presentation, talking about how he saw the game. His model was Barcelona and he occupied our complete attention.'

Mike was also contacted by someone who knew Dyche well and he was able to share that knowledge when the candidates' merits were being discussed.

'I was driving home from work and got a call from a business associate who said he had known Sean for a long time and was a close personal friend. He said he couldn't recommend him for his abilities as a football manager as he knew little about that. But, he could certainly say that he was a person of real integrity, had real motivation, organisational and general managerial talent and felt this guy was something special. I can't possibly put a price on how valuable that reference was.'

Living in the Watford area, Mike knows many Watford fans and was assured by them all that Burnley had made a great appointment.

'The final round of interviewees had included Keith Hill, Ian Holloway and Steven Pressley. The fans' choice seemed to be Holloway as he was a big, known name but I felt we had to pick who we thought was the best man for the job regardless of how fans would interpret the appointment.

'Like many, it was when Burnley beat Nottingham Forest and Derby that the realisation grew that this could be "real" but it was not until five minutes before the end of the Wigan game did I think this IS it.'

Sean Dyche said it was the Wigan game that for him was a real nirvana moment when everything came together on the day that confirmed promotion. Well before that, it was the home win against QPR when he first thought that they really could be on to something.

When he was asked for five key matches he said it was difficult to think of individual ones because it was a run of three against Nottingham Forest, Derby and Blackburn, that he saw as a critical and defining period. It meant that instead of Derby overtaking them, and Forest being just two points behind, suddenly Burnley were clear.

He saw Leeds as a key encounter because that was a game when Burnley went behind, but the crowd stayed with them, never became impatient and that was so important to both him on the touchline and the team on the pitch where they could feel the support. They went on to win the game. But if Wigan provided the nirvana moment, it was the match before, the 1-0 win away at Blackpool, when he thought confidently, 'That's it, done it.'

He finally allowed himself to say the 'p' word after the Wigan game and then in his programme notes for the final home game against Ipswich, which are kindly reproduced here. 'There you go,' he wrote, 'I've finally said the "p" word.

'In fact, I think I'll say it again, promotion, promotion, promotion. Ha ha. I don't think I'll tire of saying it all summer long. I might even bore the kids with it in answer to their every question.

'In all seriousness, last week's events were amazing for all concerned with this great football club and a fantastic achievement.

'To achieve promotion in front of your own supporters is the pinnacle and to see Turf Moor jumping was something that will remain with me throughout my days. I was a very proud man following the victory over Wigan which I understood took us to a record points total; the latest in a season of historical markers. It wasn't the fact that we won the game, it was the manner in which we did it, when others have been making noises and questioning us.

'We never wanted to achieve our goals by default with someone else doing us a favour. We always wanted to do it on our terms and there could be no better way than beating one of the strongest teams in the division comprehensively. Monday (against Wigan) was also the culmination of so much hard work by my staff and the players dating back to pre-season when we gathered and headed to Cork with one goal.

'That was to go hard each week, in every game and not lose focus. I salute the players because they have been absolutely relentless in their daily routines. Our unity has also been a great strength. Other clubs may have a bigger budget but we have shown that if you have a clear mentality and no shortage of quality you can still achieve great things.

'I'd like to think the generous comments we are receiving as a club are because we have not abandoned our principles. This is a club rooted in the community and living within its means. That is to be applauded in a game awash with cash.'

Dyche concluded by thanking everyone for their support and wished everyone a relaxing summer before coming back refreshed ready to roar the team on in the Premier League.

Of that he may be certain – ONE GAME AT A TIME.